BACKLASH

The Killing of the New Deal

BACKLASH

The Killing of the New Deal

ROBERT SHOGAN

Ivan R. Dee
CHICAGO 2006

BACKLASH: THE KILLING OF THE NEW DEAL. Copyright © 2006 by Robert Shogan. All rights reserved, including the right to reproduce this book or portions thereof in any form. For information, address: Ivan R. Dee, Publisher, 1332 North Halsted Street, Chicago 60622. Manufactured in the United States of America and printed on acid-free paper.

www.ivanrdee.com

Library of Congress Cataloging-in-Publication Data:
Shogan, Robert.
  Backlash : the killing of the New Deal / Robert Shogan.
    p. cm.
  Includes bibliographical references and index.
  ISBN-13: 978-1-56663-674-2 (cloth : alk. paper)
  ISBN-10: 1-56663-674-4 (cloth : alk. paper)
  1. Roosevelt, Franklin D. (Franklin Delano), 1882–1945. 2. United States—Politics and government—1933–1945. 3. New Deal, 1933–1939. 4. United States. Supreme Court—History—20th century. 5. Judges—Selection and appointment—United States—History—20th century. 6. Sit-down strikes—United States—History—20th century. 7. Labor unions—United States—Political activity—History—20th century. 8. Working class—United States—History—20th century. 9. Political culture—United States—History—20th century. I. Title.
E806S54 2006
973.917092—dc22   2006003863

For Ellen

Contents

Preface

THE DEATH OF THE NEW DEAL in Franklin Roosevelt's second term, hard upon his great reelection triumph in 1936, was one of the great collapses in American political history. Its importance was somewhat obscured by Roosevelt's subsequent reelection to third and fourth terms, due in large part to the outbreak of World War II. Nevertheless the debacle of 1937–1938 remains a signal happening, with far-reaching significance for American politics. Most studies of this episode have concentrated on Roosevelt's attempt to overhaul the Supreme Court, which plagued him at every turn, as the prime cause of his defeat. My narrative, drawing on more than thirty years of experience as a political journalist, takes a broader view and thus, I hope, contributes fresh insight.

For help in various forms along the way, I thank Tom Allen, Zach Courser, Alonzo Hamby, Joseph McCartin, David Wigdor, and Zena Mason and Quintell Freeman, librarians of the Johns Hopkins University Washington Center.

I salute my publisher, Ivan Dee, for his confidence in this work, for his keen editorial eye, and for resisting the prevailing tides of an industry where judgments are too often distorted by the concerns of commerce.

Finally, and most important, I am grateful to my wife, Ellen Shogan, who read every sentence in this manuscript and helped improve many of them, for her generosity and uncommon common sense.

R. S.

Chevy Chase, Maryland
April 2006

BACKLASH

The Killing of the New Deal

1

The President

The presidential flag with its shield, eagle, and white stars waved from its staff above the portico of the imposing house overlooking the Hudson. Within the walls of the Roosevelt family home in Hyde Park on election night 1936, confidence was running high, so much so that the celebrating began well before the polls closed. After dinner, while the president himself withdrew to the privacy of his study to keep his own reckoning with the aid of a news ticker, friends and family gathered in the parlor to listen to the radio.

Betsy Cushing Roosevelt, wife of the president's eldest son, James, served drinks while Sara Delano Roosevelt, matriarch of the household, ensconced in an armchair as if it were a throne, presided over festivities. Tommy Corcoran, one of the brightest and most engaging of the New Deal's young lions, broke out his accordion and began to sing a ballad with newly invented lyrics. He dubbed it "Oh, Landon Is Dead," in honor of the anticipated defeat of the president's Republican challenger, Kansas governor Alfred M. Landon.

By 9 P.M. whatever suspense about the outcome might have existed had been buried under the avalanche of Roosevelt's victory.

Franklin D. Roosevelt, now assured of a second term in the White House, swept into the room in his wheelchair to join his guests. Corcoran promptly struck up "Happy Days Are Here Again," the Tin Pan Alley tune that had become the New Deal's unofficial anthem.

Corcoran was soon drowned out by the blaring of a brass band. Roosevelt's admirers in Hyde Park had come to pay tribute, and the reelected chief executive went out to greet them.

As the clock ticked away the last minutes of election day on November 3, Roosevelt's margin grew ever larger. It would ultimately reach 61 percent of the popular vote. Then came the phone calls—most from supporters and allies, like Postmaster General James Farley, Roosevelt's prescient campaign manager, who had accurately predicted that the president would win every state but two, tiny Maine and Vermont.

But probably Roosevelt relished no call more than the one that came from St. Simeon, citadel of his archenemy, William Randolph Hearst. Once the newspaper mogul and FDR had been among the strangest of the bedfellows politics often makes. In 1932, on his route to the Democratic presidential nomination, Roosevelt had steadily wooed Hearst, chiefly by repudiating his earlier support for the League of Nations and more broadly for any U.S. involvement in European affairs. This courtship was consummated at the 1932 Democratic Convention in Chicago where Hearst brokered a deal assuring that Roosevelt would be the party's standard-bearer. As part of the bargain, FDR made John Nance Garner of Texas, speaker of the House of Representatives whom Hearst had boomed for the presidency, his vice-presidential running mate.

The Hearst-Roosevelt marriage of convenience did not survive Roosevelt's first term. By the time of the 1936 campaign, Hearst's papers had taken to rendering the New Deal as the "Raw Deal," and to proclaiming that Roosevelt, along with being the Democratic nominee, was the unofficial candidate of the U.S.

Communist party. The Chief staked his reputation on his prediction that Landon would prevail. But the publisher was not so great a fool as to allow his passions to blind himself to reality. In the closing weeks of the campaign he sent word to his editors to abandon their shameless proselytizing for Landon, and the Kansan's name almost disappeared from the Hearst press.

Now on election night, with Roosevelt's triumph undeniable, the Lord of St. Simeon saw the wisdom of a gesture to the victor. In hopes of softening the reception at the other end, he had Marion Davies, his longtime paramour, put through the call to Hyde Park. John Boettiger, husband of Anna Roosevelt, the president's only daughter, took the phone and heard the fading actress introduce herself and say, "I just wanted to tell you that I love you. We know that a steamroller has flattened us out, but there are no hard feelings on this end. I just wanted you to know that."

Then before Boettiger could relay that message to his father-in-law, Hearst himself took the phone. "I just wanted to repeat what Marion said," the publisher intoned, as FDR later recalled the conversation for his interior secretary and sometime confidant, Harold Ickes, "that we have been run over by a steamroller, but that there are no hard feelings on this end."

Even then Hearst was not done making amends. In 1932, when FDR had tried to get the publisher to accept his private reassurance that he was quit of the League of Nations, Hearst had insisted on a public acknowledgment. Now he was no less forthcoming himself. ". . . Roosevelt's victory," he wrote in his papers two days after the election, "is absolutely stunning to those who opposed him, and utterly astounding even to his supporters. . . . I believe we should all not only comply cheerfully with the will of the majority but that we should endeavor to understand and appreciate and apply the wisdom embodied in it. . . ."

And just for good measure, Hearst hired Boettiger, the president's son-in-law who had been a Washington correspondent for the *Chicago Tribune*, and made him publisher of one of his newspapers, the *Seattle Post-Intelligencer*. These efforts at ingratiation did little to impress either the president or members of his inner circle. Both Farley and Ickes urged FDR to avoid a renewal of his old friendship with Hearst. Indeed, Roosevelt told his aides that he was thinking of excluding Hearst's correspondents from his future travels.

But the truth was that the president could not afford to indulge himself in petty feuds. He had more serious adversaries to face.

Not that there was any denying the magnitude of his victory. The thirty-second president had won by a greater popular and electoral vote margin than any of his predecessors except George Washington. Moreover his triumph extended beyond his own personal success, endowing his party with almost an embarrassment of riches. Adding to their already substantial majorities in both branches of the seventy-fourth Congress, the Democrats gained twelve seats in the House of Representatives, giving them three-quarters of that body in the seventy-fifth Congress. And with that bounty came seven new seats in the Senate, establishing for the president's party almost 80 percent control of that chamber. When he returned to Washington promptly on the day after the election, tens of thousands, many of them Democratic job holders, others simply admiring citizens, lined the streets cheering wildly as the smiling president waved at them from his open car.

The panoply of triumph underscored the humiliation of the big corporations and newspapers who had opposed the president and reminded two veteran capital journalists of the glories of imperial Rome. "One wondered," Joseph Alsop and Turner Catledge wrote, "why the vanquished Republican candidate, accompanied by a selection of Du Ponts and newspaper editors, did not follow the presidential cortege in chains."

In the wake of his victory, Franklin D. Roosevelt was riding higher than any president in American history. The doorway to America's political future was wide open to him and his New

Deal, or so it seemed. Yet within the year two seismic events would transform the political landscape. A nationwide outbreak of labor unrest, particularly the spread of a new and potent labor union weapon, the sit-down strike, and FDR's launching of a scheme to overhaul the Supreme Court would combine to generate a fierce public backlash that tarnished Roosevelt's mystique and drained the lifeblood from the New Deal. Roosevelt himself would be the principal protagonist in these events and would be hailed by some as their champion, reviled by others as the villain of the piece. But before history had run its course, nearly every major figure on the public scene would play a role, including the chieftains of a new power base, organized labor, and the leaders of both political parties. The clash of rhetoric and stratagems would test the will and nerve of all involved, expose the rude realities underlying the struggle for power, and redirect the future of American politics.

The defeat of FDR and his allies was one of the great unexpected collapses in the history of American politics. But it should not have been so surprising. The truth was that the court fight and the labor turmoil exposed weaknesses in the New Deal that had been obscured by the scope of the president's victory and his personal élan.

To begin with, the New Deal had not conquered the depression, not by a long shot. About nine million still walked the streets in search of work, nearly 15 percent of the labor force, and across the land countless children still went to sleep hungry. Moreover, though the New Deal had forced the old economic order to give ground here and there, in other quarters resistance to change persisted, as strong as ever. Big business remained an unbowed adversary, newly emboldened to resist New Deal policies by the recent economic improvement that those same policies had helped generate.

Roosevelt had sought to turn this opposition to his advantage during the campaign. In accepting renomination he had declared war on the "economic royalists" who, he said, "complain that we seek to overthrow the institutions of America." Drawing an approving roar from the Democratic Convention delegates, he added: "What they really complain of is that we seek to take away their power."

Corporate America returned his animus, with interest. In a bitter *Fortune* article published as the campaign neared its climax, the steel magnate Ernest T. Weir wrote of Roosevelt: "he is opposed not by 'a small minority' as he says, but almost unanimously by the business and professional men of the country." Reflecting the resentment of Weir and other business leaders at Roosevelt's intrusion into their hitherto sacrosanct domain, Weir added scornfully of the president, "His experience with business has been narrowly limited. . . . He never went through the grim competitive battle that every man must endure who fights his way from scratch."

"I am not criticizing the New Deal," Henry Ford, the patriarch of the assembly line, had insisted unconvincingly, as he endorsed Landon for president. "I only say that we have had enough of it; we have had about all the country can stand."

In taking on big business, Roosevelt was also incurring the enmity of big newspapers, about 75 percent of whom backed Landon. By one analysis of 150 major papers, those supporting Landon counted 14 million subscribers against only 7 million for those backing Roosevelt. And while, like Hearst, many opposing publishers were temporarily silenced by the thunder of FDR's reelection landslide, no one imagined this would last for long.

In addition to these formidable opponents, Roosevelt in his drive for change also had to contend with the peculiar architecture of the government, carefully designed by the founders to curb the popular will by using the courts and the Congress to check the executive. Roosevelt had usually managed—though not without some difficulty—to get his way with Congress, whose members, like himself, were obliged to respond to the popular will or find some other means of livelihood. But the judiciary, particularly the Supreme Court with its "nine old men," as FDR's allies called them, protected by the security of lifetime appointments, was another matter. By handing down a series of decisions disrupting the New Deal, the high court had made itself the bane of FDR's existence. Indeed, finding a solution to this problem, as many people suspected, had become the number one priority on FDR's postelection list of things to do.

The court's decisions were particularly threatening to the president because they gave tangible expression to perhaps the most significant of all obstacles to the aggressive dynamic for change that energized the New Deal. This was America's middle-class tradition with its inherent respect for property, attachment to the established order of things, and mistrust of government. These feelings were rooted in the nation's infancy. In those early days the abundance of land and the absence of the class distinctions common to the Old World promised opportunity for all, elevating individualism and the rules of the marketplace above all other public values. The role of the Supreme Court in defending the supremacy of individualism and of free enterprise, in the face of grave inequities, had made the Court the natural enemy of the New Deal. This antagonism set the stage for the confrontation that would eventually overshadow Roosevelt's great victory.

The strife that would now engulf him would cast into bold relief the personal assets and failings that had marked Roosevelt's ascent to the summit of American politics. At fifty-four, his handsome, patrician features, regal bearing, and strong, resonant voice all reflected his invincible self-assurance. "He must have been psychoanalyzed by God," a spellbound aide once remarked. The president's strengths stemmed more from his character than his convictions, which, while firmly held, were often ill defined and sometimes at cross-purposes. "A second-class intellect, but a first-class temperament," was the famous judgment of Oliver Wendell Holmes after a brief visit with Roosevelt at the onset of his presidency.

Roosevelt's equanimity was sustained by an iron will, demonstrated most vividly by his refusal to submit to the paralysis that had threatened years before to destroy his career. But above all else he was a master of indirection and misdirection, a gift that permitted him to escape the normal penalties for inconsistency and self-contradiction, and allowed him to appease and assuage his friends and befuddle his foes. "His mind does not follow easily a consecutive chain of thought," the venerable statesman Henry Stimson, who would become his secretary of war, once noted in his diary, "but he is full of stories and incidents and hops about in his discussions from suggestion to suggestion and it is very much like chasing a vagrant beam of sunshine around a vacant room."

In view of his healthy margin of victory in his first bid for the presidency in 1932—when he won 57 percent of the popular vote and all but six states—his close adviser Rexford Tugwell would later view it a waste that Roosevelt had not been bolder and more explicit as a candidate. "The fact was that Franklin was continually accused by Hoover and others on the Republican side of intentions that were precisely those he should have proclaimed," he would later write. "He denied the accusations, only to reverse himself embarrassingly later on."

Similarly, in his 1936 reelection bid FDR avoided discussion of specific issues, including problems he knew he would have to face in his second term, most notably the Supreme Court. Instead he offered *himself* to the voters as the crucial reason for their support. "There is one issue in this campaign," FDR told Raymond Moley, one of his early Brain Trusters, as the election approached. "It's myself, and people must be either for me or against me."

Flexibility was his lodestar. "It is a little bit like a football team that has a general plan of game against the other side," Roosevelt told reporters early in his presidency, explaining his approach to economic policy. "Now the captain and the quarterback of the team know pretty well what the next play is going to be and they know the general strategy of the team, but they cannot tell you what the play after the next play is going to be until the next play is run off."

After vainly trying to get a straight answer out of the president on a key appointment, his interior secretary Harold Ickes exploded. "You won't talk frankly even with people who are loyal to you and of whose loyalty you are fully convinced," Ickes told Roosevelt. "You keep your cards close up against your belly. You never put them on the table."

Roosevelt cloaked his guile with a personal charm reputed to be so overpowering that some political foes were said to shrink from private encounters with him lest they succumb to his wiles. At Harvard, editor Roosevelt got along so well with other *Crimson* staffers that his co-editor recalled, "in his geniality was a kind of frictionless command." His distant cousin, Anna Eleanor Roosevelt, had been so captivated by his gaiety and natural ease that she married him in 1905, soon after his graduation from Harvard.

But after a while some found that his personality began to wear thin. Eleanor Roosevelt had to recast her life and their marriage after she learned her handsome husband had been unfaithful to her. Tugwell thought that Roosevelt's charm ultimately became "part of a whole apparatus of defense" designed to conceal his true beliefs. "He had a trick of seeming to listen, and to agree or to differ partly and pleasantly, which was flattering," he recalled. "This was more highly developed as he progressed in his career and it was responsible for some misunderstanding. Finally no one could tell what he was *thinking*, to say nothing of what he was *feeling*."

Although FDR's artfulness did him no good with the Supreme Court, it was not for the lack of trying. As governor of New York he had made it a point to get along well with the justices of the state's highest court, the Court of Appeals. And he came to Washington, as he wrote one of the high court's justices,

Benjamin Cardozo, "hoping that I can have at least in part the same type of delightful relations I had with the Court of Appeals in Albany."

Accordingly, in advance of his inauguration Roosevelt wrote Chief Justice Charles Evans Hughes, remarking on their common background as governors of New York, adding the hope of "seeing more of you than I have had the opportunity of seeing for many years." As a fellow former New York governor, Hughes might be expected to understand the sort of rapport with the judiciary that Roosevelt had enjoyed in Albany, or so Roosevelt apparently thought. At any rate, he subsequently proposed to the chief justice a sort of consultative relationship between them. He would like the chance to talk things over with the chief, he indicated, so as to get the Court's view on his own plans for policy before going forward with them.

But Hughes was unmoved by FDR's charm or this opportunity to share the chief executive's leadership role. "Mr. President," he told FDR, "the court is an independent branch of government." The barrier between the Court and the president was required by the Constitution, and Hughes for one would have no part in breaching that wall.

Despite his overture to Hughes, Roosevelt brought strong suspicions of the federal judiciary with him to the White House. In the final month of campaigning for the presidency in 1932 he declared: "After March 4, 1929, the Republican party was in complete control of all branches of the government—the Legislature, with the Senate and Congress; and the executive departments and I may add, for full measure, to make it complete, the United States Supreme Court as well." Republicans immediately pounced on the remark, hoping to spark their incumbent president Herbert Hoover's forlorn bid for reelection. Pennsylvania Congressman James M. Beck, a former solicitor general, told the press that "it saps the foundation of our government to impute to the highest court of the land a statement that in spirit or actions it is partisan."

Herbert Hoover, the incumbent Republican president, his candidacy hopelessly mired in the depression, was eager to find a fresh issue that he could use against his challenger. Joining in the chorus of indignation, Hoover claimed that Roosevelt's statement should serve as a warning that if elected, Roosevelt would "reduce the tribunal to an instrument of party policy."

In the face of the Republican protests, Roosevelt who had ad-libbed his aspersion against the Court into the prepared text of a speech, stood by his guns. "What I said last night about the judiciary is true," he told a fellow Democrat afterward. "And whatever is in a man's heart is apt to come to his tongue—I shall not make any explanations nor apology for it."

The flare-up had no measurable influence on the campaign, but there is evidence to suggest that FDR's words would come back to haunt him by spurring the Court's assault on the legislative underpinnings of the New Deal. In 1936, when the Court and the president were at each other's throats, no less an authority than Justice Harlan F. Stone, more sympathetic to the New Deal than many of his colleagues, revealed that Roosevelt's provocative remarks had not gone unnoticed by his colleagues on the bench. Some of the brethren, "being only human, were much offended," Stone confided in private conversation, and Stone thought they "were going too far during their anger."

Whatever the repercussions, Roosevelt's complaint was not without foundation. Indeed, even a year after his controversial remarks, during which time as president he had enjoyed the power to nominate his own judges, a Justice Department study of the partisan allegiances of the 266 sitting federal judges found little more than a quarter of them were Democrats. This reflected the fact that Republicans had controlled the White House for twelve unbroken years before 1933. Just as troubling as the Democratic disadvantage in numbers was the incumbent judiciary's deep-rooted devotion to laissez-faire economic doctrines in the face of the New Deal's penchant for economic planning. This attitude had been most recently illustrated in

1932, the year before Roosevelt took office, by the Supreme Court's overturning an Oklahoma law denying licenses to new ice companies to protect the ability of existing companies to survive. The justices held Oklahoma had overreached in seeking to regulate business "not affecting the public interest."

The philosophy underlying that opinion—disapproval of government action even when it was intended to aid the free-enterprise system—seemed to many to be a dagger aimed at the heart of the New Deal, which had pushed through a flood of new laws expanding government's role during Roosevelt's First Hundred Days. The lawmakers, said longtime Democratic wheelhorse and former Wilson cabinet colleague of FDR, Newton Baker, "had bundled up and passed over more power than any man ever had before him." But as Roosevelt well knew, he could count on wielding that power effectively only at the sufferance of the Supreme Court.

Although mindful of the threat the Court posed to his plans, Roosevelt from the first appeared to approach this problem with characteristic buoyancy and optimism. In his first inaugural address he set the stage for his memorable admonition that Americans had nothing to fear "but fear itself" by seeming to dismiss the idea that judicial intransigence might stand in the way of needed reform. "Our Constitution is so simple and practical that it is possible always to meet extraordinary needs by changes in emphasis and arrangement without loss of essential form," the president declared. This rhetoric, as Americans would soon learn, was vintage Roosevelt, demonstrating a gift for mellifluous fluency that fell pleasingly on the ear but camouflaged far more of reality than it revealed.

But Roosevelt's actions belied his words, making clear that he himself was far from convinced that the court would share his blithe view of constitutional expediency. Even as Congress continued to churn out New Deal–prescribed statutes that challenged existing judicial doctrine, the administration put off testing their constitutionality in the courts. The president's strategy was to give the New Deal experiments time to work and build popular support before placing their fate in the hands of the black-robed justices.

With the 1934 congressional elections approaching, New Deal critics sought to make the constitutionality of Roosevelt's remedies a campaign issue. In October conservative groups organized the Constitutional Protection League "to expose and resist internal and external socialism and communism and the promotion of these doctrines." With a healthy budget, the new group deployed its agents into the hustings to sound the alarm against the drastic expansion of government's role in the economy wrought under FDR.

Roosevelt's strategy of delay seemed vindicated by Democratic successes in the 1934 election. Not since the Civil War had either party won a presidential election without losing ground in the election two years later. Despite this precedent, in 1934 FDR's Democrats increased their ranks in both the Senate, where they picked up nine seats, and in the House, where they added ten, gains made even more impressive because they came on top of already substantial majorities.

But conservatives paid no heed to the election returns. The courts, as they saw it, were intended to serve as a protection against what Democrats might call the will of the people but which conservatives viewed as the tyranny of the majority, implemented by a chief executive lusting for power. Given the New Deal's energy and passion in assaulting the established order, and given the dedication of the Supreme Court under Chief Justice Hughes to its perceived role as guardian of the constitutional status quo, a collision was inevitable. The only questions were when it would come and how it would turn out.

The first skirmishes, in the early months of 1935, were inconclusive. In January the administration lost its first New Deal case, involving one aspect of the National Industrial Recovery Act, the centerpiece of the First Hundred Days, which created the National Recovery Administration. Under its Blue Eagle logo, the NRA sought to revive the economy by establishing wages and price "codes" for each major industry, a process involving collaboration between business, labor, and government. The same law also gave labor unions a big boost by providing for the first time a federal guarantee of the right of collective bargaining. But the Supreme Court's decision against the NRA was on procedural grounds. So New Dealers took comfort in a belief that the Court's technical objections could be resolved if only the justices upheld the major sections of the act which were still under constitutional challenge.

In February 1935 the White House breathed a sigh of relief when the Gold Reserve Act, enacted the previous year, which reduced the gold content of the dollar to help stabilize the currency, barely survived a challenge. The Court's favorable ruling staved off economic chaos for the government and millions of businesses and homeowners. But the Gold Reserve decision, like the NRA case, was decided on narrow grounds and by only a 5 to 4 majority. That left New Dealers still brooding over the question of how their most important handiwork would stand up in court.

The answer came crashing down on May 27, 1935, with a series of decisions that confirmed the administration's deepest misgivings. On that day, known for long after among New Dealers as Black Monday, the court struck three blows against the New Deal on issues that ranged from the near trivial to the most profound.

In a ruling more important for its symbolism than its substance, the Court held illegal the president's dismissal of a federal trade commissioner, a holdover from previous Republican administrations, who disagreed with FDR's policies. Since the high court itself had in the past recognized presidential authority to remove such officials, a favorable outcome had been taken for granted by the administration. So much so that the new solicitor general, Stanley Reed, had chosen to make the case his maiden appearance before the Supreme Court in his position, confident he would thus be assured of getting off on the right foot in his new job. As it turned out, though, Reed was stunned by the Court's unanimous decision that Roosevelt's action was illegal because he had not given a proper reason for the dismissal. Whatever disappointment Reed felt, it was exceeded by the anger of FDR who considered that by denying him a right accorded to other presidents the justices had gone out of their way to embarrass him. And his resentment did not soon fade.

Of broader significance was the second decision announced that day, this one overturning the Federal Farm Bankruptcy Act, designed to help bankrupt farmers reacquire land lost through foreclosure. The Court held that in giving the farmers a break, the government had violated the rights of mortgage holders, thus repudiating a New Deal initiative in the one area of the economy that had suffered longer than any other.

But both these rulings were overshadowed by the day's final decision, also unanimous, overturning the legal basis for the National Recovery Administration. For the Blue Eagle and the elaborate codes it symbolized were the bedrock of Roosevelt's entire program to overhaul the economy. The case involved a poultry company whose owners, the Schechter brothers, had been found guilty of violating NRA rules by filing false sales and price reports and selling diseased chickens. In reversing the Schechters' conviction, the Court held that the wide regulatory net cast by the NRA far exceeded the boundaries of interstate commerce, the only area in which the Constitution permitted the federal government to regulate. Chief Justice Hughes also hit hard at the codes the new agency had established under power delegated by Congress to govern the nation's major industries. "This is delegation run riot," Hughes wrote. "No such plenitude of power is susceptible of transfer."

Newspapers around the country hailed the ruling in the "sick chicken case," as it came to be called. "Constitutional government has returned to America," exulted the *Chicago Daily News*. Even many New Dealers privately saw a silver lining in the Court's action, which they suggested had relieved the president of having to defend the NRA's cumbersome and inherently arrogant system. Organized labor, however, did not share those feelings. To union leaders, the NRA, for all its high-handedness, represented the first action by the federal government to protect the right of workers to organize. Many were particularly outraged at Justice Brandeis's vote with the majority. Sidney Hillman, then a leader of the needle trades unions in New York, recalling Brandeis's long battles on behalf of social reform, railed, "Having closed the sweatshops, he now clears the way for their reopening."

Roosevelt himself was stunned by the decision and uncomprehending of the depth and breadth of opposition on the bench. When his aides brought him word of the ruling he asked, "Well, what about Old Isaiah?" the honorific that New Dealers affectionately accorded to Justice Brandeis, long the patron saint of liberal reform.

If the president had better understood Old Isaiah's judicial philosophy, he would not have had to ask the question. One of the cornerstones of Brandeis's thinking was his hatred of centralized authority, which he opposed not only in big business but in big government. This attitude brought him firmly in line with the rest of his brethren and against the NRA. Indeed, no sooner had the decision been read from the bench than he spelled out its meaning in even blunter language than Hughes.

Summoning to the justice's robing room New Deal lawyer Tom Corcoran, whom Brandeis had known since Corcoran clerked at the Court for Justice Holmes, Brandeis told him: "This is the end of this business of centralization, and I want you to go back and tell the president that we're not going to let this government centralize everything. It's come to an end." While Corcoran listened obediently, Brandeis added, "As for your young men, you call them together and tell them to get out of Washington . . . tell them to go home, back to the states. That is where they must do their work."

Brandeis's scolding only added to Roosevelt's dismay. The broad thrust of the Court's ruling was such that FDR and his close aides felt, as one of them, Jerome Frank, put it, "that it was going to be impossible for him to carry out his program."

Roosevelt brooded privately for a few days, venting his rage at two of his top lieutenants, Hugh Johnson, head of the NRA, and Felix Frankfurter, the Harvard legal savant and presidential confidant. The country, he told them, was with him, not the Court. He would bring the Court into line, he vowed, if he had to "pack it." Finally on May 31, in a clearly calculated expression of his resentment, Roosevelt delivered a lengthy excoriation of the Court at his press conference.

The NRA decision, he said, "was more important than any decision probably since the Dred Scott case." He and his advisers had been struggling with the nation's number one problem, the Great Depression. "We thought we were solving it," the president told the journalists, "and now it has been thrown straight in our faces." And he added, in a phrase that it turned out few headline writers could resist, "We have been relegated to the horse and buggy definition of interstate commerce."

One of FDR's great strengths was his skill at communicating his ideas to the American public, a gift that relied heavily on his flair for expressing himself in vigorous and colorful language that resonated with the popular idiom. But on this occasion that talent would prove his undoing. He might as well have taken the Lord's name in vain or used barnyard epithets to smear the justices. The "horse and buggy" phrase seemed to millions of Americans on the same scale as an expression of contempt and disdain for the institution many viewed as the chief guardian of their liberties.

Conservative foes were quick to take advantage. "I don't think the president has any thought of emulating Mussolini, Hitler or

Stalin," remarked Michigan GOP Senator Arthur Vandenberg. "But his utterance as I have heard it is exactly what these men would say." It tells all that needs to be told about the mood of the hour that Vandenberg's outlandish remark did not even raise an eyebrow.

Roosevelt was stunned into public silence by the overwhelming defense of the Court and the attack on himself. But in private the Court was never far from the president's mind. Early in his presidency, anticipating that the New Deal's innovations would face major legal challenges, FDR had instructed his attorney general, Homer Cummings, to look into ways to curb the Supreme Court's power. Without the knowledge of anyone else in government, Cummings quietly began doing research and collecting memos from his staff. In the wake of Black Monday, on orders from the president, Cummings's project gained impetus.

At first most of the attorney general's efforts, all shrouded in deepest secrecy, concentrated on ways to limit the Court's power to declare acts of Congress unconstitutional. But a broader question hanging over these deliberations was whether the Court's hands could be tied by legislation or whether a constitutional amendment would be required to restrict judicial power.

Roosevelt himself hinted at the amendment approach in a story he carefully planted in *Collier's* magazine in the summer of 1935. The article was written by George Creel, whom Roosevelt had known since his World War I days as assistant secretary of the navy, when Creel served as chief propagandist for the war effort. Creel's article, "Looking Ahead with Roosevelt," concluded with a paragraph that did not purport to quote Roosevelt directly but nevertheless was widely understood to be faithful to FDR's thinking. It asserted that if the Court continued to interpret the Constitution in ways that left the government powerless to deal with current social problems, "the president will have no other alternative than to go before the country with a constitutional amendment that will lift the dead hand." After dictating that paragraph to Creel, as the writer later revealed, Roosevelt told him, "Fire that as an opening gun."

But Creel's shot turned out to be a dud. Whether the article was intended to cow the Court or arouse the public, it did neither. The justices continued to slap down the New Deal, and most Americans simply ignored the article. And a Gallup poll taken around that time showed that by a margin of 63 to 37 percent most were opposed to limiting the Court's power to declare legislation unconstitutional.

Given the public mood, Roosevelt realized he had little choice but to bide his time. Either the Court would change its tune or it would wreak more havoc on the New Deal, in which case he believed the resulting public uproar would provide momentum for him to move against the Court.

If the Court were to overturn all New Deal reforms, the consequence would be "marching farmers and marching miners and marching workingmen throughout the land," FDR told a New Deal lawyer that summer. Roosevelt was particularly concerned about the fate of the Agriculture Adjustment Administration, which was intended to revive farming much as the NRA had been designed to boost industry. To farmers who agreed to curtail production in order to reduce chronic crop surpluses, the AAA offered subsidies, paid for by a tax on processors of farm products. "Of course if the Supreme Court should knock out the AAA, then the constitutional amendment would be *the* real issue," the president added. "If the court does send the AAA flying like the NRA there might even be a revolution."

Roosevelt's expectation of public response to court rulings unfavorable to the New Deal turned out to be remarkably unrealistic. In January 1936 his worst fears were borne out when the Supreme Court, in *U.S. v. Butler*, overturned the AAA, ruling that the tax on processors was unconstitutional because it amounted to "the expropriation of money from one group for the benefit of another." But the president said nothing and did nothing—perhaps because the revolution he had anticipated did not develop. While some farm leaders denounced the decision, others applauded it. And a Gallup poll released the day before the decision was handed down showed that Americans were opposed to the AAA by a margin of 3 to 2.

While the president maintained his strategic silence, he continued to consider possible moves against the Court. He told Harold Ickes that rather than a constitutional amendment he favored some form of legislation, mentioning as one possibility a law that would require the Supreme Court to offer an advisory opinion on the constitutionality of a bill before it was enacted. That way Congress could then either change the bill to conform to the Court's advice or pass the original bill a second time, after which, under this proposed statute, it would then become the law of the land. But if the Supreme Court declared this new law unconstitutional, as it almost certainly would, Ickes pointed out, FDR would be back to square one.

Roosevelt had an answer for that. He would go to Congress and ask whether he should obey the law they had passed or obey the Court ruling overturning it. If Congress told him to follow the statute, not the Court, the president would rely on U.S. marshals to implement the will of Congress and ignore the Court.*

Similar schemes were hatched on Capitol Hill where the New Deal's allies offered more than a hundred proposals to counteract the Court. Some measures aimed at expanding congressional power to enact social and economic reforms. Others, anticipating Roosevelt's own as yet unformed intention, sought to expand the membership of the Court, thus allowing the president to pack it with justices to his liking. Yet another type of re-

---

*Roosevelt may have had in mind the response of an earlier Democratic president, Andrew Jackson, to a decision by Chief Justice John Marshall denying the state of Georgia sovereignty over land claimed by the Cherokee nation. Disagreeing, Jackson is supposed to have said, "John Marshall has made his decision, now let him enforce it." The decision was rendered moot.

vision sought to eliminate or limit the power of judicial review. The sponsor of one such measure, Senator George Norris of Nebraska, longtime leader of the once-potent Senate contingent of progressive Republicans, claimed that he had scoured the Constitution carefully, "but nowhere in that great document is there a syllable, a word or a sentence giving to any court the right to declare an act of Congress unconstitutional."

He was right about that, of course. But for more than 130 years, since *Marbury v. Madison* when John Marshall established the precedent that "it is emphatically the province and duty of the judicial department to say what the law is," the Supreme Court had been doing just that, though not without occasionally provoking furious protests from presidents.

The controversy over the Court subsided briefly when the justices surprised some of their critics by upholding another New Deal creation, the Tennessee Valley Authority (TVA). But in the spring of 1936 the Court renewed its judicial assault on the New Deal. First the justices undercut the regulatory authority of the Securities and Exchange Commission, established in 1934 to curb the excesses in stock dealings that had contributed to the crash of 1929. The very idea of such government regulation of the securities industry outraged many conservatives, a disapproval that seemed reflected in the Court's 6 to 3 decision. The majority held that it could find "no support in right principle or in law" for the commission's probing of a questionable transaction in oil securities, and labeled the agency's conduct "wholly unreasonable and arbitrary."

Then the Court rejected outright two other major pieces of New Deal legislation. The Guffey Coal Act, by which the administration had sought to stabilize the soft coal industry by salvaging some of the codes of the ill-fated NRA, was found to exceed the reach of federal power under the Constitution's interstate commerce clause. The Municipal Bankruptcies Act, aimed at relieving the plight of the nation's depression-ridden cities, was held to violate the rights of states. This despite the fact, as dissenting justices pointed out, that the statute stipulated that no city could invoke the federal law unless the state's laws permitted it.

Finally in its last session, by a 5 to 4 majority, in what would become its most infamous decision of the year, *Morehead v. New York*, the Court overturned a minimum-wage law for women, enacted not by the federal government but by the state of New York, as interference with contract rights. Justice Roberts, considered to be more or less of a middle-of-the-roader, joined with the Court's steadfast conservatives, McReynolds, Van Devanter, Sutherland, and Butler, to make the majority. To attempt to regulate the conditions of women's bargaining with their employers, Justice Butler wrote, denied them constitutional equality with men, and their freedom of contract, "part of the liberty protected by the due process clause." In dissent, Justice Stone, allied with the Court's other two liberals, Brandeis and Cardozo, and Chief Justice Hughes, asked bitterly, where was the freedom for "those who because of their economic necessities give their services for less than is needful to keep body and soul together?"

Stone was not the only one to dispute the *Morehead* decision. The ruling was not just a blow against the New Deal but also a self-inflicted wound for the Court. This was particularly so because in the *Adkins* case in 1923, involving the District of Columbia, the Court had denied to the federal government the authority to establish minimum wages. *Morehead* thus embarrassed many of the Court's supporters, one of whose most consistent claims was that the New Deal represented federal authority run amok, transgressing on terrain that should be left to the states. Now the Court was saying that not even the states could regulate the working conditions of women because doing so would infringe on their freedom of contract.

Even Herbert Hoover joined in the national outcry against the decision, calling for a constitutional amendment to restore to the states "the power they thought they already had." In the staunchly Republican *New York Herald Tribune,* the columnist Franklyn Waltman called the decision the biggest break the New Deal had received in many months, potentially "the turning point in the entire controversy over the Supreme Court and the necessity for amending the Constitution." In the same vein, Felix Frankfurter wrote FDR: "And what am I to reply to Frank Buxton of the Boston *Herald* who calls me up and asks, 'is it true that the president bribed Butler and his four associates to decide the minimum wage case for him the way they did?'"

In the wake of the ruling, FDR for the first time in a year, since his "horse and buggy" comment following the NRA decision, broke his silence on the Court. But considering the uproar provoked by the voiding of the New York law, the president was remarkably circumspect. All he said at his regular press conference was that the *Morehead* case, together with other recent decisions, had created "a no-mans land where no government—state or Federal—can function."

"How can you meet the situation?" a reporter asked.

But Roosevelt backed away. "I think that is about all there is to say about that," he said.

The president continued to steer a cautious course even in the midst of the ensuing 1936 presidential campaign. So unpopular was the *Morehead* decision that Alf Landon, about to be nominated by the GOP, felt obliged to set himself apart from the party platform which accused the New Deal of flouting "the integrity and authority of the Supreme Court." In a telegram to the Republican Convention, which met in early June in Cleveland, the Kansas governor advocated a constitutional amendment to protect working conditions for women and children if congressional legislation along those lines were held unconstitutional.

In advance of their own convention later that same month in Philadelphia, many Democrats came forward with a variety of specific platform proposals to curb the Court. But at Roosevelt's insistence the delegates settled for a plank notable for its tortured ambiguity, even when judged by the high standards for blurriness traditionally established by such documents. If national problems "cannot be solved by legislation within the Constitution," the Democrats promised, "we shall seek such clarifying amendments" that would assure to the states and to Congress the power to enact laws necessary to protect the public welfare. What that meant exactly, no one could be certain—which was exactly the way Roosevelt wanted it.

To be sure, it would not have been hard to infer the president's thinking about the Court from the convention keynote speech delivered by Kentucky Senator Alben Barkley, every word of which Roosevelt had approved. After inveighing against the Court for rejecting laws enacted to save the country from economic distress because of "the rigors of legal technicality," Barkley insisted that he respected the tribunal "as an institution." But, he asked the assembled delegates, "Is the court beyond criticism? May it be regarded as too sacred to be disagreed with?" To both of which questions he predictably got resounding "No's." During the campaign, Republican supporters of Landon did what they could to stir concern over Roosevelt's intentions toward the high court. They repeatedly pointed out that if reelected Roosevelt would have the potential power to reshape the Court to his liking. And they continually declaimed their reverence for the Constitution, in contrast to the incumbent progenitor of schemes that defied that sacred document. They even set this point to music in a tune sung at GOP campaign rallies around the country.

> Alf Landon learned a thing or two,
> He knows the right solution
> And in the White House he will stay
> Within the Constitution.

But none of this was enough to draw Roosevelt out on this issue. He was determined to avoid a controversy over the Court and the Constitution which might detract attention from the campaign themes he thought most favorable to his candidacy: the accomplishments of the New Deal, the dastardly record of the last Republican administration, and, finally and foremost, his own compelling persona. He himself was the dominant issue, as he told Moley, "and the people must be either for me or against me."

Yet another reason for not arguing the Court problem in the campaign was that the president had no political strategy for solving it that could win public support. Even the cantankerous Harold Ickes, who had rarely seen a political brawl he did not ache to join, counseled FDR to avoid debating his problems with the Court in the campaign. "The groundwork had not been laid," Ickes told the president shortly before the Democratic Convention. "The issue should be built up over the next few years."

But it was by no means clear that the president had that much time. His reelection victory, sweet as it was, and the end of the campaign made it difficult for him to continue to avoid the problem. In the coming months the Court would be deliberating and deciding on cases testing the validity of laws that were crucial to the success of the New Deal—among them the Social Security Act providing government insurance to the elderly, and the Wagner Labor Relations Act providing guarantees of collective bargaining that had been erased by the overturning of the NRA. The future of the Roosevelt presidency hung in the balance.

Still, Roosevelt did not reveal his intentions, even after he had been assured a second term. "Now that the election is over, will you discuss your attitude toward amending the Constitution to carry out the purposes of the New Deal?" he was asked at his first postelection press conference.

"Why spoil another happy day?" the president replied.

At his cabinet meeting that same day, much was said about the Court, none of it good. Solicitor General Stanley Reed, the number two man at the Justice Department, who appeared in the absence of Attorney General Cummings, mentioned to the president that Justice Harlan Fiske Stone, one member of the Court relatively sympathetic to the New Deal, was ill. The 64-year-old

Stone had contracted amoebic dysentery while vacationing in Mexico and would be away from the Court for months. That one of the younger and more moderate justices was ailing while his older and more conservative colleagues continued to enjoy robust health apparently struck the president as the essence of painful irony. With mordant humor he mused that he expected Justice McReynolds, ten years Stone's senior and one of the anchors of the court's right wing, to survive and remain on the Court until he was 105. (In the event, McReynolds died ten years later at 84.)

On a more serious note, Roosevelt advised Reed that the New Deal had abandoned its erstwhile strategy of delay. Now he instructed the solicitor general to push ahead as rapidly as possible on all cases testing the constitutionality of New Deal laws. FDR left the impression, with Harold Ickes for one, that he expected the Court to overturn the laws and that he intended to use these anticipated reversals to make a case against the justices in a higher tribunal, the court of public opinion. "I am keen myself that this question should be raised," Ickes wrote, "and I hope to be able to take part in that fight, if and when it came."

That fight was coming sooner than Ickes realized. Two days before the cabinet meeting, FDR had called in Attorney General Cummings for a report on his secret Supreme Court research project, urged him to step up his efforts, and reminded him to keep whatever he did to himself. About two weeks later, just before Roosevelt boarded the USS *Indianapolis* for a nearly month-long combination vacation and goodwill tour of Latin America, the two met again. Cummings turned over to the president two bulky packages for him to take along on his excursion—one contained proposed constitutional amendments, the other draft legislation. More material would be sent to the president at every port of call on the twelve-thousand-mile voyage.

But it was FDR who had the real news at his meeting with the attorney general. For the first time the president gave Cummings definite word about what would happen to his research. FDR would make a proposal to Congress as soon as one could be readied, and he hoped that would be right after the return from his trip.

For his part, Cummings was elated that his months of labor would soon bear fruit. But he was in for a disappointment. When he next met with Roosevelt on December 15, after the president's return, he was told that he had not yet found the solution that FDR wanted. Meanwhile events were pressing in on the president. Congress would return the first week of January, and the president would need to present his budget and make his annual report on the state of the Union. Only two weeks after that would come his inaugural and the beginning of his second term. If Roosevelt was to move against the Court, it would become his priority and needed to be ready at the start of the term. Press on, the president told his attorney general.

Mindful of the need for haste, Cummings returned to his law books and legal pads. Christmas was coming, but he had little time for gift buying.

That year the Roosevelt family spent the holiday not at Hyde Park but at the White House. On the next day, December 26, 1936, Cummings called the White House to say he was ready with an answer. Roosevelt wasted no time. Cummings arrived, laden with documents and briefing books, at 5 P.M. For the next two hours, interrupted only by tea and toast served to them by the president's son James, the two laid the groundwork for their surprise assault on the Court.

In preparing for this challenge, Roosevelt had taken into consideration a broad range of political factors and gone to great lengths to maintain secrecy in order to gain the advantage of surprise. But this was not the only battle on the horizon, nor the only surprise. Roosevelt would be blindsided by the eruption of a bitter conflict in another arena where, as in Washington, the established order was under challenge.

2

Captain of a Mighty Host

I have always found that if I could not make a living in one place, I could in another," John L. Lewis told a convention of Illinois miners early in a career that would take him to the top of what at the time was the largest and most powerful labor union in the country. A plan to use union funds to provide for unemployment benefits was up for a vote, and Lewis was arguing against it, using a logic about the work ethic that he might have borrowed from the local chamber of commerce. "Many men do not hunt work if they can make a living without it," he declared. Lewis's views in the years before the Great War reflected his own experience in life and the labor movement. Born in 1880, he was the son of an Iowa miner who moved from one coal town to another to provide for his family. Following a few youthful years as a miner and construction worker in the West, young Lewis returned to Iowa where he tried to find a place for himself in the middle class, marrying the schoolteacher daughter of a local doctor and trying his hand at business and then as a politician.

For Lewis these frustrating years roughly resembled the experience of "Uncle Sol," anti-hero of e. e. cummings's sardonic paean to the perils of free enterprise, "Nobody Loses All the

Time." A vegetable farmer until "the chickens ate the vegetables," Uncle Sol then started a chicken farm until "the skunks ate the chickens." This misadventure led Sol to launch a skunk farm, but this too failed when the skunks "caught cold and died." Sol then emulated the skunks by doing himself in. After he was laid to rest, cummings wrote, Sol "started a worm farm."

In Lewis's case he started a grain and feed venture that went sour, then entered politics only to lose a race for mayor. He must have been discouraged. But he was made of sterner stuff than Uncle Sol, and instead of surrendering to despair he decided to return to coal mining and make a career for himself with the United Mine Workers of America. With the active support of his father and five brothers, Lewis quickly became president of one of the largest locals in the state.

By the time he voiced his opposition to unemployment benefits, Lewis was already embarked on an upward path that relied less on comradely proletarian zeal than on his energy and gift for ingratiating himself with members of the union hierarchy. Friendly union leaders in Illinois helped him get a post as a UMW lobbyist in their state. His work caught the eye of Samuel Gompers, who had helped found the American Federation of Labor and whose straight-ahead dollars-and-cents unions had established the AFL as the dominant force in America labor. Gompers appointed Lewis as a national organizer for the federation, a job that helped him cultivate useful contacts in the labor movement around the country. In 1917, when the office of UMW vice president suddenly became vacant, Lewis was tapped to fill the job, the number two post in the union. "Our ship made port today," Lewis wrote presciently in his journal. He was only thirty-seven years old. Without ever standing for election for office in the international union, he had positioned himself to be its leader.

In 1919, with the union's president Frank Hayes rendered hors de combat by alcoholism, Lewis in effect took charge of the UMW just as the nation's trade unions plunged into a savage struggle with management for advantage amidst the economic turmoil that followed the Great War. Hard-pressed by inflation, fearful their jobs might disappear after the wartime boom, more than four million workers that year staged an unprecedented three thousand walkouts.

Lewis's UMW, whose half-million members made it the nation's largest union, led the way. In the White House was Woodrow Wilson, elected with labor support in 1916. But Wilson, who had long since forsaken the liberal beliefs he once championed, managed to break the strike with an injunction even before it started. Lewis at first tried to tough it out. Then, in the face of public outrage backed by the legal muscle of the federal government, he ordered the miners back to work after winning the promise of a commission to arbitrate the miner's wage demands. The commission ultimately awarded the miners a hefty 27 percent increase. This success helped Lewis gain election as UMW president in his own right in 1920, winning, by the estimate of longtime Wilson aide Joseph Tumulty, "more votes than the Democrats" in the presidential election.

Lewis would hold on to the presidency with all its power for years to come. But the impact of the union's gains in the 1919 strike was limited and short-lived. The huge increase in production stimulated by the demands of the Great War left the country with a glut of coal and of coal miners. In coal as in other major industries, Big Business ruled, aided by a government that exalted market forces and the profit motive above all other values.

Lewis held his ground. "No backward step," he told his membership, vowing not to yield any of the hard-won contract gains. But the coal companies that had once worked hand in glove with the union to maintain high production now turned their backs on Lewis. They reneged on existing contracts, refused to bargain further with the UMW leader, or in some cases simply shut up shop and moved south where they were safe from unionism.

By the fall of 1929 the UMW's ranks that had once reached a half million had shrunk to double digits. And the union's treasury was so depleted that Lewis was forced to cancel the union's annual convention. Some miners grumbled at his failed strategy of rejecting compromise. "No backward step was taken," Fred Mooney a West Virginia UMW leader later wrote, "but the ground lost by the union became a landslide into the gutter for the miners."

Yet even as his union staggered into a seemingly hopeless decline, its membership dwindling as paychecks shrank, Lewis himself grew stronger. Each year in office he used his position to enhance his power, exploiting the patronage of his office to enlist henchmen, systematically rooting out dissenters, smearing opponents like the tenacious John Brophy as tools of communism. Technology boosted his efforts. At the UMW's 1924 convention Lewis introduced a loudspeaker system, whose use was restricted to himself and his favored friends and denied to insurgents on the floor. In its first thirty years of history the UMW had been led by ten different presidents. That was before Lewis. By 1929 he had enjoyed ten years at the top, and his hold on the UMW was considered as secure as the pope's grip on Holy Mother Church.

His domineering personality and imposing appearance made Lewis a figure to be reckoned with outside the union hall as well. When he was in his forties a journalist described Lewis's appearance as "a cross between William Jennings Bryan and James J. Jeffries"—a hulking figure of a man with broad shoulders, a high forehead, heavy jowls, a square jaw and bushy eyebrows that would endear him to political cartoonists for decades. His deep baritone commanded attention, a weapon he could use to bully or charm with equal ease.

Lewis had a theatrical flair first honed as an amateur actor on the stage of his hometown in Iowa and had learned how to comb the Gospel as well as *Bartlett's* for material. He was a master both of caustic invective and soaring rhetoric, replete with biblical and Shakespearean allusions. He argued labor's cause, Lewis told a UMW convention at a dark hour in the union's history, "not in the quavering tones of a feeble mendicant asking alms, but in the thundering voice of the captain of a mighty host." He was quick on the uptake too. When a carping congressman complained during the Lewis-led 1922 anthracite strike that the miners had received a 75 percent wage increase since 1913, Lewis snapped: "The miners of the United States are gifted with a number of talents, but they cannot eat percentages." The miners got the contract they wanted.

In a laudatory profile in the 1920s, *Time* magazine, no great friend of organized labor, hailed him as "one of the most able leaders that the labor movement has yet produced: shrewd, adroit, resourceful, a dangerous opponent either at the bargaining table or on the industrial field of battle." And it added reassuringly— and significantly in terms of Lewis's own hopes and dreams, "he is not a radical." To prove that last point Lewis, with the help of a brainy economic consultant, W. Jett Lauck, built a case for a union role in the business-dominated world, an argument based on mutual self-interest. Labor and capital could work side by side to the benefit of both, Lewis argued in his book *The Miners Fight for American Standards*, published in 1925.

When the coal operators turned a deaf ear to his proposal for cooperation, Lewis sought to gain acceptance for his views in the political world. A lifelong adherent of the GOP, he tried to insinuate himself among the Republicans who now ruled the nation. Among the targets of his often heavy-handed flattery were Calvin Coolidge, whom Lewis endorsed in his 1924 campaign for the White House, and Coolidge's commerce secretary, Herbert Hoover, also endorsed by Lewis when he ran for the presidency in 1928. Stumping for Hoover, Lewis credited the great engineer's imaginative policies at the Commerce Department with the "present era of unprecedented prosperity."

Republican leaders accepted Lewis's obsequiousness as more or less their due. But they were no more responsive to his preachments about a labor-management partnership than the coal operators had been. Neither was willing to provide the help to labor that Lewis sought from them.

The Great Depression transformed Lewis's fortunes, opening broad new horizons for his ambition and reshaping his outlook and his rhetoric. Trouble had been brewing for years beneath the complacent surface of boom and prosperity that dominated the so-called Roaring Twenties. But with the stock market crash of 1929, the problems could no longer be ignored. "Wall Street lays an egg," jeered *Variety*, in what would become one of the most celebrated and trenchant headlines of the century.

Day after day, gilt-edged securities tumbled in value while the bulls who had ruled Wall Street for most of the decade panicked and ran. "The present week has witnessed the greatest stock market catastrophe of all the ages," the *Commercial & Financial Chronicle*, a publication not given to overstatement, reported in its November 2, 1929, edition. But the stock market crash was only the tip of the economic iceberg that ravaged the nation's prosperity.

The market, which had briefly recovered after its initial collapse, began careening downward again in April 1930 and did not stop until July 1932, when it was almost impossible for it to sink any lower. By the end of that year more than 5,000 banks had gone under, 86,000 businesses had failed, and $74 billion in investments had vanished—three times the cost of World War I. *Fortune* calculated that in September 1932, 34 million Americans, more than a quarter of the population, had no income, an estimate that did not include the millions of destitute farm families. The economic malaise deepened and spread, sending shock waves rippling through the nation's political and social structure. Commerce and industry ground to a halt, bankruptcy was rife, and farmers saw land they had tilled all their lives forfeited under the sheriff's hammer.

With jobs almost nonexistent and workers plentiful, employers lowered wages to a dime an hour for lumberjacks, a nickel an hour for sawmill workers, eighty cents a week for hatmakers in

New York sweatshops. Teachers endured "payless paydays"; without rent or meal money, many "boarded around" with their students' families. Layoffs created an army of 13 million jobless. Some sold apples and some sought a way out. When the government of the Soviet Union announced openings for 6,000 skilled workers, 100,000 Americans applied.

Despair hardened into violence. After months without paychecks, miners in West Virginia looted the company stores. From the prairies to the plains, farmers burned bridges and turned over trucks to stop the flow of goods to market. In a once-peaceful Iowa town, an angry mob surged into a courtroom in the midst of foreclosure proceedings, dragged the judge from the bench, threw him in the dirt, tore off his clothes, and stopped just short of a lynching.

"No one has starved," President Hoover claimed. But in Harlan County, Kentucky, miners' families lived on dandelions and blackberries, and in Pittsburgh, steelworkers recalled to the mills by a brief flurry of orders collapsed from hunger at their machines. In New York City in 1932, when the depression hit its nadir, twenty-nine Americans actually did starve to death.

No wonder, then, that in the presidential election of that year Americans turned their backs on twelve years of Republican presidents and sent Democrat Franklin D. Roosevelt to the White House. Lewis had personally supported Hoover. But others in his union had backed FDR, allowing the UMW president entrée to the new Democratic White House. More to the point, given the crisis and the new administration's struggles to find a coherent blueprint for meeting it, the door was open to anyone who grasped the causes of the disaster and possessed at least the glimmer of a solution. Now Lewis at last had an audience for the doctrines of labor-business partnership and progressive capitalism that he had argued to deaf ears for most of the preceding decade. But in these parlous time the words he now placed his emphasis and his hopes on were labor and progressive rather than business and capitalism. He no longer dwelled on the virtues of the chamber of commerce work ethic that he had extolled in his younger days. Instead he became a clarion voice for the labor movement, calling for greater militancy by workers and larger responsibilities for government.

In the bleak, grim winter of 1933, two months before FDR was sworn in as the nation's thirty-second president, Lewis argued eloquently in testimony before the U.S. Senate finance committee for bolstering the purchasing power of workers and their families as the key to reviving the economy. Emergency relief could do only part of the job. The crucial step that government must take, Lewis contended, was to promote labor unions by protecting the rights of workers to join them. Drawing on past UMW proposals for government to stabilize the coal industry by establishing safety and conservation standards and regulating marketing (which had been long ignored), Lewis urged that similar steps be taken now not just for coal but for all major industries.

"Let us stop uttering pious platitudes about the need to balance the budget," Lewis said, scorning much of the conventional wisdom of the day. "The balancing of the budget will not in itself place a teaspoonful of milk in a hungry baby's stomach or remove the rags from its mother's back."

Lewis's blueprint for recovery was grist for the mill of FDR's brain trusters. Not only did they tap into his ideas, they called upon his wide contacts with businessmen and on Capitol Hill for advice and support. It was no surprise then, that FDR's National Industrial Recovery Act, cleared by Congress in June 1933, embodied many of the principles Lewis had advocated for years.

The new law "will suit our purposes," Jett Lauck wrote to Lewis. That was putting it mildly. Thanks largely to the NIRA's section 7A, guaranteeing the right to organize and bargain collectively, applauded by Lewis as the greatest single advance for human rights in the United States since the Emancipation Proclamation, the UMW flourished.

The authority of the new law and the prestige of the new president swept away many of the obstacles that had crippled the union for more than a decade. "The President wants you to join the union," UMW organizers told the rank and file as they swarmed through the fields of Appalachia where sheriff's deputies and company guards had once barred their way. The partnership of the country's chief executive with their own president was a powerful force. "John L. Lewis is having beer and sauerkraut with President Roosevelt," was the word that spread through coal country, "and to hell with the company guards."

In McDowell County, in southern West Virginia, a longtime bastion of anti-union coal operators, miners paid tribute to this alliance with a ballad.

> Some people don't know who to thank,
> For this "State of McDowell" that's so free;
> Give part of the praise to John Lewis,
> And the rest of it to Franklin D.

Those were heady days. But even as his union's membership swelled at a rate that a year or two earlier scarcely seemed possible, Lewis realized that the UMW could not continue to grow, indeed might have trouble surviving, without increasing the strength of the overall labor movement. Roosevelt was a formidable force but only a sometime friend. As he sought some formula to achieve the economic recovery that still eluded him, the president frequently found it expedient to favor business over the unions.

As a pragmatist, Lewis dealt in realities. One reality was that his most dependable allies were in the labor movement itself and that he needed more of them. Another truth was that the only way to build those numbers was to organize the great bulwarks of the economy—autos, steel, and other mass-production industries. And the decisive reality was that this could be achieved only by industrial unionism, the great bugaboo of the American Federation of Labor.

The UMW itself was an industrial union, where all the workers in a mine, regardless of their particular task, were part of the same union. It had grown up that way as a result of the idiosyncratic nature of coal mining, particularly the remote locations of some mines. But the UMW, for all its power and influence, was an aberration within the AFL, nearly all of whose major unions, such as the Carpenters, the Machinists, and the Plumbers, were identified by a particular skill.

The leaders of the AFL unions had grown up with craft unionism and adapted to it. They viewed any departure from this pattern as a threat to their existence. When mass-production workers, encouraged by the changes in Washington, sought to emulate the success of the UMW and organize their own unions, the AFL stood by while these efforts perished in their infancy. Indeed in some cases the AFL craft unions, viewing these upstart organizations as intrusions on their own turf, did what they could to speed their dissolution. Despite the New Deal, in some of the nation's biggest industries organized labor was getting nowhere.

Lewis spoke out, urging the Federation to make a greater effort in the mass-production industries, utilizing the backing of the New Deal. The Supreme Court's overturning of the NIRA with its clause 7A had been almost immediately remedied by the adoption of the Wagner Act, sponsored by New York Senator Robert Wagner, which Lewis pointed out provided the same protections for organized labor. But his arguments were ignored by the Federation's hierarchy, which was less interested in organizing the unorganized than in protecting the ground already held by the unions.

Matters came to a head at the AFL convention in October 1935 in Atlantic City. Looking for a way to dramatize his cause, Lewis found it on the last day of the convention. Ohio rubber workers trying to promote industrial unionism were denied the floor on a point of order raised by "Big Bill" Hutcheson, the head of the Carpenters Union, one of the most intransigent of the AFL oligarchs and a fixture on the Republican National Committee's labor committee. Summoning his theatrical instincts, Lewis took up the rubber workers' cause, deliberately provoking Hutcheson by branding his objections "rather small potatoes."

"Well, potatoes is what I was raised on," retorted Hutcheson, who stood about six foot three and weighed more than three hundred pounds. Lewis, no puny figure himself, replied in kind, continuing to goad Hutcheson, once a poker-table pal, until the Carpenters' boss called Lewis a "bastard."

Responding as if he had never been called such a name before, Lewis vaulted a row of chairs and uncorked a right jab to the jaw that sent his old chum sprawling. While his friends helped the bleeding Hutcheson from the hall, Lewis dusted himself off, adjusted his tie, relit his cigar, and made his way to the rostrum. "You shouldn't have done that," William Green, the AFL president who had presided over the fracas remarked. "He called me a foul name," Lewis said.

"Oh, I didn't know that," Green muttered.

Lewis's haymaker not only floored Hutcheson, it reverberated through the world of American labor. Lewis was widely acclaimed as "the John L. Sullivan of the labor movement." For millions his haymaker gave vivid meaning to the conflict between craft and industrial unionism, wrote Len De Caux who witnessed the episode as a journalist. One of Hutcheson's own members, a Kansas City union carpenter, wired Lewis: "Congratulations, sock him again."

Lewis lost no time taking advantage of the moment. The next day he met with a handful of allies from other AFL unions, setting in motion plans that within a month resulted in the birth of the Committee for Industrial Organization within the AFL. For a time Lewis tried to continue to operate within the Federation, but the leadership shunned his new group. Ultimately the AFL expelled the CIO and its member unions. Meanwhile Lewis went ahead on his own, using funds from the UMW and allied unions to lay the groundwork for CIO organizing efforts.

But one item took priority on Lewis's agenda, coming ahead even of his push into the mass-production industries. This was the reelection of Franklin Roosevelt. Lewis and the CIO went all out in the 1936 presidential campaign, providing massive backing for the president. Not that Lewis was blindly devoted to FDR. "I've been sold down the river by too goddamn many politicians to trust any of them," he told one New Dealer who tried to persuade him to put his faith in Roosevelt to serve the best interests of the labor movement. For that reason much of the CIO's campaign effort in 1936 was channeled through a new organization, Labor's Non-Partisan League. It was created by Lewis to provide support not just to FDR but to other pro-labor candidates down the ballot—and perhaps, many believed, to serve as the foundation for a future independent labor party. But that was no more than a vague possibility. "We cannot forecast the future," Lewis told the *New York Times*. "There may well be new alignments in the next few years."

For the present, Lewis was enough of a realist to recognize that labor's best chance for success lay in another term for Roosevelt. The issue to be decided by the election, Lewis declared, in one of a series of radio campaign addresses, was whether working people "should have a voice in determining their destiny or whether they shall serve as indentured servants for a financial and economic dictatorship." Freedom could only be won, Lewis declared, by joining the CIO and voting for Roosevelt.

For his part, Roosevelt was by no means shy about seeking labor's support. In June the president, who had no hint at the time that he would gain a landslide victory, and believed he needed every vote labor might win for him, called Lewis to the White House to assure him that he would look after the interests of labor. Roosevelt pledged to help Lewis unionize the steel industry, famous for its antagonism to any tinge of unionism. And he read Lewis portions of the draft party platform with its reference to a constitutional amendment to curb the Supreme Court. In the next few days that language would be softened at Roosevelt's behest. But by then Lewis had given the platform his hearty public embrace. In the campaign's closing weeks Lewis stumped the country, praising Roosevelt to the skies and deriding Landon before an overflow crowd in Madison Square Garden as "just as empty, as inane, as innocuous as a watermelon that had been boiled in a bathtub."

In the argot of the working people who made up the mighty host he captained, Lewis put his union's money where his mouth was. In addition to giving more than $200,000 directly to the Democratic National Committee, the UMW spent even more on the campaign through Labor's Non-Partisan League, adding up to an unprecedented total of $600,000 in union money expended on Roosevelt's reelection.

In the wake of the president's great victory, which some in the CIO considered as much a triumph for Lewis as for FDR, the labor leader made no secret of what he expected. "We must capitalize on the election," he told the CIO executive board just after the election. "We wanted a President who would hold the light for us while we went out and organized."

In some areas FDR and the energized labor movement seemed headed down the same track. Fewer than three weeks after the election, the UMW executive board issued a public demand on Congress to limit the power of the Supreme Court to obstruct economic reforms backed by the New Deal. The high court, of course, was exactly the problem uppermost in Roosevelt's mind as he pondered the suggestions of Homer Cummings for doing just what Lewis sought.

But the success of Roosevelt and his labor allies in the election had generated a momentum of its own within the labor movement, forcing FDR and Lewis to deal with problems that neither had foreseen. From the inception of the CIO, Lewis had given steel, the nation's most basic industry, priority in the CIO's efforts to break into the mass-production industries. As for the auto industry, it seemed like an even tougher target than steel. General Motors, the nation's wealthiest corporation, was richer and more powerful than ever, thanks to the New Deal–aided economic recovery. In its obsessive determination to resist unionism it topped even U.S. Steel, its counterpart in the steel industry. In the past two years GM had spent about $1 million for private detectives to spy on union activities, making itself the largest corporate client of the Pinkerton Detective Agency. The Committee on Civil Liberties, set up under Progressive party Senator Robert M. La Follette, Jr., of Wisconsin in 1936 to probe interference with union organizing efforts, called GM's ties to Pinkerton "a monument to the most colossal super-system of spies yet devised in any American corporation."

Moreover auto workers still remembered an abortive 1934 AFL-led strike against GM when intervention by FDR did more to help the company than the union. Under the president's compromise, all union groups in the plant were given proportional representation on the bargaining committee—including the company unions set up by GM. Union members were so disgusted with the outcome of the negotiations that thousands burned their union cards.

Still, by 1936 the union movement had been reborn at GM, operating through a new group calling itself the United Auto Workers which affiliated with the CIO. In theory, if the UAW could shut down GM plants in Flint, about fifty miles north of Detroit, it could cripple production and force the company to the bargaining table. But even union activists were skeptical about the UAW's chances, given that the union could claim only 1,500 members out of GM's 42,000-man Flint labor force—and no one knew how many of those 1,500 were Pinkerton agents. After the militant UAW organizer Wyndham Mortimer took over leadership of the GM locals in Flint, he discovered, for example, that Flint GM's delegate to the most recent UAW convention had been a Pinkerton agent.

Under the circumstances, Lewis and his collaborators agreed to put off plans for assaulting the GM bastion. But their reasoning did not take into account the mood of the rank and file auto workers and the union organizers on the scene in Flint: they were driven by a combination of hope and desperation. The hope was stirred by Roosevelt's victory over Landon, despite GM's all-out backing for the Republican ticket. The desperation was fueled by the speedup in production enforced by GM as the company sought to meet the rising demand for Chevrolets in the improving economy.

The assembly line had always been an ordeal for autoworkers. "The men worked like fiends, their jaws set and eyes on fire," one observer reported in 1929 on the eve of the depression. "Nothing in the world exists for them except the line chassis bearing down on them relentlessly."

Now, as GM sought to make up for the profits it had lost during the depths of the slump, the tempo became even harder to bear. Some young workers, unused to the frantic pace, couldn't eat until they threw up their previous meal when they arrived home. One Buick worker, Gene Richards, told the *Atlantic Monthly* that he had been made so dizzy by the constant noises of the assembly line that when he left the plant he could not remember where he had parked his car.

Spurred by unrest among the autoworkers, Homer Martin, president of the fledgling UAW, wired General Motors on December 16, 1936, asking for a meeting. Martin wanted GM to bargain with the UAW as the representative for all its workers over such issues as seniority, wage scales, and the speed of the production line. The company made clear it had no intention of doing any such thing. It would bargain only on a plant-by-plant basis, GM told Martin, a procedure that would fragment the union and undermine its basic goal of gaining recognition as the sole bargaining agent for GM's workers.

UAW leaders figured they had no alternative but to call a strike. But while they pondered over when and where to force the issue, their members answered these questions on their own. They did so by resorting to a relatively novel weapon for unions — the sit-down strike. Instead of throwing a picket line around a factory, the strikers simply sat down at their machines, bringing production to a halt. This tactic offered great advantages to the UAW in its incipient stage of development. It was particularly efficient in the mass-production industries where a relatively small number of workers could shut down a factory by disrupting the assembly line. To be sure, sit-down strikers often assigned patrols to picket plant gates in small numbers, mostly for reconnaissance. But by dispensing with mass picketing the UAW avoided overburdening its limited membership.

The sit-down prevented companies from using strikebreakers to reopen their factories since the strikers stood guard at their machines. And employers were more reluctant to resort to strikebreaking violence because it might endanger millions of dollars' worth of their own equipment. Employers could get a court injunction against the strike, as they had often done in the past; but enforcing the court's order would mean driving the sit-downers out of the plant they controlled.

Sit-downs were by no means a brand-new tactic. As early as 1906 General Electric workers sat down at a Schenectady, New York, plant, and European workers staged various forms of sit-ins in the years after the Great War. But it was amidst the hard times and frustration of the depression years that sit-downs became particularly attractive devices in a number of industries, notably among Akron rubber workers as well as autoworkers. In 1936 the Labor Department recorded forty-eight sit-downs around the country. From the first, employers claimed they were illegal, but legal precedents were few and of little interest to GM's hard-pressed workers.

The nominal head of the UAW was its president, thirty-five-year-old Homer Martin, but he had many limitations in that role. A onetime Baptist minister, he was known as the "Leaping Parson" because of his skill in track and field events. Fired from his pulpit in Kansas City because he had urged autoworkers in the local Chevrolet plant to join the union, Martin found his second calling in the labor movement. His great strength was oratory. Drawing on his clerical background, he preached the union cause with religious fervor. His talks, enriched with biblical allusions, struck a chord with the thousands of Southern-born autoworkers who had found work in the auto factories of the North. Aside from his ability to preach the union gospel, Martin was a flop as leader. He lacked management skills, could not be relied upon, and too often was governed by impulse.

Thus most of the union's serious work was carried forward by a group of talented organizers, more disciplined and wiser in the ways of the auto industry than Martin. These included Wyndham Mortimer; the three Reuther brothers, Victor, Roy, and future union president Walter, then a member of the union's executive board; and Robert Travis, who had earned his spurs organizing the Chevrolet plant in Toledo.

The unorthodox approach of the sit-downs suited the aggressive attitude of these men. "They want things done right now, and they are too impatient to wait," a CIO official remarked of the UAW leaders. As Arnold Lenz, manager of the Chevrolet plant, told Roy Reuther, "The trouble with all you fellows is that you are young and full of piss and vinegar."

The UAW leadership mix also included a handful of resourceful and dedicated Communists, of whom Wyndham Mortimer was probably the most influential. Later foes of the UAW and the CIO would claim that the sit-downs were part of a Communist plot. But as even fierce anti-Communists such as Roy Reuther later agreed, the strike stemmed from worker resentment of the conditions at GM, not from Communist scheming. Later Mortimer and other Communists would become targets in bitter internecine battles within the union and would be driven out. But in Flint as the showdown with GM neared, whatever Mortimer's ties to the American Communist party, no one questioned his commitment to the UAW cause.

Overshadowing ideology was the realization shared by the Reuther brothers and Mortimer that if the UAW was to gain a foothold among the desperate autoworkers, it could not afford the luxury of patience. The union would have to take on GM, which Mortimer acknowledged to be the auto industry's "citadel of power," and it would have to move fast and hit hard.

A ballad composed by a UAW loyalist caught the mood of the men.

> When they tie the can to a union man,
> Sit down! Sit down!
> When they give him the sack they'll take him back,
> Sit down! Sit down!
> When the speedup comes, just twiddle your thumbs,
> Sit down! Sit down!
> When the boss won't talk don't take a walk,
> Sit down! Sit down!

Two dates shaped the UAW's timing: December 18, 1936, when GM workers would collect an eighty-dollar bonus, which would help tide them over during the strike; and January 1, 1937, when Frank Murphy the new governor of Michigan, elected in the 1936 Democratic landslide and known to be a friend of labor, would take office. That meant no strike until 1937, or so the UAW leaders and CIO chief Lewis agreed.

To the union strategists the targets were obvious. Production of all of GM's models depended on body dies produced at only two plants, the Fisher Body installation in Cleveland and Fisher Body No. 1 in Flint. At these factories, particularly Fisher No. 1 in Flint, the auto giant was most vulnerable.

Events moved faster than the UAW had reckoned, though not so much faster as to make an important difference. On December 28 a squabble over layoffs in one department at the Cleveland Fisher Body factory triggered a sit-down which shut the plant and idled seven thousand workers. Two days later, UAW leaders in Flint learned that GM was moving its crucial dies, focal point of the union's strike strategy, out of Fisher No. 1 in Flint and preparing to ship them to other plants that were relatively free from UAW penetration.

That night, December 30, at their 8 P.M. lunch hour, UAW leaders assembled their members at the Flint plant and laid out the situation. The response was unanimous. "Well, them's our jobs," said one man about the dies. "We want them left right in Flint."

"Shut her down, shut the goddamn plant down," another worker shouted, and others took up the cry and began sitting down at their machinery. Within an hour, when the starting whistle blew, there was no response from the production line. "She's ours," one of the strikers shouted in jubilation. For good measure, sit-downers also seized control of Fisher Body No. 2, a much smaller plant in another section of Flint.

A song called "The Fisher Strike," written by the workers to the tune of the old West Virginia folk ballad "The Martins and the Coys," told the story of the event and served to lift the spirits of the men during the long ordeal inside the factory they endured that memorable winter.

> Gather round me and I'll tell you all a story,
> Of the Fisher Body Factory Number One:
>> When the dies they started moving,
>> The union men they had a meeting,
> To decide right then and there what must be done.

These four thousand union boys,
Oh, they sure made lots of noise,
They decided then and there to shut down tight.
In the office they got snooty,
So we started picket duty,
Now the Fisher Body shop is on a strike.

The immediate exultation of the strikers did not last long; it soon became clear that they were in for a protracted fight. The conflict between the UAW, not much advanced beyond its embryonic stage, and the nation's richest corporation became the centerpiece of a national struggle that pitted the labor movement, chiefly the CIO, with the sometime help of President Roosevelt whom it had just helped reelect, against American business—and many believed against the free-enterprise system itself. For many in the business community viewed the sit-down strike as a much greater threat than any ordinary walkout because it involved the seizure of private property and rendered useless many of the weapons employers had traditionally used against conventional strikes.

John L. Lewis lost no time in entering the fray. The strikers at Flint had not followed his preferred timetable nor sought his advice on their actions. But the issues involved were too crucial for Lewis to allow those factors to make a difference. On New Year's Eve 1936, barely twenty-four hours after the Flint sit-downs began, Lewis took advantage of the radio networks' willingness to provide a platform for public figures. He bought time on NBC to bolster the strikers' cause and to demand the help of Franklin Roosevelt. By a huge majority, he contended in a nationally broadcast address, the American people had "voted for industrial democracy and reelected its champion, Franklin D. Roosevelt." That meant, as Lewis read the returns, that the days of the billy club and the tear gas grenade and other violent measures that had been used to combat unions had come to an end. In pursuing its objectives, Lewis declared, "labor will expect the protection of the federal government."

For GM the stakes were equally as high as for Lewis, the CIO, and the New Deal. The automaker could not ignore that the strike was spreading through its vast empire. In the week following the seizure of the Flint plants, with sit-downs and walkouts the UAW had shut down the Guide Lamp works in Anderson, Indiana; Chevrolet plants in Norwood and Toledo, Ohio; Chevrolet and Fisher Body factories in Janesville, Wisconsin; and the Cadillac plant in Detroit. But none of these were as menacing to the company's welfare as the three sit-downs at the Fisher Body plants in Cleveland and Flint, which among them produced bodies and parts for about three-fourths of all GM production. The shortage of these materials forced GM to shut down other plants around the country that the union had not struck.

Even before the strikes spread beyond Flint and Cleveland, GM had begun to act to squelch the union. As Lewis was putting the finishing touches on his New Year's Eve speech asking FDR's help, William Knudsen, GM executive vice president, sent word to UAW President Martin that the company regarded the sit-downers as "clearly trespassers and violators of the law of the land." There would be no bargaining, Knudsen declared, so long as the strikers remained in "illegal possession" of property.

Backing up its rhetoric, on the first working day of the New Year GM lawyers obtained an injunction from Genesee County Judge Edward D. Black, ordering the sit-downers out of the two Flint plants. They trooped into the Fisher No. 1 cafeteria to hear the local sheriff read the court's writ. When he was finished they serenaded him with "Solidarity Forever" and stayed put. Soon thereafter, union lawyers burrowing through GM's stock records found that Black owned 3,665 shares of the company's stock, worth $219,000, a holding that appeared to contravene a Michigan conflict-of-interest statute. Unfazed, Judge Black claimed that his holdings would in no way influence his judgment. But GM was discomfited enough to put its injunction strategy on the back burner, at least for the time being.

GM's next move relied on brute force and was aimed at Fisher No. 2, the more lightly held of the two UAW bastions. On January 11, the twelfth day of the strike, a platoon of company guards rushed a group of workers handing food in through the main gate of the plant, overpowered them, and slammed the gate shut. At the same time, with the temperature 16 degrees above zero, GM turned off the heat in the plant.

After union headquarters was alerted, hundreds of workers rushed to the scene to reinforce the picket line outside the plant. Some were from Buick and Chevy, some were bus drivers who had been helped by the autoworkers during their own recent strike, and some were "flying squads" in town from Toledo and Norwood, Ohio, to help out in just such emergencies.

Finding themselves outnumbered, the company guards surrendered the plant gate and took refuge behind barricades in the plant ladies room. Flint police soon arrived in force, brandishing revolvers and tear gas guns, and laid siege to the plant. But the strikers inside dragged fire hoses to the windows and drenched the police while bombarding them with two-pound door hinges and the like. To make matters worse for the cops, the wind blew the tear gas they had fired at the strikers back into their faces.

The lawmen retreated, regrouped, and made a second rush at the plant, only to be greeted by another hail of auto parts. Now the pickets, armed with missiles given to them by the sit-downers inside the plant, charged the police and drove them back. Frustrated, the police opened fire, wounding a dozen or more strikers and their allies. But when the shooting stopped, the union forces remained in command of the battlefield. On the other side, nine lawmen, including Genesee County Sheriff Thomas Wolcott and one of his deputies, were injured.

From the sound truck that served as a union command post, Victor Reuther shouted: "Let General Motors be warned; the patience of these men is not inexhaustible. If there is further bloodshed . . . we will not be responsible for what the workers do in their rage! There are costly machines in that plant," Reuther pointed out. "Let the corporation and their thugs remember that!"

In celebration of their victory at the Battle of the Running Bulls, as it came to be called, the strikers created yet another commemorative ballad. One verse, sung to the tune of "There'll Be a Hot Time in the Old Town Tonight," went like this:

> Tear gas bombs
> Were flying thick and fast
> The lousy police
> They knew they couldn't last
> Because in all their lives
> They never ran so fast
> As in that hot time
> In this old town last night

The battle was more than a tactical defeat for GM; it would have far-reaching strategic implications. The company's resort to violence and the success of the strikers in beating back the GM assault energized the strikers and bolstered their support among autoworkers in Flint and elsewhere. On the day after the battle, January 12, 1937, eight thousand workers massed in front of Fisher No. 2 to celebrate the victory. Many were from Flint, but others poured in from the other auto centers in Michigan—Detroit, Pontiac, and Saginaw—and from Toledo, Cleveland, and South Bend, Indiana.

Even more important, the fracas at Fisher No. 2 brought Michigan's newly elected governor Frank Murphy into the fray. Good news in itself for the union, Murphy's new role in Flint carried with it the hope of an even more positive development— the increasing involvement of Murphy's patron, Franklin Roosevelt, in the workers' struggle.

Murphy was a man of many parts, some of them seemingly contradictory. A devout Roman Catholic, he was also deeply committed to social welfare and to civil liberties for all, not excluding Communists. With his blue eyes, red hair, and soft-spoken charm, this lifelong bachelor was also a notably success-ful ladies man.

Murphy was born in 1890 in Sand Beach, in the Michigan Thumb, to Irish-Catholic parents who exercised distinct influ-ences on his future. His father, John Murphy, a successful lawyer who was active in Democratic party affairs, encouraged his son to study for the law and involve himself in politics. His mother Mary, said to be the ruling spirit of his heart, convinced the young man he was destined for greatness and instilled in him a willingness to abide views different from his own. Friends be-lieved that his unusually strong attachment to her accounted for his never marrying, despite his attraction for women.

After service during the Great War as an army first lieutenant, Murphy got his start in public service when friends wangled an appointment for him as an assistant U.S. attorney for the Eastern District of Michigan. He lost his first try for elective office, run-ning for Congress in 1920. But after a brief stint in private prac-tice, he won election as a judge on Detroit's recorder's court, where he handled a heavy load of criminal cases. Judge Murphy acquired a reputation for tempering justice with mercy, helping him gain the support of Detroit's liberals, blacks, and white eth-nic groups. He used moderate bail procedures to reduce the jail population and was friendlier toward organized labor than most jurists in Detroit, a city at the time dominated by the open-shop approach to labor relations.

It was Murphy's style to deprecate his own abilities and pro-fess to dislike publicity. But in reality he welcomed attention be-cause he was a man of powerful ambition, reaching as high as the White House. His aspirations were aided by his oratorical skills which helped him win applause from a broad range of audiences.

In 1930, when Detroit's mayor was ousted for incompetence in a recall election, Murphy seized the opportunity and defeated four opponents to take control of city hall. In his two years as mayor of what was then the nation's fourth largest city, Murphy reinforced his friendship with organized labor but also got along famously with auto company executives, including Walter Chrysler and Lawrence Fisher, for whose family the Fisher body plants were named. When the sit-down strike erupted, Murphy owned more than $100,000 in GM stock.

Overshadowing all this in importance for the struggle in Flint was Murphy's strong bond to Franklin Roosevelt. As the pro-labor mayor of Detroit—who some said had done more to help the unemployed than any other city official in the nation—and Michigan's leading Democrat, his support for Roosevelt's 1932 candidacy was well remembered by the president. As a reward, FDR offered the mayor the chairmanship of the Federal Trade Commission. Murphy, whose fiery idealism in no way dimmed the flame of his hopes for advancement, said he preferred to be attorney general. Since that job was already promised, Murphy settled for the governor generalship of the Philippines.

Murphy thrived in Manila and helped smooth the islands' transition from a U.S. possession to status as a commonwealth with the promise of independence. Then in 1936, at Roosevelt's urging, Murphy left his post in the Philippines and returned home to run for governor of normally Republican Michigan. FDR was counting on Murphy's popularity to help him gain reelection. As it turned out, Roosevelt scarcely needed him. The president won the state by 300,000 votes, helping pull to victory Murphy, who won by only 50,000.

Murphy's involvement in the sit-down strike, with his ties to the White House, was good news for Lewis, whose objective from the start of the strike had been, as he later put it, to dump this dispute "in the lap of one man, the President." If Roosevelt had needed any hint of Lewis's purpose, the labor leader had surely provided it in his New Year's Eve speech when he pointedly reminded Roosevelt of labor's contribution to his reelection victory.

But just as much as Lewis hoped to engage him, the president wished to stay out of the fray. Even after four years of depression, Roosevelt knew that labor unions and strikes made voters nervous. While about half of those queried in 1936 had told pollsters they favored stronger labor unions, this support tended to fade when unions went out on strike. The same month the UAW struck GM, only 17 percent of Americans said they felt sympathy for the strikers when they saw a picket line. And even in the wake of his landslide reelection, FDR was no more eager to risk his popularity than most politicians. Right now his plan to deal with the Supreme Court was bound to create as much risk as he could handle.

Given his predicament, Roosevelt must have had mixed feelings about Murphy's involvement in the clash between GM and the UAW. The president could reasonably expect Murphy to do what he could to protect the interests of labor unions and thus spare FDR from having to deal with their complaints for the moment. But he also knew that at some point Murphy might not be able to handle the struggle between the aggressive union and the intransigent company without putting his own political future at risk. At that point FDR might have to step in and bail Murphy out—which was exactly what John L. Lewis was hoping for.

For the time being, Murphy was in charge and behaved much as FDR and the union expected him to. Rushing to Flint in the wake of the January 11 violence, the new governor vowed to preserve the peace. He immediately mobilized twelve hundred National Guardsmen, a number that would increase threefold before the next month was out, and dispatched them to Flint. GM officials were at first elated. They expected, based on the past history of governors and presidents calling out troops, that the soldiers would be deployed to break the strike.

Company officials must have been astounded when they learned that the strikers cheered the very news that GM regarded as its salvation. The workers had a better sense than their bosses of how Murphy would use the Guard. It was not the troops themselves the workers cheered, explained Henry Kraus, editor of the *United Auto Worker* and the *Flint Auto Worker*, "but the arm of the governor that they trusted would be used to re-establish peace, and halt the violence of General Motors."

Murphy did not let them down, but he had to walk a tightrope. On the one hand he made it clear that he regarded the strike as an illegal trespass and that he would preserve order. "This is not going to be a brawl," he announced as soon as he arrived. But he also let it be understood that he did not intend to use the Guard to evict the strikers, only to quell violence that the local police could not control. Indeed the Guardsmen spent their time standing by and scrubbing floors at the abandoned junior high school where they bivouacked.

Murphy's first accomplishment was to persuade union leaders and GM officials to meet in his office in Lansing and reach a preliminary agreement: the strikers would evacuate the plants, after which the company would meet with the union officials to discuss their demands.

But just as the January 17 deadline neared for the Flint sitdowners to leave their posts, the deal fell through. A journalist tipped union leaders that GM had already agreed to meet with the Flint Alliance, a group of workers backed by GM and loyal to the company, which the UAW regarded as the equivalent of a company union. Charging betrayal by the company, union leaders called off the evacuation. The strike dragged on.

Typically Homer Martin, missing the significance of the GM strategy, at first wanted the evacuation to go forward as scheduled. But when Robert Travis, the union official in charge at the struck plants ignored his advice, Martin delivered a fiery speech denouncing GM's breach of faith.

With the UAW and GM at an impasse, FDR's involvement increased gradually but steadily. Striving to stay out of the line of fire, at first he sought to use his labor secretary, Frances Perkins, as a proxy. This would have been a severe challenge for anyone; it was particularly difficult for Perkins, or Madam Secretary, as she was often referred to in public, the first woman to serve in a presidential cabinet.

A thoughtful and dedicated public servant, Perkins had a solid grasp of the issues that confronted the labor movement. But she lacked experience at this level of high-pressure, high-level negotiations. And for reasons that had probably more to do with the prevailing male chauvinism of the day than with her own abilities, she did not command the full respect of the parties involved.

Born and raised in New England to conservative Republican parents, Perkins was fifty-one years old when Roosevelt appointed her to his cabinet and had already battled for the rights of workers for three decades. Equipped with a master's degree in sociology from Columbia, and inspired by witnessing firsthand the horrors of the 1911 Triangle Shirtwaist fire, she lobbied the New York legislature for stronger safety laws for women.

Perkins married Paul Wilson, a New York City official, but defying the conventions of the day she continued to use her maiden name professionally. In 1916 she gave birth to a daughter and thought her career was over. But two years later Al Smith, whom she had known as a promising legislator from her lobbying days, won the New York governorship and made her chairman of the state's Industrial Commission. Franklin Roosevelt, when he succeeded Smith in the governor's mansion, chose her to head the state's labor department.

Determined to be taken seriously, Perkins dressed modestly, habitually wearing a simple black dress with a white bow and a small tricorn hat that became her trademark. Despite her demure manner she was not easily browbeaten, and her dry sense of humor helped ward off gender bias. When a reporter asked if being a woman was a handicap, she answered coolly: "Only when climbing trees."

But her critics were not easily disarmed. When her cabinet appointment was announced, labor leaders complained loudly because she had never been affiliated with a trade union. "Labor can never become reconciled to the selection made," said AFL president William Green. And despite Perkins's obvious dedication to the union cause, she remained underappreciated within union ranks. Lewis, for example, doubted that she had the ability or the prestige to challenge the big corporations, a skepticism that unfortunately for Perkins tended to validate itself.

Her efforts to bring the fledgling union and the giant automaker to the bargaining table began January 19, 1937, and ran into difficulties immediately. Asked to order the strikers out of the plants as a prelude to negotiations, Lewis flatly refused. GM, for its part, refused to meet with Lewis as long as the sit-downers were in control of the company's property. As a concession, GM did agree to meet in Washington with Perkins and Governor Murphy on January 20, 1937, which happened to be the day FDR was sworn in for a second term.

Perkins left the inaugural stand to attend the meeting; Murphy never got to attend the inauguration at all. For all that they accomplished, they could have stayed and watched the parade. Alfred P. Sloan, the sixty-year-old president of General Motors, was adamant that he would not bargain while the strikers controlled the plants in Flint. Sloan was said by many to have perfected the art of managing a behemoth corporation during his thirteen-year tenure at the top of GM. First he created a corporate office, whose job was to allocate resources and coordinate the company's operating divisions but not to run them. From this nerve center, every branch of the auto company got whatever it needed—money, factories, sales forces—to operate autonomously. To link the divisions, Sloan promulgated a set of "standard procedures" for budgeting, hiring, forecasting, reporting sales, and the like. Under Sloan, GM appeared to have the proper amount of central control, divisional independence, and plenty of ways to share ideas. One thing it did not have was a union, and Sloan was determined to keep it that way.

GM and the DuPont Company, the principal GM shareholder since the company nearly went belly-up in the postwar slump of 1920, had done all they could to defeat Roosevelt in the 1936 campaign. After the vote, GM had been warned by one of its own executives, Stephen DuBrul, that because of its stand in the election it would be "particularly vulnerable" in any showdown with the UAW. GM would have to bend over backward to appear fair, but by doing so it could put the union "on the defensive both with the public and the Administration." The objective for the auto company, DuBrul advised, should be to make Lewis, whom DuBrul rated as "probably the keenest labor strategist in the nation," seem to be an "obstructionist." But if Sloan had ever read DuBrul's advice, he chose to disregard it. And by his hard-line tactics he created for Lewis an opening that the labor leader would exploit to the fullest.

At a post-inaugural press conference Lewis boldly appealed directly for FDR's intervention to break the logjam over the Flint strike. This was no time for "neutrality and pussyfooting," Lewis declared. He pointed out that during the campaign the "economic royalists" of General Motors—a phrase coined by FDR himself in accepting nomination to a second term—"contributed their money and used their energy to drive this administration out of power."

Then, in the unlikely circumstance that anyone might forget the CIO's massive financial and organizational support for Roosevelt, he added: "The administration asked labor for help to repel this attack and labor gave its help." The time to return the favor had now arrived. "The same economic royalists now have

their fangs in labor," Lewis said. "And the workers expect the administration in every reasonable and legal way to support the
autoworkers in their fight with the same rapacious enemy."

That was enough for Sloan, who had never wanted to come
to Washington in the first place. Now he told Perkins he was leaving town and that further meetings were futile in view of Lewis's
remarks.

FDR himself delivered a mild reproof to Lewis. "I think in
the interest of peace, there come moments when statements,
conversation and headlines are not in order," he said.

The CIO leader had no trouble shrugging that off. "I do not
believe the president meant to rebuke the working people of
America who are his friends and who are only attempting to obtain rights guaranteed to them by Congress," he said. Instead
Lewis concentrated his ire on General Motors and Sloan's refusal
to bargain. "Perhaps," he needled, "he feels his intellectual inferiority to me."

Despite the flap over Lewis's comments, the pressure was
now on Sloan and the administration. Perkins issued a formal invitation to Lewis and Sloan to meet in Washington "without condition or prejudice." Lewis shrewdly accepted. Sloan, as Lewis
probably guessed he would do, refused.

With the help of Lewis, Perkins, and FDR, Sloan had managed to make himself seem unreasonable, a circumstance Roosevelt quickly pointed out. Sloan, the president informed his
January 26 press conference, "had made a very unfortunate decision." Told that the GM president had indicated he would accept
an invitation directly from the White House, Roosevelt seemed
personally offended. "A representative of the president did ask
him to come down," he snapped.

Perkins was more vehement. Her face flushed, she called
Sloan and GM "high-handed" and charged that they had "made
the mistake of their lives in failing to see the moral issues here."
As to the illegality of the sit-downs alleged by GM, a charge

unanimously backed by other corporations, that issue, Perkins said, was "unexplored." Her remark, suggesting ambiguity about an issue that many regarded as clear as the distinction between good and evil, would bring down on her head the wrath of business leaders and conservative politicians.

Meanwhile, though, Madame Secretary soldiered on. The very next day after chastising Sloan, Perkins asked Congress for authority to deal with strikes by subpoenaing the principals and requiring them to negotiate. GM did not need private detectives to figure out who that measure was aimed at.

Still Perkins did not give up on persuasion. She pressured Sloan to come back to Washington to meet with her and union leaders on January 29. Sloan agreed, or so Perkins believed. But there was no meeting. Sloan did not appear and claimed he had never really committed to the idea. Perkins thought otherwise. In a comment that delighted headline writers everywhere, she snapped: "He ran out on me." On the verge of tears, the champion of the downtrodden confessed to reporters: "It seems that all of my work has gone to waste."

The rhetorical battle in Washington gave some hope to the strikers. "Sloan has been criticized by Roosevelt and Perkins," the January 27 minutes of the Cleveland sit-down strikers noted. "We are in a better position now."

But that was by no means clear. Even if GM had embarrassed itself, it was no more willing to give ground, any more than the union was.

The stalemate continued, posing a sizable problem for Franklin Roosevelt at a time when he did not need additional headaches. For as FDR well knew, his determination to put the U.S. Supreme Court in what he believed was its proper place was about to test his leadership skills at least as severely as the struggle between GM and the CIO in Michigan.

3

Answer to a Maiden's Prayer

For millions of Americans, the Great Depression was a disaster, stealing their jobs and their savings, ruining their dreams. But for Homer Cummings the nation's economic collapse turned into a burst of personal good fortune, reviving his dormant political life and elevating it to heights he would never even have dared imagine. The rise of Homer Stillé Cummings could serve as a gauge of the standards and values that had all too often shaped American politics, underpinning the system that Franklin Roosevelt tried to control and manipulate. Intellectual toughness and philosophical conviction did not carry Homer Cummings to the upper echelons of the New Deal; these were not his strengths. He relied instead on the conscientious application of his energies to whatever task was at hand, a talent for ingratiating himself with his peers and superiors, and a flair for self-promotion.

Until the events that followed the 1929 crash opened the way for Roosevelt and the New Deal, Cummings appeared to have reached the zenith of his career a decade earlier, in the criminal courts of Connecticut. There as a county prosecutor he won national attention by clearing an innocent man charged with murder.

From the start he did not lack for the advantages and ambition that normally lead to success. Cummings was born to affluence in the home of a prominent Chicago cement manufacturer and educated in private schools and Yale University, which awarded him both a bachelor's and a law degree. With the help of his Yale contacts he set up practice in what was then the small Connecticut town of Stamford, and then as soon as he could entered politics as a Democrat. He claimed to have been attracted by the idealism of William Jennings Bryan's populist rhetoric with its promise of social justice. But it may well have occurred to him that in Connecticut, as in most of New England, there was more room in the Democratic party than among the dominant Republicans.

In 1900, when he was only thirty, Cummings was elected mayor of Stamford, then a town of about five thousand, and twice reelected. But it was hard for him to climb much higher than that—he was beaten three times, once running for Congress and twice seeking a Senate seat—until he gained the Fairfield County prosecutor's post in 1914, a ten-year job. He did much better with his colleagues in the Democratic party, who made him their national chairman in 1919. At the 1920 convention, where he was the keynote speaker, he put in a good word for an upcoming New Yorker with a famous name, Franklin D. Roosevelt, and may have helped Roosevelt win the vice-presidential nomination. In any event FDR was said to have thought so, and to have remembered this support long afterward.

After the Democratic debacle in the 1920 elections, Cummings returned to his post as prosecutor in Fairfield County. In his final year the murder of a popular local priest, Father Hubert Dahme, led to his most memorable courtroom achievement. Father Dahme was shot down as he walked the streets of downtown Bridgeport for no apparent motive, and the senselessness of the crime shocked and terrorized the community. A week later a vagrant named Harold Israel was arrested, and after being questioned and identified by witnesses as the killer, ultimately confessed to the crime. It seemed, as the saying goes, an open-and-shut case.

But as Cummings began to prepare for trial, his own investigation turned up one fact after another that contradicted the supposedly ironclad evidence against the suspect. Another prosecutor might have issued a statement clearing Israel, released him, and let it go at that. But not Cummings. Given the opportunity to free an innocent man, he decided to do it with a flourish. He let the case go to trial, and on the first day he rose to make his opening statement. A tall, stooping figure of a man who wore a gold-rimmed pince-nez and usually a melancholy expression, Cummings held everyone's attention as he first presented the case for the prosecution—then, with his customary slow delivery, proceeded to demolish it point by point. The trial was over, the defendant would soon be released, and Cummings became a hero in Connecticut and around the country. The Wickersham Commission on Law Enforcement cited Cummings's handling of the charges against Israel favorably, and years later it would become the basis for a popular movie, *Boomerang*.

All the glory Cummings collected did him no good in national politics. Before the next month was out he endured what was probably the most frustrating and humbling experience of his life, as platform chairman of the infamous Democratic Convention of 1924. At that gathering the search for a nominee was overshadowed by passionate disagreements over prohibition, the Ku Klux Klan, and fundamentalist religion. It was Cummings's task somehow to patch together a platform that would reconcile these schisms. His usually morose countenance seemed even sadder than ever as, despite his efforts, the debate over the platform descended into chaos after a proposal to condemn the Ku Klux Klan was defeated by one vote. Only a thousand-man contingent of New York's finest avoided what probably would have been a full-scale riot. Even so, things were bad enough. Delegates went beyond name-calling to brawling in the aisles while the galleries howled and stomped.

The convention dragged on for a record 14 days and 103 ballots, finally nominating John W. Davis, a handsome Wall Street lawyer with only limited political talent and experiences, who failed to win 30 percent of the popular vote in the 1924 election. Like nearly everyone else prominently involved in that disastrous conclave, Cummings suffered for it. His failure to bridge the deep intraparty divisions, and his support for the early front-runner, William Gibbs McAdoo, who had somehow gotten involved with the defenders of the Klan, made him persona non grata in many party circles. Absent from the political stage, he concentrated on his law firm and his personal life. In 1928, when the Democratic party nominated for president Al Smith, whom Cummings had opposed in 1924, Cummings was not on the scene. Nor did he have much to say in his own state of Connecticut, where Smith's backers ruled.

For Cummings the main event of the year was a divorce, his second in two years, followed the next year by his third marriage. To some in Fairfield County this behavior seemed out of keeping with prevailing mores and standards. Indeed, when Cummings took his third wife, Mary Cecillia Waterbury, in 1929, the Episcopal bishop of Connecticut, Edward Campion Acheson, the father of Dean Acheson, was sufficiently troubled to deny the happy couple the sanction of the church. Cummings found church blessing for his nuptials in another denomination, but he did not forget this slight.

By 1932, however, with the brightening of Democratic prospects and the fast-emerging presidential candidacy of another New York governor, Cummings returned to the political game in earnest. Whatever debt Roosevelt may have believed he owed to Cummings as a result of the 1920 convention, Cummings was

determined to increase that obligation several fold. Scouring the
country, calling in every chit owed him from the past, he re-
cruited no fewer than twenty-four senators and an even greater
number of House members for FDR's bandwagon. As convention delegates assembled in June 1932 in Chicago, Cummings,
taking on the mantle of Roosevelt's floor manager, swung into
high gear. But his enthusiasm sometimes blurred his judgment.

At the convention Cummings displayed a tendency to over-
play his hand, which would have troublesome consequences a
few years later. First, he went all out in his home state of Connecticut, determined to get all its delegates for FDR. Had Cummings been willing to bargain, Roosevelt might have come away
with half. As it was, under the unit rule, all the Nutmeg State's
sixteen votes went to Al Smith and stayed with him for all four
ballots.

Roosevelt survived that. But he might not have been able to
withstand the impact of another Cummings maneuver had
Cummings not been talked out of pursuing it. In 1932, as in
nearly all the party's previous history, Democratic conventions
required a two-thirds majority for nomination, one of the causes
of the 1924 deadlock. Fearing that something of the sort might
happen again, Cummings planned to address the convention
and ask for a change in the rule. But cooler heads in the Roosevelt camp prevailed. They feared that such a speech would
boomerang by inflaming the South, which viewed the rule as a
safeguard for its regional interests, and wind up turning Dixie's
delegates against FDR.

In the end Roosevelt overcame the two-thirds rule by cutting
the deal that gave the vice-presidential nomination to Garner and
gained FDR the votes from California and Texas that put him
over the top on the fourth ballot. As for Cummings, his spirited
seconding speech for Roosevelt drowned out the grumbles about
his mistaken advice on strategy.

Cummings campaigned hard for his candidate that fall, and with FDR's election launched another campaign—for his own appointment as attorney general of the United States. For two solid months he contacted nearly everyone he knew of influence. Among them were Joseph Davies, later to become the first U.S. ambassador to the Soviet Union. Playing coy, Cummings asked Davies if he did not think "anyone was foolish to want to be attorney general." Davies, going along with Cummings's artifice, agreed with emphasis, calling such an ambition "perfectly idiotic in view of what the attorney general is going to be up against." But, he added, "it is a sort of a responsibility that has to be assumed when the time comes."

No one doubted that Cummings thought himself ready for that burden. But two formidable obstacles stood in his way. One was the fact that for all his efforts during the fall, he had been unable to carry his own state, Connecticut, into the Democratic column on election day. Another more formidable problem was the imposing presence of Montana Senator Thomas J. Walsh, one of the most distinguished and respected public figures of his time. Sent to the Senate in 1912, Walsh rewarded Montanans with twenty years of unstinting though unspectacular service on behalf of such progressive causes as the banning of child labor and the granting of woman suffrage.

Walsh's work was little known outside Capitol Hill until 1922 when, as a result of his reputation for probity, he was chosen by his peers to head the Senate investigation into the Teapot Dome scandal. His work exposed the sordid details of the various oil-lease transactions that stained the Harding administration and led to the conviction of Harding's interior secretary Albert Fall on bribery charges.

As chairman of the 1924 Democratic National Convention, the same gathering that had damaged Cummings's political career, Walsh's poised oversight of the tangled proceedings so impressed the delegates that they offered him the vice-presidential nomination, which he prudently refused. In 1932, when he chaired the Democratic Convention that nominated FDR, he was able to draw on his experience of 1924 to help avoid another such disastrous deadlock.

It did not take Roosevelt long to select Walsh as his attorney general. Cummings would have to settle for the governor generalship of the Philippines. None of the choices Roosevelt made for his cabinet seemed more logical or stirred wider approbation than did the selection of Walsh, who was generally recognized for standing apart from most of his fellow practitioners. Said the solidly Republican *New York Sun*: "No wise Democratic politician is likely to go to him in his new job looking for special favors. It would be like asking the statue of Civic Virtue for a chew of tobacco."

This was not the sort of observation that would be made about the man who ultimately took the position that fate snatched from Walsh. For the seventy-three-year-old Walsh a new life seemed to be dawning in more ways than one. Ten days before FDR's inauguration the attorney general–designate, a widower for fifteen years after a twenty-seven-year marriage to a schoolteacher he met in the Dakota Territory, traveled to Havana to take a new bride. She was Señora Maria Nieves Perez Chaumont de Truffin, the widow of a Cuban banker and sugar grower. The excitement may have been too much for the old reformer. As he prepared to travel to Washington for the inauguration, Walsh became ill for several days in Florida. He died on a northbound train early on the morning of March 2, 1933.

Roosevelt got the news that same day as he was boarding a train from New York to Washington. The very next day he called Cummings to his hotel room in the capital and told him that the job he had sought and failed to get was at last his. Yet he hedged the decision, telling Cummings he had not given up on sending him to the Philippines. Roosevelt claimed the job in Manila was sensitive because of tensions brewing in the Far East. Worries stemmed from the new militarist regime in Japan, which had seized Manchuria the year before and was now greedily eyeing China.

It would have taken a far more obtuse man than Homer Cummings not to get the point of this conversation. However much the president was troubled about the threat of war in Asia, Cummings was not exactly the man to deal with that, having never lived outside the United States in his life and having spent zero days on diplomacy. What was clear was that Roosevelt was putting Cummings on notice: he had been tendered the job that Walsh was supposed to get, but he only had it on probation. It was not the sort of thing that even Roosevelt would have broached to Tom Walsh, the elder statesman. But dealing with Cummings, the eager supplicant who had only recently returned from the political wilderness, was far easier, and for Roosevelt more convenient. There is no reason to believe that Cummings would not have set out to do all he could to please Franklin Roosevelt no matter what the circumstances. But now he had more incentive than ever to do so.

And there was no secret about what FDR expected from his attorney general. Most presidents look to that officer to find good constitutional reasons against their doing the things they would prefer to avoid, and to find ways around the Constitution and the law to do the things close to their hearts. In this regard Franklin Roosevelt was no different from the others except he was more open about his inclinations. "If you are a good attorney general, tell me how I can do it," was the order he gave those who served him as chief legal officers of the land.

This instruction Cummings followed unblinkingly, as he demonstrated immediately after Roosevelt took office. To deal with the nation's banking crisis created by the depression, Roosevelt wanted to take bold action—to close all banks and to curb the export of gold. But what authority did he have? The only law that came to mind was the Trading with the Enemy Act, adopted to deal with the economic challenges of the Great War. Could that be applied in time of peace?

Just a few days before FDR was to take office, outgoing President Herbert Hoover was considering taking similar drastic action and was pondering the same issue. It was extremely doubtful, Hoover told FDR at a dramatic meeting just before the transfer of power, that the wartime legislation was still valid. His own attorney general thought it was not—and the use of these powers under this cloud of uncertainty could create an even more dangerous situation if Hoover's actions were challenged. Roosevelt replied that he would put that question to his own attorney general, Homer Cummings, as soon as he and Cummings had taken office.

A few days later, on Sunday, March 5, the day after he was inaugurated, the president called a meeting of his newly installed cabinet, raised the issue of the validity of the Trading with the Enemy Act, and, turning to his freshly minted attorney general, asked: "How much time will you require to prepare an opinion?"

Cummings did not hesitate. "Mr. President, I am ready to give my opinion now," he replied.

The financial disaster that now threatened the nation's banking system, Cummings said, was tantamount to the crisis of wartime, so the president could use the wartime law. Cummings had passed his first test. Within a week Roosevelt informed him that his probation was over. Michigan's Frank Murphy would handle the crisis in the Far East from the Philippines post. Cummings would stay on as attorney general.

But while he was clearly a team player on policy matters, Cummings was less tractable on matters of personnel, particularly on the question of who would be his solicitor general. As the president's litigator in chief and his envoy to the judiciary, particularly the Supreme Court, the occupant of that office is of great importance in every administration. It was anticipated, and accurately so, that the solicitor general would be particularly important in Franklin Roosevelt's administration, where the urgent perils facing the nation were bound to call for the kinds of solutions that would invite legal challenge. The background of FDR's attorney general, as a country lawyer, small-town prosecutor, and political operative, made it even more necessary—as Roosevelt's unofficial legal advisers, Felix Frankfurter and Justice Louis Brandeis pointed out—that the solicitor general be a lawyer of high quality and scholarly achievement.

Frankfurter, Roosevelt's old friend and confidant from their days together in the Wilson administration, had been FDR's first choice for the job but had turned it down; he would be of greater service to the president, he maintained, as a sort of jack-of-all-trades adviser. But Frankfurter and Brandeis soon had another candidate for the job, one of the brightest stars of one of Washington's most prestigious law firms, Dean Acheson.

A former law clerk to Brandeis and a protégé of Justice Holmes, Acheson had established himself as one of the nation's top appellant lawyers and was already a familiar figure as a litigant in the chambers of the Supreme Court. If Frankfurter and Brandeis had anything to say about it, he would soon appear before the Court as a regular. They pressed his name on FDR, who in turn asked Cummings if it would be "all right" to name Acheson as solicitor general.

"No, it's not all right," was the answer. And that was the end of it. Only later did Acheson learn why the usually complaisant Cummings had turned him down. The explanation came from Acheson's father the bishop, who told him of his disapproval of Cummings's 1928 marriage. After waiting five years, Cummings had finally gotten his revenge for this snub.

But if Cummings was determined to keep Acheson out of his Justice Department, he was nowhere near as fussy about who he let in. The department became a patronage cow for Democratic officeholders, whose party for a dozen years had had no federal jobs to award. Now party leaders, with a free hand from the attorney general, made up for lost time, staffing Justice with a flood of second-raters. Of course political patronage and the Justice Department have never been total strangers. But the challenge for every attorney general is to find party loyalists who are also skillful lawyers. Under Cummings, the latter part of the equation seemed to have been neglected. After he had been in office barely two years, Frankfurter and Harold Ickes spent part of a morning brooding over the situation, which Frankfurter had discussed with FDR. "The President now thoroughly understands the weakness of the Justice Department," Ickes wrote in his diary. "It is indeed weak. It is full of political appointees. It has some hard working earnest lawyers, but no outstanding ones."

Perhaps the weakest link in the chain of ineptness was the man who got the job that Dean Acheson did not get—a sixty-year-old North Carolina lawyer named James Crawford Biggs. He was appointed because in the early confusion surrounding the staffing of the new administration, after Acheson had been turned down, no one could think of anyone else. A trial lawyer who lacked appellate experience and grounding in constitutional law, Biggs floundered around like a ship with a hole in its side and soon exhausted the patience of the Supreme Court. In his first five months he lost ten of seventeen cases.

"Mr. Solicitor General, you have talked for 45 minutes already," Chief Justice Hughes admonished him on one occasion. "You had better take the next 15 minutes telling us what you want this court to do." Biggs resigned in March 1935 to be replaced by the vastly more experienced Stanley Reed, a former Hoover appointee who served as solicitor general until he was eventually elevated to the Supreme Court. But damage to New Deal legislation and to the administration's credibility in the eyes of the Supreme Court had already been done.

While others fretted about the mediocrity of his lawyers, the attorney general had other priorities. He set out to establish his department as a sort of legal empire in the Roosevelt administration. Whereas in the past the various agencies had conducted their own litigation in the lower federal courts, Roosevelt, prodded by Cummings, issued an executive order placing the Justice Department in charge of all federal litigation. Determined to make a name for himself as a legal reformer, Cummings overhauled the rules of practice and procedure in federal courts and extended the authority of federal law enforcement against kidnapping, bank robbery, and firearms. To enhance his department's prestige and his own, he convoked a national conference on crime and published two books, *We Can Prevent Crime* and *Federal Justice*. And all of this was in addition to overseeing the secret effort to find a way to set the Supreme Court back on its heels.

But for all his bureaucratic striving, Cummings's primary mission remained to help clear the New Deal's legal path, a role that would soon once again cause him to cross paths with Dean Acheson. Just as FDR had called upon him to bless his plan for a bank holiday on his first day in office, in September the president asked Cummings to endorse another unorthodox response to the nation's economic crisis.

This time the president wanted to buy gold at a higher value than the price set by statute. The idea was to devalue the dollar, which was tied to gold, thereby creating inflation and hopefully breathing life into the still-stagnant economy. To accomplish this, FDR's advisers concocted a complicated scheme for getting around the law by using the Reconstruction Finance Corporation (RFC), which had been established by President Hoover at the outset of the depression, to buy the gold. But Dean Acheson, in the post of Treasury undersecretary, the man who would actually purchase the gold at the new and higher price, balked. He argued that despite all the administrative hocus-pocus, the plan was illegal and also immoral since it amounted to cheating purchasers of government bonds whose securities would lose some of their value.

Facing a dilemma, Acheson went to his old mentor Justice Brandeis to ask whether, if Cummings ruled the plan legal, he should buy the gold. He could not have been greatly surprised at the response. "Dean, if I wanted a legal opinion I would prefer to get it from you rather than from Homer Cummings," Brandeis told him.

His back stiffened by these words from Old Isaiah, Acheson stood his ground until FDR would no longer tolerate his resistance. He was summoned to a meeting with Cummings, who insisted that the plan was legal and told Acheson to do his duty. After a few more days of defiance, Acheson at last consented. Soon thereafter FDR ordered him fired because the president believed that Acheson was leaking information to the press critical of the policy.

But Acheson's departure did not end the controversy over the administration's gold-buying policies. In 1934 bondholders brought suit challenging another aspect of the president's actions on gold. Cummings took over as lead lawyer in the case from other New Deal attorneys. Not only that, he went to see Chief Justice Hughes to ask special permission to make his argument to the tribunal before the petitioners presented their case, so he would not have to respond to what they said. That would have contradicted the Court's normal procedure, something Hughes was unwilling to accept, particularly since, as he pointed out to Cummings, the attorney for the petitioner was a young lawyer who would be arguing his first case before the Supreme Court. "Cummings was quite miffed," another Justice Department lawyer observed.

Such behavior on Cummings's part fed resentment of him among other New Dealers and bolstered the impression of the attorney general as a man whose ambitious reach often exceeded his professional grasp. By Raymond Moley's account, both Tom Corcoran and Ben Cohen, the two brightest stars in the New Deal legal firmament, regarded the attorney general with "undisguised intellectual disdain." Yet this negative view of Cummings held by some of his peers did not seem to disturb the New Dealer whose opinion mattered most, the man in the Oval Office. It was not so much that FDR was unaware of Cummings's limitations as that for the president they did not matter much. In a sense, Roosevelt turned to Cummings as his chief adviser on dealing with the Supreme Court—arguably the most serious crisis of his presidency—not despite Cummings short-comings but because of them.

Certainly Roosevelt had more imposing legal minds he could have enlisted, notably Corcoran and Cohen, architects of many of the New Deal's innovative remedies; Donald Richberg, the former law partner of Harold Ickes, who had been general counsel to the NRA; and the new solicitor general, Stanley Reed. These were strong minds and strong personalities, independent thinkers all. FDR's decision to include them out and instead turn to Cummings reflected his idiosyncrasies in using the people around him in decision making.

Roosevelt made it a point to collect advisers of intellectual prowess and far-reaching imagination; they helped him generate ideas and not incidentally enhanced his prestige. The president showed his recognition of that advantage when, just after his nomination, he shrewdly coined the term "Brain Trust" to describe them, a cognomen which, as his counselor Sam Rosenman wrote, "like the phrase 'New Deal' itself, would catch the popular imagination."

FDR was no intellectual himself and did not pretend to be one. He read books only on occasion; he got his information from newspapers, correspondence, government documents, brief memos from aides, and conversations with visitors he trusted. And he took care not to be dominated by any of his strong-willed advisers. Although they surrounded him, he kept them all at a distance and was wary of surrendering too much authority to any of them.

If he had a fundamental rationale for making decisions, he kept it to himself. "Franklin allowed no one to discover the governing principle," Rex Tugwell once said. To prevent overconcentration of authority in the hands of any one adviser, he blurred lines of authority and responsibility. He also took advantage of the natural competitiveness of his advisers to pit one against the other. While this was frustrating for those who served him, it protected Roosevelt's own zone of authority and increased his ability to manipulate them. "Mr. President, you should do it my way and not yours," James Rowe, an administrative assistant to Roosevelt once told the president about a personnel move Roosevelt wanted to make.

"No, James, I do not have to do it your way, and I will tell you the reason why," Roosevelt replied. "The reason is that, although they may have made a mistake, the people of the United States elected me president, not you."

Rowe, a former law clerk to Justice Holmes, a Harvard law graduate, and a brilliant lawyer, was probably Cummings's superior in credentials and ability. But he was also more likely to challenge the president. Finding a way to restrain the Supreme Court was challenge enough. It was the most difficult problem of his presidency, and Roosevelt did not want an adviser who would make it more difficult by pointing out all the flaws that would doubtless exist in whatever solution the president adopted. He simply wanted someone who would help him implement the solution he favored.

In this regard he could count on Homer Cummings. Roosevelt would not have to remind Cummings who was president. After all, it was Roosevelt who had rescued Cummings from the political wasteland of private practice in suburban Connecticut. And in return for this Roosevelt could count on Cummings's overflowing gratitude and, of more practical importance, his unswerving obedience.

Cummings's loyalty had been reinforced by his pride in the assignment Roosevelt had given him on his first day back at the

White House after his reelection victory: to look into ways to curb the power of the Supreme Court. For the next couple of weeks, as Cummings scurried back and forth to the White House nearly every day, slipping in and out through a private entrance, gathering material for Roosevelt to take on his vacation cruise, the attorney general was in a state of advanced euphoria.

By now Cummings had caught the drift of Roosevelt's thinking and learned to angle his advice in the direction where it was most likely to get attention and approval when the two met on the day after Christmas. A constitutional amendment had been ruled out by FDR for several reasons. Chief among them were that it would take too long to gain approval and would be too easy to block. Operating from that premise, Cummings had told the president that it wasn't the Constitution that needed changing — thus bolstering what the president wanted to believe. Rather, Cummings argued, the justices were the problem, the "Nine Old Men" who must be either changed or somehow diminished in authority. That much was well understood by both men before their meeting. But now Cummings had something new to bring to the table.

He had found a way to deal with these troublesome justices, a method made particularly appealing because it came right from the enemy camp, specifically from Justice James McReynolds, archest of the archconservatives. In 1913, while serving as attorney general for the most recent previous Democratic president, Woodrow Wilson, McReynolds had recommended that when any judge of a federal court, other than a Supreme Court justice, who had served for at least ten years, continuously or otherwise, failed to retire at age seventy, the president could nominate an additional judge to sit on the same court.

"This," wrote McReynolds, "will insure at all times the presence of a judge sufficiently active to discharge promptly and adequately all the duties of the court." The fact that McReynolds had specifically exempted Supreme Court justices from his proposal did not deter Cummings one bit. If the principle of compensating for aged judges with new appointments was valid for the lower courts, it would surely be just as sound for the highest court, which, he told the president, had been the subject of "a good deal of criticism" because it had failed to grant review "in many important cases."

The genius of Cummings's plan was that enlarging the lower courts "would throw more burden on the Supreme Court." Therefore, as he told the president, "it was perfectly fair" that the Supreme Court should also have a larger membership to manage this extra work. This reasoning, or so Cummings contended, would help shield the proposal against the inevitable charges of Court-packing. Inherent in Cummings's scheme was the seed of subterfuge. While he and the president had probably been "unduly terrified" by the phrase "Court-packing," he conceded that "there was a discernible and substantial objection in the country to making a deliberate addition to the Supreme Court bench for the purpose of meeting the present situation," by which he evidently meant the opposition of conservative justices to the New Deal.

But if all the president wanted was to make the Court larger and more youthful, and thus supposedly more efficient, the charge of Court packing would lose much of its weight. His plan was "not free from objection," Cummings conceded. "But it was freer from objection than any plan that had yet come to my attention."

So Homer Cummings contended. And so Franklin Roosevelt wanted to believe.

The net result, Cummings argued, would be all but certain to end FDR's troubles with the Court. If this law could be adopted, Cummings pointed out to the president, given that six of the nine justices had passed the seventy-year benchmark, FDR would be able to make no fewer than six appointments of his own. That ought to provide a majority strong enough to shepherd New Deal legislation to safety.

"We could afford to take our chances with six new judges on the Supreme Court," Cummings said, together with the three sitting justices friendly to the New Deal. "We could then look for decisions of a progressive nature and probably get all we ought to get and all we need to get to carry on our program."

If Roosevelt had misgivings about Cummings's proposal, he did not mention them. To the contrary, Cummings said, he "expressed approval of almost every sentence" in the memorandum on the plan that Cummings read to him and "began to talk of ways to put it into effect." The more FDR thought about it, the more he liked it. He came to regard Cummings's plan, he later told an intimate, as "the answer to a maiden's prayer."

Cummings made a point of telling the president that, as instructed, he had held knowledge of the plan close to his vest, sharing it with no one except Stanley Reed, the solicitor general, "just to get his reaction and under seal of strictest confidence."

Ben Cohen and Tom Corcoran were so much in the dark that they had been developing their own solution to the Court problem. Unaware that the president had agreed to Cummings's approach, they kept at it, eventually recommending a constitutional amendment that would permit a two-thirds majority of Congress to override a Supreme Court decision holding legislation unconstitutional. Their proposal was roughly similar to one later put forward by Senator Burton K. Wheeler of Montana, who was to become the chief nemesis of the Court plan.

The secrecy made the plan all the more attractive to the president and permitted him to indulge his taste for the theatrical. It would take Cummings a month or so to put the finishing touches to his creation. Given that it was the start of a new calendar year, this period would be filled with significant events, both substantive and ceremonial. And the president made sure to use each of them to set the stage for the public unveiling of his grand surprise.

The first milestone on the road to Roosevelt's confrontation with the Court was the State of the Union address on January 6.

Admiring crowds lined his route down Pennsylvania Avenue to Capitol Hill where the president, clad in a cutaway coat and matching trousers, read his talk in sonorous tones to the lawmakers. They greeted him with an ovation—and no wonder. They had every reason to be grateful to the president, just as he had every reason to be confident of their reception to his talk. In the Senate he could count 76 Democrats against only 16 Republicans and 4 independents. In the House the Democrats claimed 332 members to 89 Republicans and 14 independents. It was the greatest domination of one party over another in 134 years, since 1823 when James Monroe's Democrats vastly outnumbered the battered remnants of the Federalist party.

More than anything else, his listeners in the chamber and around the country wondered if Roosevelt would confront the Court rhetorically and, if so, how he would do it. He did not keep them waiting long. And though the president relied heavily on indirection, his underlying meaning was clear. He began by speaking of the challenges facing the government. "You and I," he told the lawmakers, "helped to make democracy succeed by refusing to permit unnecessary disagreement to arise between our two branches of government," leaving his audience to wonder about the cooperativeness of the third branch.

Indeed there was much to wonder about when it came to the judiciary. The members of the Supreme Court who normally attend such occasions, clad in their robes of office, were conspicuous by their absence. FDR later mentioned their nonappearance to Ickes and speculated that "they had gotten a tip as to the contents of the message." In his diary Cummings wrote: "I am sure they were more comfortable where they were than they would have been had they been present."

As he warmed to his oratorical task, the president provided more and more reasons for the justices to feel less comfortable, wherever they learned about the speech. Each of the many points Roosevelt aimed at the Court was read slowly and deliberately to add emphasis and to reinforce the significance of his words. And as the *New York Times* noted, "the Democrats cheered practically every remark which they could interpret as aimed at the court."

It did not take the president long to mention one of the most serious wounds inflicted on the New Deal by the Court, the over-turning of the NIRA. "The statute of the NRA has been out-lawed," Roosevelt observed. "The problems have not," he added soberly. "They are still with us."

He affirmed his support for the tenets of the Constitution: "The vital need is not an alteration of our fundamental law, but an increasingly enlightened view with reference to it."

Roosevelt now made the central point of his speech. Earlier he had praised the cooperation between the legislative and exec-utive branches. Now, in words that must have struck an ominous note when they were read by the justices, he said: "It is not to be assumed that there will be a prolonged failure to bring legislative and judicial action into closer harmony."

An expectant hush fell over the crowded House chamber. Then came the punch line: "Means must be found to adapt our legal forms and our judicial interpretation to the actual present national needs of the largest progressive democracy in the world. The process of democracy must not be imperiled by the denial of essential powers of our government."

A thunderous ovation followed, joined by the public in the galleries and the distinguished visitors, among them the mem-bers of FDR's cabinet. Interior Secretary Ickes found himself yelling on one occasion, "and that is something I do not often do." Buoyed by FDR's powerful delivery and his rousing recep-tion, Ickes was confident there would be even more to cheer about ahead. "I believe that we are on the eve of an era where the powers of the Court will be much more strictly limited than they have been in the past," he told his diary.

Roosevelt himself seemed to share that confidence. To cele-brate his triumph on Capitol Hill, he summoned Ickes and other cronies to a poker game at the White House. Fortune seemed to be smiling on Roosevelt. Not renowned for his skill at cards, that evening he was the second-biggest winner, after Harry Hopkins. It cost Ickes $8.75 for a couple of hours of entertainment and good company, topped off by caviar, cheese, "liquid refreshments," and the disclosure by the president that following his afternoon speech thousands of telegrams had poured in from all over the country cheering him on.

But while FDR exulted in the promising start for his offensive against the Court, and while his supporters on the Hill awaited their marching orders, one senior member of Congress had plans of his own. This was Representative Hatton Summers, a onetime Dallas prosecutor, who was starting his second quarter-century in the House of Representatives as chairman of its Judiciary Committee. While members of Congress could only guess what FDR had in mind to do about the Court, they all knew from the start that Hattie Summers would have a great deal to say about how it turned out.

On the floor of the House Summers liked to set himself above the prosaic concerns of his colleagues by invoking the Lord above, whom he referred to as the "Big Boss," and the grandeur of the cosmos. "God operates through nature to enlighten men," he contended. "It's the weeds that make good farmers." The men who wrote the Constitution, he said, relied upon verities provided by nature and experience. They were "not creators but discoverers, not founding fathers but finding fathers."

But for all that high-flown rhetoric, behind the doors of the Capitol's cloak rooms and committee rooms Summers relied less on theology and nature's laws than on the thrust and parry of the political jungle. Arriving in Washington in 1913, the same year as FDR's most immediate Democratic predecessor, Summers did not take long to get under Woodrow Wilson's skin. "Legalistic" was the way Wilson privately described Summers. What he meant, as Josephus Daniels, FDR's old boss at the Navy Department explained to him early in the fight over the Supreme Court, was "that 'black letter learning' influenced him more than the making of law an instrument of humanity and justice."

It did not take all the Washington wisdom that Hattie Summers had absorbed in his years in the House to see that a mighty storm was brewing over the Supreme Court. If allowed to erupt, this was a tempest that could force Summers himself to make some difficult choices between his innate aversion to meddling with the laws of nature and nature's God and his nominal allegiance to the president of his own party.

Months before FDR's reelection and his State of the Union address, Summers had seen a chance to head off such a quandary. He had been informed that two of the staunchest and oldest members of the Supreme Court's right wing, seventy-seven-year-old Willis Van Devanter and seventy-four-year-old George Sutherland, were eager to resign. All that was stopping them, or so Summers was led to believe, was money. They feared that though they were by statute entitled to full pay on retirement, a hostile Congress might shrink their salary, as miserly lawmakers had done to Justice Holmes when he left the bench in 1933. Moreover, consistent with their conservative principles, the two septuagenarians did not wish to lose their shelter from the income tax that their judicial position afforded them.

For a man of Summers's talents and imagination, this problem was no problem at all. He quickly concocted legislation which would confer upon the two potential retirees the newly created position of retired justice, and grant them, along with some routine responsibilities, the tax immunity they were reluctant to discard. Summers had steered his handiwork to the verge of enactment the previous session when it ran afoul of another lawmaker unwilling to see any justice rewarded above the level of his own prospective pension. But with a new session came a new birth of life for Summers's brainchild. And with the militant words of Roosevelt's message still ringing in his ears, he set out to push it into maturity with all the considerable resources at his command.

Summers was one of the very few lawmakers who grasped the president's intent. Others, lacking Summers's perspicacity, began promoting their own solutions to deal with the problem they believed the president preferred to sidestep. Senate Majority Leader Joseph Robinson and House Speaker William Bankhead both declared themselves in favor of a constitutional amendment to curb the Court's power. Of a similar bent, Nebraska Senator George Norris, a progressive Republican and a New Dealer at heart, met with Elmer Benson, the Farmer Labor party governor of Minnesota, about an amendment to limit the Court's power to invalidate social legislation. And Emmanuel Celler of New York, a member of the House Judiciary Committee, issued a general warning that Congress would act to curb the Court if more laws were overturned.

Another indication that, despite the sharpness of his rhetoric, Roosevelt had still managed to disguise his intentions, was the reaction of some liberal critics of the Court. "To many he will appear courageous for daring to read a lecture to the justices at all," commented the *Nation*. "But considering the temper of Congress and the country on this issue, considering the avalanche of bills ready to be introduced that would do almost everything to the justices short of deporting them, Mr. Roosevelt's words were calculated not to channel this energy into political results but to dampen the ardor of what the newspaper editors like to call 'the Congressional hotheads.'" As the *Nation* saw it, for the "ruling groups of America" FDR's speech was an occasion for rejoicing. "Mr. Roosevelt has chosen to make with them a peace without victory."

Normally FDR resented press criticism as much as any other politician. But in this case he had to be delighted with the *Nation's* complaint, because it helped maintain the secrecy that was one of the major components of his strategy.

In the ensuing weeks, once he had exposed his intentions, FDR would be criticized roundly for his clandestine approach, for not consulting members of Congress and other political allies and for not trying to build public support. But as the president realized, whatever advantages such a course offered, it also presented serious risks. In the superheated atmosphere surrounding the Supreme Court, referred to by the *Nation*, FDR knew that whatever he proposed would be second-guessed from the start. Some would say he had gone too far. Not far enough, others would contend. A few might think he had achieved just the right balance. But their comments were bound to be drowned out by denunciations from the Court's ardent defenders and its severest critics. The danger he faced would be that his proposal would be so battered that by the time he sent it to Capitol Hill it would be dead on arrival.

Besides, by keeping his own counsel FDR could maximize the benefits of his skill in framing the issue on his own terms and at a time of his own choosing, and addressing the public directly. And when it came to that, as even his foes would have to agree in the wake of the last election, he had shown himself to be remarkably gifted.

Strategic reasons aside, the president seemed to take a sort of boyish satisfaction in the idea that he was nurturing a secret plan that would shock the nation. To Felix Frankfurter, whose advice on jurisprudence he probably valued more than anyone else's, he wrote on January 15: "Very confidentially, I may give you an awful shock in about two weeks." Then he added a comment which revealed his own concerns on how his "awful shock" would be received. "Even if you do not agree, suspend final judgment," FDR wrote, "and I will tell you the story."

If he had to worry about Frankfurter's reaction, what concerns must FDR have had about the response from others less favorably inclined to him and his works?

Whatever inner doubts he might have harbored, they were not apparent on January 20, 1937, when Roosevelt was sworn in to serve his second term as president. There he stood on this cold and rainy day on the east portico of the Capitol, the nation's chief executive, triumphant but embattled, face to face with the leader of the institution that had become the blight of his presidency, Chief Justice Hughes. Would he, Franklin Delano Roosevelt, "preserve, protect and defend the Constitution of the United States?" Hughes asked in a tone so emphatic that it amounted to a challenge.

Roosevelt, buffeted by a mean wind and soaked by the steady rain, threw the challenge back in the chief justice's face, repeating the oath word for word, giving as much stress as Hughes to the words as he swore on the Bible to "preserve, protect and defend the Constitution of the United States."

Reciting this litany, Roosevelt later told his speechwriter Sam Rosenman, "I felt like saying; 'Yes, but it's the Constitution as *I* understand it, flexible enough to meet any new problem of democracy—not the kind of Constitution your court has raised up as a barrier to progress and democracy.'"

The rain kept coming down as FDR delivered his inaugural address. He had ordered the removal of a temporary shelter installed to protect him from the elements as a bond with the thousands of spectators in the Capitol Plaza.

Although these remarks were much briefer than his State of the Union speech, Roosevelt managed to find room for a barb at the Court. Speaking of the challenges that still lay ahead of the country, he recited a list of economic and social hardships, concluding with the address's most memorable phrase: "I see one third of a nation ill-housed, ill-clad, ill-nourished." Seeing these injustices, Americans were determined to correct them, he declared. And he added: "They will insist that every agency of popular government use effective instruments to carry out their will."

With that the time for rhetoric was over, the hour for action was drawing near. As the day approached for the public unveiling of his plan, Roosevelt made only three exceptions to his rule of secrecy. Two of his choices might have been expected. One was his close adviser Tommy Corcoran, with whom he had been reluctant to discuss the Court plan because of the low esteem in which Corcoran held Cummings. The second was Charlton Cogburn, a trusted ally, chief counsel of the AFL, who had helped draft the National Labor Relations Act. By far the most surprising was the third choice—John L. Lewis, himself in the midst of his struggle with General Motors over the Flint sit-down. "The President told me he had a talk with Lewis on the plan," Cummings wrote in a postscript to his diary entry of January 24. The labor leader, Cummings added, "agreed to support it and thought it better than the amendment plan."

Thus did the president bind the CIO chieftain to his cause and link the sit-down strikes to the Court packing. It was a maneuver that, had they known of it, would only have bolstered the darkest fears and suspicions of his foes.

By this time Cummings had completed work on the proposed legislation and had drafted a message from the president, along with a letter from himself, to accompany the proposed bill when it was sent to Congress. After looking over Cummings's effort at a message, Roosevelt decided to call for help, mainly polishing the prose to bring it to presidential standards. He summoned Sam Rosenman to the White House on January 30, which happened to be FDR's fifty-fifth birthday.

It had become traditional for Roosevelt to celebrate by lunching with a bevy of movie stars. They came to Washington each year for the president's annual Birthday Ball, staged to help raise funds for the March of Dimes charity. Roosevelt of course had a great interest in the event, whose main purpose was to help fight polio, the disease that had altered his life. And he enjoyed hobnobbing with the Hollywood luminaries. But this year he passed up the diversion of lunching with the likes of Robert Taylor and Jean Harlow for a working lunch to discuss the Supreme Court problem.

On hand in addition to Rosenman and Cummings were two of the New Deal's most experienced legal troubleshooters, Donald Richberg and Solicitor General Stanley Reed. Richberg and Reed had at least some inkling of what was to be discussed, having been involved peripherally in discussions about solving the administration's Supreme Court problem. But Rosenman was totally in the dark.

He was in no way enlightened when during the meal FDR remarked that the peaceful lunch reminded him of a story from his days as Navy undersecretary during the Great War about the anti-submarine exploits of the "Q" ship *Santee*, which was camouflaged to look like an ordinary merchantman. When a German sub closed in on the seemingly easy target, a false section of the *Santee*'s hull would come down, uncovering enough deadly naval guns to blast the sub into Davy Jones's locker. Rosenman was bewildered until the luncheon dishes were cleared away and FDR revealed his own hidden guns by reading aloud his message and Cummings's letter on the Supreme Court proposal.

The president's guests brought up various alternative approaches to dealing with the Court, all of which were quickly discarded as they had been by FDR during his three months of discussion with Cummings. Rosenman soon realized that "the President had finally made up his mind once and for all."

But what bothered Rosenman, and Reed and Richberg, was the message's reliance on the claim that the federal judiciary from bottom to top was overworked and its dockets congested as the chief justification for appointing additional judges. The three outsiders, Rosenman, Richberg, and Reed, all suggested that stress should be placed instead on the argument that the courts, including the Supreme Court, "could be given a fresh and more resilient outlook by the addition of younger men." Cummings, however, insisted that the premise for his argument about overworked judges was based on solid evidence.

As for Roosevelt, Rosenman observed, he was drawn to Cummings's plan as " a subtle device" for changing the Court while avoiding the charge that he was acting because he was unhappy with the way the justices were deciding cases.

Rosenman prodded Roosevelt and Cummings into agreeing to tweak the language of the message to include allusions to the advantages of new blood on the Court. This would be introduced in the revised draft of the president's message with a throat-clearing phrase, as "a subject of delicacy and yet one which requires frank discussion." The new version went on to explain, in Rosenman's graceful language: "A lowered mental or physical vigor leads men to avoid an examination of complicated and changed conditions. Little by little new faces become blurred through old glasses fitted, as it were, for the needs of another generation. . . ." But as Rosenman noted, even in the final version the main point remained what Cummings wanted it to be—the need to correct delays caused by overworked judges and crowded calendars.

To Rosenman it seemed unlikely that the president could persuade the public "that he was suddenly interested primarily in delayed justice" rather than in ending "a tortured interpretation of the Constitution." But this was just the issue that Roosevelt did not wish to confront, as Rosenman finally realized.

Rather than making substantive changes to his message, the president was interested in stylist improvements; the prose would have to be "pepped up," he told Rosenman, who went about his task with the assistance of Tom Corcoran. The job was complicated because the president, mindful of the ill feelings between Cummings and Corcoran, instructed Rosenman to make sure that Cummings did not know of Corcoran's role. As they refined and strengthened the message's language, Corcoran and Rosenman faced a deadline. Roosevelt had set February 5, less than a week away, as the date for the plan's public unveiling.

Only one public occasion intervened in the period that remained. This was the president's annual dinner for the judiciary, a gathering that this year would be heavily laden with irony. Rosenman later pronounced it the most memorable of all the formal dinners he had attended during his thirteen years as a close adviser to Roosevelt in the White House. The ninety guests included Woodrow Wilson's widow and former heavyweight champion Gene Tunney and his wife. But most of the attention and tension focused on the justices. First Lady Eleanor Roosevelt had Chief Justice Charles Evans Hughes on her right and senior Associate Justice Willis Van Devanter on her left. All the other members of the Court, except for Brandeis, who at eighty did not attend evening functions, and Harlan Fiske Stone, still recovering from his bout with dysentery, were seated according to precedence. Senator Henry Ashurst of Arizona and Representative Summers, heads of the Senate and House Judiciary Committees, were also at the table, as were Cummings, Reed, and Richberg, all of whom had been plotting dramatic changes in the Court's future.

If the justices had any inkling of what their host held in store for them, they gave no hint of it. The chief justice was jovial. McReynolds was dour, but, as Rosenman noted, this was his usual mood. Roosevelt seemed completely at ease as he bantered with the chief justice and Van Devanter during the postprandial entertainment. But the tension was hard to ignore for those who knew what impended, and the attorney general for one claimed to be troubled by the unfolding melodrama. "I wish this message was over and delivered," Cummings whispered to Rosenman at one point. "It makes me uncomfortable; I feel too much like a conspirator."

But the tension continued to mount, and by the next day, February 3, even Roosevelt felt it as he worked with his aides on the message. That night, as Rosenman was preparing to return home to New York, FDR's secretary Missy LeHand called him aside.

"The president is terribly nervous about this message," she told him. "I think it would be helpful and comforting to him if you stayed over until the thing is finally completed and put to bed."

Rosenman of course agreed. He had already noticed FDR's uneasiness himself. "While he was convinced he was right about the step he was taking, he was nervous," Rosenman later recalled. "It is the only time I can recall that he seemed worried after once deciding upon a course of action."

What Rosenman did not realize was that more weighed upon the president's mind than the forthcoming confrontation with the Court. The contest between General Motors and the new autoworkers union had entered its second month and apparently a new phrase as a result of a startling development in Flint. On February 1, as the president was deep in contemplation of his Supreme Court message in Washington and GM was pressing for a court injunction to end the strike, the union, by a bold stroke, had taken the initiative and put the giant auto company at a disadvantage. The sit-downers had seized control of Chevrolet plant No. 4 in Flint, producer of a million engines a year, largest unit in the worldwide General Motors empire, and supposedly "impregnable" against attack.

Next morning the local leaders of the union called John L. Lewis in Washington and urged him to come to the front lines in Flint. As he boarded the train to Flint that morning, Lewis responded to reporters in typically dramatic and cryptic fashion with a line from Tennyson: "Let there be no moaning at the bar when I put out to sea." Just as the aging poet had signaled in his quatrains his acceptance of the death that soon awaited him, Lewis seemed to be implying that he too was just a wayfarer on the ocean of life, borne by tides beyond his control.

Whatever Lewis meant, neither GM nor the Roosevelt administration had time to decipher it. As Lewis headed for Flint, Labor Secretary Perkins called Michigan Governor Murphy and urged him to arrange a meeting between Lewis and GM executive

unto you," she had lectured him. "Agree with thine adversary quickly, forgive us our trespasses."

But Sloan responded to the secretary's biblical plea in the language of the boardroom and the courtroom. "We propose to demonstrate that the trespassers who have seized our plants and who have taken from you the privilege of working have not the right to do so," he told GM workers. Backing up its rhetoric with action, GM vigorously promoted a back to work movement among its plants that had been forced to shut down because of shortages of parts produced by the struck plants in Flint and Cleveland. On Monday, January 27, 1937, forty thousand Chevrolet workers returned to their jobs, including almost eleven thousand in Flint, the storm center of the strike. Moreover, though Governor Murphy had so far refrained from using the troops he had called out against the strikers, no one could be sure how long he would resist the unrelenting pressure on him from GM and its allies.

On January 28, as GM renewed its effort to gain an injunction, Murphy was presented with a resolution allegedly representing the views of fifty thousand GM employees in Michigan charging that his continued toleration of the strike would lead to "the destruction of the right to private property" and "the further invasion of communism." The next day two delegations of workers loyal to the company visited him in Lansing and threatened a sit-down of their own in his office, calling upon him to enforce the law against the strikers. "You ought to be ashamed you are being used in this way," Murphy told them. "There are agent provocateurs at work on an adroit plan to embarrass me and to compel the use of force."

Meanwhile the greatest concern to the strike leaders was the condition of their own followers. Their steadfastness had been the union's most potent weapon. Now it was in danger of being eroded. The UAW 156 set up outside pickets, which allowed sit-downers to take leave and visit friends and families. Even so, the strength of the sit-downers fluctuated widely. The number of strikers holding Fisher No. 1 ranged from a high of something over 1,000 to fewer than 100; in Fisher No. 2, from more than 450 to as few as 17. The large number of married men in Fisher No. 2 was a particular vulnerability because of the men's concerns about their families.

Especially damaging to morale had been the false peace of mid-January when the union had agreed to leave the plant in return for an agreement from the company to negotiate. One of the Fisher No. 2 sit-downers, Francis O'Rourke, kept a diary during the long ordeal which reflected the emotional roller-coaster ride. "We are to leave the plant, Diary," O'Rourke had written on Saturday January 16, when news of the agreement first broke. "Sunday evening we will all be in our homes and are the boys pleased? I wonder how the furniture looks and the children's toys. I'll be so glad to be with them again. Boy, I'm even anxious to see Mike the cat."

Next morning O'Rourke and his comrades had gotten up early to be ready for their departure. "Clean shirts, faces that show marks of an early morning shave. Most of the fellows have neckties on today. Some are washing their clothes, others are trying to make their shoes shine. Everyone is in a happy frame of mind."

Then a sound truck pulled up and blasted out the unwelcome news. "What is that announcement?" O'Rourke wrote. "We have been double-crossed? We are not going to leave the plants? Gee! I feel dizzy. Not going home? Not going home after all these preparations. General Motors would not keep an honest agreement." The smiles vanished. "Discouraged men," O'Rourke wrote of himself and the other strikers. "Heart-sick men. Men who had planned to go home, but who have decided to stay for our own interest."

To keep up their spirits, the men holding the plants had to depend upon each other. From the beginning they had prepared for a long ordeal. They organized themselves into committees to deal with food, sanitation and health, safety, and entertainment. Every worker had a specific duty for six hours a day, which they performed in two three-hour shifts.

In this situation cleanliness was indeed on a par with godliness. Each day at 3 P.M. at Fisher No. 1 no matter how cold the January weather, all windows were opened wide as teams of workers moved in waves on and between the assembly lines for the entire length of the plant, sweeping and scrubbing. Each man took a shower daily or had to answer for it before the strikers' kangaroo court.

The strikers divided themselves into social groups of fifteen and set up housekeeping in whatever corner of the plant they could make comfortable. They made mattresses of car cushions, removed the seats from the vehicles and made the car floors their beds. Alcohol, gambling, even smoking, except in restricted areas, were prohibited under rules posted by the strike committee. All questions from the press and other queries from the "outside world" had to be written out in advance and answered only in the presence of the strike strategy committee.

A sixty-five-man police committee guarded all entrances to the plant against incursions by company spies or other troublemakers. Seeking to provoke a scandal, GM smuggled a prostitute into the plant, but she was discovered and quickly sent on her way. A special patrol made regular rounds of the plant, on the lookout for violators of the rules, who were tried and initially given minor punishment. Repeat offenders were expelled.

A handful of journalists were admitted to Fisher No. 1, but only after intensive vetting. "A 'reception committee' of five searched my party and car for weapons outside the plant," wrote Bruce Bliven of the *New Republic*. Then "we walked up to the plant itself. All doors were shut and barricaded. I climbed onto a pile of packing bags and swung over a heavy horizontally hinged steel door into the plant. On a platform inside there was another reception committee which checked credentials again."

Another visiting journalist, Charles Walker of the *Nation*, was impressed by "the almost military control and discipline that prevail among the strikers in the whole area. Machinery in the plant is scrupulously protected. And there are sentinels on the roof."

Loneliness and boredom, more or less in that order, were the most serious problems for the sit-downers. Wives came to the plant windows to pass in laundry and food, which went immediately into the general commissary. Women were not allowed to enter, but children were passed through the windows for brief visits with their fathers. Every night at eight the strikers' six-piece band—three guitars, a violin, a mouth organ, and a squeeze box—broadcast their music over a loudspeaker for the strikers and the women and children outside. Spirituals and country tunes made up most of their repertoire. But they always closed with "Solidarity Forever," the anthem of the labor movement. And for once there seemed, at least to the sit-downers, as much truth as poetry in Ralph Chaplin's powerful lyrics: "We can break their haughty power, gain our freedom when we learn, that the union makes us strong."

The sit-downers themselves were all males, but women played a major role in their effort. The UAW's women's auxiliary organized dancing performances, representing different national groups, in front of the plant. They formed "living formations" or mass charades to pantomime phrases like "Solidarity Forever." They even devised an arrangement to symbolize the union's crucial demand to be "Sole Collective Bargaining Agent" for General Motors.

Starting with the Battle of the Running Bulls, some women had become more directly—and dangerously—involved, under the leadership of Genora Johnson, the wife of a strike leader. At one point during that bloody skirmish, the twenty-three-year-old Johnson, a mother of two, had grabbed a microphone and denounced the police firing on the union men. "Cowards! Cowards! Shooting unarmed and defenseless men!" she cried.

Then she sought to rally the other women, some of them workers in the plant, the others wives of union men: "Women of Flint!" Johnson cried. "This is your fight! Join the picket line and defend your jobs, your husband's job, and your children's home."

Her resolve strengthened by that experience, Johnson organized the women's emergency brigade as a vanguard detachment of the women's auxiliary, ready to respond to critical situations on short notice. Some 350 women responded to her call and were assigned to squads under captains who had access to autos or phones.

"If we go into battle, will we be armed?" Johnson asked her red bereted troops rhetorically.

"Yes," she said, answering her own question, "with rolling pins, brooms, mops and anything we can get. We will form a line around the men, and if police want to fire then they'll just have to fire into us."

"There isn't a flaming-eyed Joan of Arc among them," wrote Mary Heaton Vorse, a leading woman radical and pioneer in labor journalism about the brigade. "One and all are normal, sensible women who are doing this because they have come to the mature conclusion it must be done if they and their children are to have a decent life."

Yet for all the courage and determination of the strikers and their women, the union leaders saw the need for a dramatic action to regain momentum. Something "really spectacular" was needed in the view of Robert Travis, who had taken over from Wyndham Mortimer as leader of the strike. "We felt the strike was inevitably weakening because of its static condition, which seemed to indicate that the union had long since demonstrated its major strength," Henry Kraus, the *Flint Auto Worker* editor, wrote later.

The impression was accentuated by the reopening of those plants free of sit-downs, a program that had been carried out in apparent defiance of the union's desire or power to resist it.

Meanwhile the anti-strike Flint Alliance turned out eight thousand citizens for a mass meeting at which Lewis and other strike leaders were truculently denounced. More troublesome, anti-strike violence mounted. In Detroit five picketers were injured in a scuffle with police when some company officials tried to enter the closed Cadillac plant. In Saginaw a gang ran six strike organizers out of town. As four of the organizers were proceeding to Flint under police escort, an automobile swerved into their path, forced their speeding taxicab off the road into a telephone pole, seriously injuring all four. In Anderson, Indiana, a mob of two thousand broke up a UAW meeting with rotten eggs, then moved on to wreck the union headquarters.

Against this background, Travis and Victor Reuther decided to make their move. The target would be Flint's giant Chevy No. 4 plant, which GM believed understandably to be invulnerable. The plant's superintendent, Arnold Lenz, was known for his ruthless suppression of attempts at organizing by firing any worker suspected of UAW sympathy. In addition, Lenz had a contingent of armed guards on round-the-clock duty to forestall any UAW incursion. But the very strength of the plant's defenses created an opportunity for the union forces. No one expected the strikers could take over this fortress, least of all GM.

Cloak-and-dagger tactics were part of the union plan. Making use of a Pinkerton spy, "Frenchy" Dubuc, who had been pressured into serving as double agent, Travis had Dubuc tipped off his Pinkerton boss, Arthur Pugmire, that the union was considering an assault at Chevy No. 4. But Pugmire laughed off the tip. He told Dubuc that Travis was putting him on, perhaps because he had caught on to his being a spy.

"He knows goddamn well the union couldn't take Chevy 4," Pugmire said.

That was just what the strike leaders were hoping to hear. Now they were confident the company could be caught unawares. But to heighten their chances they decided to create a diversion at a smaller plant, Chevrolet No. 9. First they made sure that GM's spies carried word to the company that the union intended to stage a sit-down at No. 9. Consequently when the sit-down actually began at No. 9, at shift change on the afternoon of February 1, just as lawyers for GM were making their case for an injunction in a Flint courtroom, GM dispatched two hundred of its security guards who had been held in readiness to oust the strikers. To help, the company also sent a contingent of workers loyal to GM from Chevy No. 4, thus stripping that plant of all its company partisans. A violent melee ensued, with the company forces using clubs and tear gas against the outnumbered strikers. Shots were fired and fifteen were injured.

Outside, a member of the women's brigade saw her husband gasping for air at one of the few open windows and shouted, "They're smothering them! Let's give them air." She and her red-bereted comrades set about smashing all the windows in the plant. The battle was over in about forty minutes, when the union men marched out of the plant, bruised and dejected by their failure.

As it turned out, though, they had accomplished their mission: setting the stage for the takeover of Chevy No. 4. Just as the battle for No. 9 was reaching its climax, the struggle for No. 4 began.

A picked force of union shock troops invaded No. 4 and soon found allies from among two hundred or so union members already inside. In little more than an hour of hand-to-hand combat the strikers, using fire hoses and auto parts, overcame the company guards and their billy clubs, chased out the supervisors, and took control of the plant.

For the once disheartened strikers it was a moment for rejoicing. "Tonight, fellows, we can have some peaceful rest," Francis O'Rourke wrote in his diary that night. "General Motors has asked for another injunction, but we can worry about that tomorrow. Peace on Earth, Good Will toward Men."

While the seizure of the plant was a triumph for the strikers, it made even more difficult the political and legal predicament facing Governor Murphy, the man whose goodwill was critical to the strikers' chance of ultimate success. With both Flint Mayor Harold Bradshaw and Genesee County Sheriff Thomas Wolcott calling for troops to avoid an escalation of the violence, the governor might have demanded that the strikers leave Chevy No. 4. Instead he used the National Guard to cordon off the Chevy plant and nearby Fisher Body No. 1, which had been under control of the union from the start of the sit-down. And he called for reinforcements, bringing the total Guard strength to about 3,500.

As Sidney Fine pointed out in *Sit-Down*, his definitive chronicle of the strike, of all the actions realistically open to the governor this was probably the least damaging to the union cause. By ringing the plant with troops Murphy had in effect protected the strikers from a counterattack either by GM guards or the local police, or both. To be sure, he also denied them access to their supporters, and for a while to their food supply.

But a day later, after receiving assurances that outsiders— union men not regularly employed in Chevy No. 4—had been sent out of the plant, the governor allowed food deliveries to resume. Perhaps more important in the long run, Murphy assured John Brophy, Lewis's second-in-command at the CIO, "The military will never be used against you. I'd leave my office first."

This was an assurance that during the next stormy fortnight Murphy was to have reason to regret offering. Yet ultimately it was a pledge he stood by, almost against his will.

While Murphy did what he could for the strikers, in ruling on GM's injunction request Genesee County Circuit Judge Paul V. Gadola gave the union the back of his hand and GM everything it asked for. Not only did he order evacuation of two Fisher Body plants where the sit-down had started by 3 P.M. the following day, February 3, he also commanded an end to picketing and other strike-related activities. Failure to comply would result in a $15 million fine against the union. The amount was so out of proportion to the union's finances that the strike leaders simply laughed it off. Defying the evacuation order, the union instead staged a mammoth rally outside the struck factories. Some three thousand pickets and seven thousand spectators, who had descended on Flint from all corners of the state, gathered outside Fisher Body No.1, spilling over into the main street of the town. Spearheaded by the women of the emergency brigade and the women's auxiliary, they marched around the plant singing and cheering on the strikers who leaned out of the windows of the plant to join in the hullabaloo.

Judge Gadola's deadline came and went with no action against the strike. Demonstrating the better part of valor, Sheriff Wolcott decided that GM needed to obtain a writ from the judge against the strikers for failure to comply with the evacuation order before action could be taken. CIO director Brophy called it a "gala day," a sentiment shared by the thousands of demonstrators.

Middle-class citizens in Flint and elsewhere felt differently. In a letter to the *Flint Journal*, a local minister expressed their feeling. "I have witnessed the abdication of the law and the rule of the pug-ugly, by the law of the jungle the law of club and fang," he wrote. It was a reaction that was to swell and expand during the months ahead, with ominous implications for the union movement and its friends, particularly those in elective office—like Frank Murphy and Franklin Roosevelt.

Such condemnations were not limited to Michigan. On February 6 the Federal Council of Churches of America, in a report on the GM strike, said its investigators had turned up evidence that GM had pressured employees to join the Flint Alliance, the company sponsored anti-UAW group. Even "conservative citizens" believed that the speedup imposed by GM was "an unreasonable strain" on the worker, the report added. Nevertheless, in the section of the document that captured headlines, the church group branded the sit-down "a dangerous weapon," adding, "It can be employed in a wholly tyrannical way by a minority of workers who happen to be in position to tie up a huge concern by taking possession of key plants."

On the same day the massive demonstration rocked Flint, GM resumed bargaining with the union it was trying to crush. The company had made sure to point out that it made this concession only at the command of the President of the United States. The sessions took place in Detroit, removed from the hubbub in Flint, in Detroit's dreary Recorder's Court building, where justice was meted out to all manner of offenders against the public safety, from traffic violators to murderers.

To say the two sides negotiated would be an overstatement. The GM team, headed by Knudsen, conferred among themselves in one of the jury rooms. Lewis and the UAW representatives were quartered in the office of Murphy's brother, George, a Recorder's Court judge. Murphy shuttled between them, carrying such proposals and counteroffers as were made. "The governor is jumping around like a jackrabbit," said UAW President Homer Martin.

Martin himself did not have much more to say about the bargaining. His energies had been drained by weeks of tension. To rest him, and to avoid having him snarl the talks, Lewis pulled him out of the meetings and dispatched him on a tour of GM plants to explain the strike to autoworkers, accompanied by another union official to monitor his health and behavior.

Most of the participants on both sides were showing signs of wear and tear. Murphy had not had a full night's sleep for five weeks. GM's Knudsen, according to a close friend, had "aged ten years in the past month." Of all the principal bargainers, only Lewis, hardened by the experience of many such sessions, seemed imperturbable.

Time and again Murphy would call Lewis aside and plead that he get the sit-downers to withdraw voluntarily. Finally Lewis told the governor he would not order the men out until there was a settlement. "What are you going to do?" he challenged Murphy. "You have the bayonets," Lewis said, as the CIO leader later recalled the episode. "Which kind do you prefer to use—the broad double blade or the four-sided French style? What kind of bayonets, Governor Murphy, are you going to turn around inside our boys?"

He would never do any such thing, Murphy insisted.

"Then why bellyache to me about my getting those boys out to save you?" Lewis snapped.

From the beginning it was clear what the major stumbling block to an agreement would be—the union's insistence on exclusive bargaining rights. Without that status the union leaders realized they would not have the leverage to deal with the giant corporation.

In fact the union had backed off from its original demand that it bargain for *all* GM workers. Instead it insisted only on the right to represent the workers in the twenty GM plants then on strike, which included the vital operations in Flint and Cleveland that were the keys to auto production.

But GM turned that down. It would recognize the union in those plants as the agent only for its own members, a restriction that would severely limit the union's clout at the bargaining table and therefore cast a shadow over its future.

There were other differences too. But the issue of exclusive representation was the chief bone of contention, a fact that was driven home to FDR when he once against sought to assert his influence in the dispute. On February 4, 1937, the night before he was to unveil his Supreme Court plan, Roosevelt called Murphy to tell him to urge the union and the company that the public welfare demanded they settle their differences.

The next day, after FDR had finally revealed his scheme for the Court to his cabinet, Congress, and the country, the president was back on the phone to Murphy, telling him that the two sides seemed "awfully close." The deadlock could be broken,

FDR suggested, if GM would agree to bargain on national issues only with the UAW. But as Murphy soon discovered, that idea would not do the trick. The UAW still wanted its exclusive representation.

With the help of Secretary Perkins, Roosevelt developed a new pitch which he advanced on February 6 in phone conversations with both Knudsen and Lewis. The idea of exclusive representation would be postponed for a set time. During this interval the UAW would be able to bargain for its autoworkers who already were members and be able to organize others. Lewis was not being asked to give up his demand, just delay it. Around the same time, either on its own or in response to Roosevelt's initiative, GM came up with a variation of FDR's idea, offering not to bargain with any other organization in the struck plants for a period of 90 days without first informing Murphy.

Lewis was tempted but at first did not agree. Then, on Monday, February 8, he told Murphy he would accept the corporation's pledge if the period of exclusive bargaining rights was extended from the three months offered by GM to six months. Knudsen said he lacked the authority to grant that concession. Approval would have to come from higher-ups.

That, Murphy realized, would call for White House intervention. "The Boss has got to get in touch with Sloan or the DuPonts—tell them this is okay," he told FDR's appointment secretary Marvin McIntyre. "This strike has got to go through tonight or we are done."

But FDR did not make the call to GM, at least not that night. Murphy meanwhile decided to put the heat on the union. He was by this time under great pressure himself. On February 5 GM's lawyers had obtained from Judge Gadola the writ of attachment commanding the removal of the sit-downers from the struck plants and the arrest of supporting pickets. Murphy had put off responding in the hopes that a settlement could be reached. But on February 8, after being told by Flint's

Democratic congressman Andrew Transue that there was no congressional support for the sit-down, the governor vowed to "do something on it tonight."

What Murphy did was to prepare a stern letter which he read the next day to Lewis, who was still insisting on the six-month waiting period. In fulfillment of his constitutional duties as governor of the state, Murphy told the union leader, he had no choice but to comply with the court order and "take the necessary steps to restore the plants to their rightful owners. I have no alternative but to perform this duty to the best of my ability." Despite this apparently decisive language, there is little evidence that Murphy's letter and his encounter with Lewis had much to do with ending the strike. The chief significance of the face-to-face meeting between the governor and the labor leader stems from the strikingly different and revealing accounts later provided by those close to Murphy, and by Lewis himself.

Carl Muller, a Detroit reporter and good friend of Murphy, claimed that the governor grabbed Lewis by the coat collar and "in no uncertain terms told him the men would get out of the plant or else." According to George Murphy, the governor's brother, Lewis told Murphy: "Governor you win." And Murphy himself called the confrontation "the turning point" in the strike. Indeed, one Murphy admirer, noting that Lewis took to his bed the next day with the grippe, claimed that "Lewis was not sick, he was knocked out by Murphy's ultimatum."

So far as Lewis's illness was concerned, the union leader's years mining coal in the pits had left him at the age of fifty-six prone to colds and other respiratory ailments. Regarding Murphy's claim that his letter was a transforming event, circumstances show otherwise. Lewis was just as insistent on the six-month period of exclusive bargaining rights after his talk with Murphy as before.

The dramatic accounts provided by Murphy and his supporters should be considered in light of the governor's fear that he would pay a high political price for his role in the strike and was trying to save his reputation and his political life. Murphy knew that the longer the strike continued, the more condemnation he would draw. If Murphy wanted to warn Lewis, with whom he had been in frequent contact for six weeks, he did not need to write him a letter. He could just have talked to him. The letter was important not for Lewis but for the rest of the world. In fact the governor submitted it to the Senate Judiciary Committee in 1939 in support of his nomination for attorney general when his handling of the sit-down strikes came under sharp scrutiny.

As for Lewis, never a shrinking violet, he had good reason not to allow one of the crowning accomplishments of his service to the American labor movement to be diminished by another man's recounting of the event. Lewis gave his first version of the event three years after the fact, in a speech to the 1940 UAW convention. "I do not doubt your ability to call out your soldiers and shoot the members of our union out of those plants," Lewis claimed he had told Murphy. But he added: "When you issue that order I shall enter one of those plants with my own people. And the militia will have the pleasure of shooting me out of the plants with them."

Even more colorful was the recollection Lewis provided a few years later to one of his biographers, Saul Alinsky. Responding to Murphy's claim that he was trying to "uphold the law," Lewis reminded the governor of his family's ties to the Irish rebellion against the British crown. "When the British government took your grandfather as an Irish revolutionary and hanged him by the neck until dead," Lewis claimed to have said, "you did not get down on your knees and burst forth in praise for the sanctity and the glory and purity of the law, the law that must be upheld at all costs!"

But all this was merely prelude to Lewis's thundering peroration. If Murphy did in fact turn the troops on the strikers, Lewis declared he would enter the plant, "walk up to the largest window, open it, divest myself of my outer raiment, remove my shirt and bare my bosom. Then when you order your troops to fire, mine will be the first breast that those bullets will strike."

At this point in the Alinsky/Lewis chronicle, the union leader lowered his voice: "And as my body falls from that window to the ground, you listen to the voice of your grandfather as he whispers in your ear, 'Frank, are you sure you are doing the right thing?'" Whereupon, according to Lewis, a badly shaken Murphy seized the letter from Lewis's hand and fled the room.

By this rendering it was Murphy, not Lewis, who was discombobulated by the exchange between the two men. This account, surely embroidered by Lewis and quite possibly by Alinksy too, is probably closer to mythology than history. But like many myths, by evoking the passions of the moment it captures a measure of the truth absent from more literal narratives.

In actuality, just as there is no evidence that Murphy's warning in any way altered Lewis's position, neither is there reason to believe that Lewis's purported response, however impassioned, caused Murphy to change his plans. The whole notion of "shooting" the union members out of the plant was a creation of Lewis's; Murphy said nothing of the sort and had previously promised he would quit as governor before using troops against the strikers. The governor merely said he would take necessary steps, without spelling out what those steps might be.

One thing he might have done was to continue to cordon off the plants and starve the strikers into submission. But given Murphy's aversion to cracking down hard on the strikers, it seems likely he would have taken a more conciliatory course. "Our good Governor Murphy, whom we have so much faith in," was the way Francis O'Rourke referred to him in his diary. Murphy, as Sidney Fine suggests, could have tried to exploit the goodwill he enjoyed among the strikers by visiting the plant and personally appealing for them to evacuate.

In any event, Murphy had to do none of these things because GM and the union came to an agreement in the next two days, though not without a helpful nudge from FDR. While Murphy tried in vain to budge Lewis from his insistence on the six-month interval, the Roosevelt administration worked to get GM to accept that figure. Appropriately enough, since big business was involved, FDR called not on Labor Secretary Perkins but on Commerce Secretary Dan Roper to close the deal. Roper talked to GM vice president Donaldson Brown and also to S. Clay Williams, board chairman of R. J. Reynolds Tobacco, whom Roper had come to know when Williams chaired the now defunct National Industrial Recovery Board. Williams talked to Brown too, and also to GM president Alfred Sloan. As a result of all these conversations, Roper was sufficiently encouraged to report to the White House his confidence that the strike was "on the way to a successful consummation."

As the negotiations headed toward a climax on February 9 and 10, their venue shifted from the corridors of Recorder's Court to the Statler Hotel on Detroit's fashionable Washington Boulevard, where Lewis lay abed, nursing *la grippe*. Sensing the tide was moving in his direction, Lewis continued to press every advantage he had. The local papers had featured the latest disclosures from the La Follette Committee hearings in Washington, where senators were probing GM's massive use of spying to undermine union organizing efforts. One story focused on the activities of a Pinkerton agent on the prowl in Alexandria, Virginia, in the same neighborhood where Lewis and his family lived.

Just as GM negotiators Donaldson Brown and John T. Smith were hammering home an essential point, Lewis interrupted. "What's the basis of your statement?" he asked as belligerently as he could, as he later recounted the story to Heber Blankenhorn, a journalist and labor investigator. "Some lousy Pinkerton?"

Before the GM officials could respond, Lewis demanded to know which of them "had sent a Pinkerton bastard to spy on me. Was it you Brown? Was it you Smith?"

When both men professed ignorance of Pinkerton activity, Lewis snorted in disgust: "Well, how is this General Motors run anyway?"

By this time Brown and Smith had lost not only their train of thought but whatever momentum they had generated behind their argument. But Lewis was relentless. The next day's paper brought news of yet another GM excess: it had deployed Pinkertons to spy on an assistant secretary of labor assigned to mediate a 1935 auto strike at one of GM's Toledo plants. Time and again Lewis brought that episode up during the parley, until he was satisfied that he had left his adversaries "embarrassed, humiliated and extremely nervous" at the mention of Pinkertons.

Another breed of man might have felt disadvantaged trying to conduct negotiations while flat on his back. But Lewis seemed to convert his sickbed into the functional equivalent of a throne as he lorded it over the tycoons who tried to haggle with him over the terms of the settlement. Governor Murphy and federal conciliator James F. Dewey were seated on his bed. Smith, GM's general counsel, considered the wiliest and toughest member of the automaker's team, and his GM colleagues were in chairs nearby. Lewis glared at Smith and pregnantly cleared his throat.

"What's the matter?" Smith asked.

"Move your chair closer," Lewis asked, "so I can tell my grandchildren how close I once sat to one and a half billion dollars."

Smith tried to make GM's case for the three-month waiting period, but Lewis stuck to his guns. "Six months," he said flatly. Then he rolled over in bed, leaving Smith along with Murphy and Dewey to study the striped flannel pajamas covering his huge back.

Lewis had good reason to take a firm stand. He knew that GM's auto output was near the vanishing point. It had produced a grand total of 151 cars in the first ten days of February. The odds against dislodging the union men from the struck plant any time soon were great. And probably just as important, the Roosevelt administration was doing everything it could to get GM to give in.

No wonder, then, that on the night of February 10, in Lewis's hotel room, GM agreed to the six-month period that Lewis had demanded. While the auto company managed to avoid conceding the UAW exclusive bargaining rights in the literal terms it had sought, the six-month period, guaranteed by a letter from Knudsen to Murphy, in effect gave the union what it needed to achieve the goal it had set for itself.

At the Fisher No. 1 plant in Flint, Wyndham Mortimer read the terms of the settlement to the sit-downers. At first, when they were told that General Motors would recognize the union as bargaining agent only for its members, the sit-downers grumbled. But when they heard Mortimer read Knudsen's letter to Murphy guaranteeing that the company would bargain with no one else but the UAW for six months, the grumbling stopped and the celebrating started. Wives pulled up to the plants in the family cars, honking the horns on their Chevys. Magnesium flares burned in the streets, movie cameras ground as the sit-downers paraded out in triumph.

"We will march out as a victorious army, in a glorious crusade for a better life," bellowed a union leader. A jubilant cavalcade marched past the factories and through the streets of Flint.

The AFL's William Green was quick to sneer at the settlement. "So far as recognition of the union is concerned, the situation is practically the same as it was before the strike was called," he said. "As regards the closed shop principle, the defeat is complete."

Lewis did not seem concerned. "Now I can sleep for a while," was all he said as the negotiators left his hotel room.

The CIO chieftain could afford to relax and contemplate the future. The winds of victory were at his back, and the fruits of the union success in Flint were soon at hand. In elections supervised by the new National Labor Relations Board at several smaller automakers, Hudson, Packard and Studebaker, the UAW quickly won majorities, leading to contracts with management at all these companies.

Even more dramatic was the CIO's success in the steel industry, which had been Lewis's initial target until the aggressiveness of the Flint autoworkers altered his timetable. Most remarkable was that the triumph in steel was achieved without a single worker going out on strike—the economic equivalent of winning a battle without firing a shot. The initiative came from Myron Taylor, president of U.S. Steel, which had long been just as dead set against unions as had General Motors. Impressed by the determination and energy of the Flint unionists and the CIO, as well as by their political clout in Washington, Taylor agreed to a deal with Lewis and his Steel Workers Organizing Committee little more than a fortnight after the UAW's triumph in Flint.

Just as Lewis flourished in the glow from the Flint victory, so did Frank Murphy, or so it seemed for a while. In the immediate aftermath of the settlement, *Time* offered a jaunty prediction. Noting the credit Murphy was drawing from all sides, the magazine said: "It was soon apparent that the first vehicle to roll off General Motors' revived assembly lines will be a bandwagon labeled 'Frank Murphy for President in 1940.'" Even opponents of the sit-down, such as the *Flint Journal*, hailed the governor for having managed the conflict in such a way that, in contrast to many past labor struggles, not one life was lost on either side. A high-ranking conservative Democrat, later revealed to be Vice President Garner, told columnist Arthur Krock of the *New York Times* that Murphy's compromise with property rights was "in the spirit of wise statesmanship at the present time."

But the conflict over labor's right to unionize was escalating, just as the battle over FDR's Court plan was under way. And the heat generated by both struggles would greatly change the way Garner, among others, judged the spirit of the times.

5

If Men Were Angels

On February 4, 1937, the same night that Roosevelt called Frank Murphy to urge that GM and the sit-down strikers reach agreement, White House secretaries left phone messages for congressional leaders summoning them to the cabinet room at 10 A.M. the next morning. The lawmakers and the others invited, Vice President Garner and all members of the cabinet, were told only that the matter to be discussed was "highly confidential."

Hours before they arrived, White House staff were at work grinding out hundreds of copies of the president's message to Congress on court reform, his accompanying legislative proposal, and a supporting letter prepared by Attorney General Cummings, most of which would be distributed to a press conference following the session in the cabinet room. The legislative contingent, Senate Majority Leader Robinson, House Speaker Bankhead, Majority Leader Sam Rayburn, as well as the House and Senate Judiciary Committee chairmen, were men of power and influence. On the face of things they should have been expected to deploy their assets on behalf of their president in the forthcoming struggle. After all, they were Democrats every one.

And Roosevelt had given their party the greatest victory and the greatest advantages it had ever possessed.

Yet Roosevelt would discover, as other presidents of both parties before him had found, that his personal success could not assure him of the allegiance of his fellow partisans in the separate legislative branch of government. The meeting that FDR had planned as the launching of what would be the greatest triumph of his presidency would instead sow the seeds of his worst debacle, inflicted in large part by the congressional eminences he had counted on to do his bidding.

A number of reasons accounted for this reversal of expectations, but the most fundamental causes for the harsh treatment inflicted upon Roosevelt by the leaders of his own party could be traced back to the founding of the Republic. The men who gathered in Philadelphia in the sweltering summer of 1787 to remake the ramshackle Articles of Confederation into a durable structure were vexed not only by the heat but by a substantive dilemma. Although wary of government, they felt obliged to strengthen the existing feeble system. Committed to the principle of popular sovereignty, they nevertheless mistrusted human nature and doubted the wisdom of the populace. Fearful of monarchy and dictatorship, they also dreaded the tyranny of the majority.

Madison, the chief architect of the Constitution, best described the anxieties plaguing its framers. "If men were angels, no government would be necessary," he wrote in No. 51 of the *Federalist Papers*. "If angels were to govern men, neither external nor internal controls on government would be necessary."

Since heavenly assistance was beyond reach, Madison, who had a front-row seat at the convention hall, devised a worldly compromise. He designed the structure of government in a way that would convert the human frailty that worried him and his colleagues into a self-generating restraint on power. A lifelong hypochondriac, he was short, slim, and introverted, an unlikely figure to dominate a gathering of dynamic and powerful personalities. But the little Virginian compensated for his unprepossessing appearance with disciplined rhetoric and meticulous reasoning.

To curb the will of the majority, which might come to dominate the legislative or executive branch of the government, Madison gave the Congress and the president separate constituencies and terms of different length. Members of the House of Representatives would stand for election every two years, each answerable to a different majority of voters—segregated by district and scattered around the country—whose needs and concerns varied with the differences in latitude and longitude, not to mention their diverse history, tradition, and ethnography. In the other legislative branch, senators would enjoy six-year terms and an entire state to represent. The chief executive faced the voters only every four years and had to appeal and respond to a national electorate, which became a political reality only with each quadrennial. Madison also armed each part of government with power to check and balance the other. One house of Congress could reject legislation approved by the other house; even if both passed a bill, the president could veto it. As the ultimate safeguard, Madison and his colleagues created the Supreme Court whose justices, to the great frustration of Franklin Roosevelt, ultimately assumed for themselves the power to checkmate either or both of the other branches.

The inevitable clash of personal rivalries produced by this design, Madison believed, would make these restrictions work. "Ambition must be made to counter-act ambition," he wrote. "The interest of the man must be connected with the constitutional rights of the place." He was right about that, as the later President Madison himself learned when a rebellious Congress would not allow him to shape his own cabinet, leading him to complain to his old collaborator, Jefferson, that the Congress had become "unhinged."

In addition to hamstringing the presidency, the Constitution created a wasteland for political parties. If they are to amount to much, parties must be able to win support from the voters and deliver results in government. But the Constitution undermines political parties by ordaining a permanent antagonism between the executive and the legislative branches, which transcends party allegiance. Efforts by the parties to get the presidents and the lawmakers they help elect to office to work together generally founder on the Madisonian devices designed to drive them apart—and often to set them at each other's throats. In the face of all this, parties manage to survive, but barely, serving mainly as agencies for collecting votes, distributing patronage, and filling offices.

Meanwhile the powers of government and the demands upon it have expanded beyond anything imagined by Madison and his colleagues. But their eighteenth-century legacy has lingered on in the strictures of the Constitution, warping the political system over which Franklin Roosevelt presided.

The Great Depression led to the aggrandizement of federal power during Roosevelt's first years in the White House. But a lifetime in politics had made him fully mindful of the structural limitations on his authority. Nor was he very different from his predecessors in his relationship with his party. In his first term Roosevelt tried to cast himself above mere party concerns. He installed Bull Moose Republican Harold Ickes in his cabinet, urged Democrats to invite Republicans to their Jefferson Day dinners, and gave his unofficial but public support to Progressive Senator Robert La Follette of Wisconsin against his Democratic challenger. "If we have the right kind of people, the party label does not mean so very much," he explained.

With his insight into the American system, Roosevelt should not have been greatly surprised when in 1935, with the national economy struggling to come back to life, he struck out at the power of entrenched interests and ran into a hailstorm of opposition, even within his own party. One FDR proposal that stirred great controversy aimed at the much deplored and much abused system of public utility holding companies. These entities were operated so as to assure exorbitant profits for a few manipulators while imposing extravagant costs on the public. The bill's so-called death penalty provision allowed the federal government to eradicate any utility holding company that failed to cooperate with rules administered by one of the New Deal's creations, the Securities and Exchange Commission. The massive lobbying effort against the measure by the utility companies thrust a corporate executive named Wendell L. Willkie, hitherto little known outside the world of business, into national prominence and set him on the path that was to lead to the Republican presidential nomination in 1940.

More important at the moment, it drew into opposition a score or more of moderate Democratic senators who had not previously opposed the New Deal but who were disturbed by this latest government intrusion into the corporate world. Ultimately Roosevelt persuaded Congress to agree on a compromise which watered down the death-sentence provision but still forced the breakup of the old utility company empires. But his bullying of many in his party into compliance created tensions that would fester and reemerge during the battle over the Court. Meanwhile the opposition had learned they could resist the New Deal and survive to fight another day.

That day was not long in coming. A few weeks after the death-sentence bill was introduced to reform public utilities, FDR targeted wealth across the board. Impelled in part by the increasing attention gained by Louisiana Senator Huey Long's "Every Man a King" populism, the president demanded that Congress make sweeping changes in the tax code that would greatly boost levies on giant corporations and rich individuals.

Roosevelt had done nothing to prepare the public or Congress for his drastic proposal. But the prospect of catching the barons of Capitol Hill off guard seemed to intrigue the president, much as it would two years later when he hatched his plans for dealing with the Supreme Court in absolute secrecy. "Pat Harrison's going to be so surprised he'll have kittens on the spot," Roosevelt told Raymond Moley, referring to the Mississippian who chaired the Senate Finance Committee.

What accounted for the outrage against FDR's soak-the-rich proposal was that it was aimed at the structure of wealth and power that in good times and bad, for better and worse, shaped the national destiny. The wealthy and the powerful had been willing to accept the New Deal as long as, as Moley put it, it seemed intended to help stabilize the turbulent conditions created by the depression. But taxing the rich and big business on the scale Roosevelt proposed would, in the view of those who would bear the burden, create even more havoc than the depression itself.

A bitter debate raged on Capitol Hill all summer of 1935. Finally, aided by connivery and compromise engineered by Democratic congressional leaders, a tax bill of sorts was patched together. Enough of Roosevelt's original proposal, such as an increase in surtax rates on high incomes and graduated corporate taxes, survived for the president to be able to claim victory. But once again, as with the death-sentence fight, it was a costly success with a fallout in exasperation and antagonism almost everywhere in the Congress.

Along with Roosevelt's quirky willfulness, something more fundamental had contributed to the rise of resistance among the lawmakers, a feeling that the New Deal had already done enough, and maybe too much, to change the way the country was run. In a sense Roosevelt was a victim of the New Deal's accomplishments. Whatever their limits, the programs FDR pushed through had served to stave off the panic that had gripped the nation during Hoover's final days in office. Absent the sense of overwhelming crisis, FDR no longer had a blank check to proceed at will with making over the government and the economy.

"Throughout the country many businessmen who once gave you sincere support now are not merely hostile, they are frightened," the publisher and sometime friend Roy Howard warned the president soon after the turbulent 1935 congressional session adjourned. Howard suggested "a breathing spell" and "a recess from further experimentation." Roosevelt responded, quickly agreeing with Howard's diagnosis and mimicking his terminology. His basic program was now substantially complete, the president said, adding reassuringly that the "breathing spell of which you speak is here—very decidedly so." When released to the public, the exchange of correspondence set off a binge of near euphoria.

Approving letters and telegrams flooded the White House, stocks soared to their highest level in four years, and Roosevelt's poll ratings climbed too. The next year, 1936, he extended the "breathing spell" in part because with the election dominating political thinking, both he and Congress sought to avoid unnecessary acrimony. But once the returns were in, Roosevelt decided to terminate the honeymoon. He took off after the Supreme Court while giving aid and comfort to the newly aggressive labor movement.

In launching his Supreme Court initiative the president once again, as in 1935, forfeited whatever benefit he might have gained by consulting congressional leaders in advance in favor of the advantage he hoped to gain from surprise. In fact, instead of dealing with these personages as they saw themselves, as the lords of Capitol Hill, Roosevelt treated them more like poor relations. When they gathered at the White House on February 5 in response to his summons, FDR had little to say to them. Hurrying into their midst in his wheelchair while clerks strewed the output of the mimeograph machines around the table, the president uttered a cheerful good morning, and cautioned that he would have little time since his press conference was scheduled in half an hour. The papers that lay before them, he said, had to do with a proposed bill to resolve, once and for all, his problems with the Supreme Court.

He mentioned, almost in passing, that he had considered the idea of a constitutional amendment but had rejected it in favor of legislation. "Give me ten million dollars," he explained, "and I can prevent any amendment to the Constitution from being ratified by the necessary number of states."

After reading a few paragraphs from his message, the president hurried off to his press conference, leaving his guests to ponder the material he had presented them. Vice President Garner said not a word, the first time, Harold Ickes noted, "that I have seen him at a cabinet or any other meeting sit entirely silent." Speaker Bankhead's "pokerish" expression betrayed nothing of what he thought. Loyal old Joe Robinson indicated what Ickes thought was "mild assent." The most positive reaction came from Senate Judiciary Committee chairman Henry Ashurst, who remarked that he thought Roosevelt's approach better than his own idea for a constitutional amendment. House Judiciary Committee chairman Summers seemed pleased, Ickes thought, because the president's message endorsed his judicial retirement bill.

But as they looked over the material that would allow the president to tame the Supreme Court by adding six justices of his own choice, FDR's distinguished guests were struck by the fact that the most significant aspect of the bill and accompanying documents was what was left out. Nowhere was there any mention of what everyone knew to be the driving force for the bill, the profound differences in political and constitutional philosophy between the president and the Court, between the New Deal and the status quo.

Instead the whole proposal was treated by Roosevelt and Cummings as nothing more than a managerial reform intended to make the court system more efficient. As Cummings put it in his supporting letter: "Delay in the administration of justice is the outstanding defect of our judicial system." Similarly the president in his message emphasized the need for reorganizing the courts and dwelled at length on "the complexities, the delays and the expense of litigation in the United States," making the courts "chiefly a haven for the well-to-do." The Supreme Court "is laboring under a heavy burden," the president lamented, noting that the Court had declined to hear 717 of 867 petitions for review brought by private litigants. It seemed clear, he contended, that the need to relieve "present congestion" required "enlarging the capacity of all the federal courts." Aggravating the problem of overcrowded dockets, Roosevelt explained, was the advanced age of many of the judges, and here he used the language Rosenman had inserted about the benefit of "younger blood" on the bench.

The combination of this ingenious deviousness with the drastic remedy proposed began to sink into the consciousness of the congressional leaders once they left the White House. Perhaps the most important and decisive reaction came from House Judiciary chairman Summers. Whatever approval Ickes may have read into his demeanor earlier, because of FDR's backing for his judicial retirement bill, was far overshadowed by the other elements in Roosevelt's scheme. This was just the sort of approach he had been trying to preempt. "Boys," Summers told his colleagues as they drove back to Capitol Hill, "here's where I cash in my chips."

Another attendee at the cabinet room meeting, Vice President Garner, was less explicit but more dramatic in his reaction. Shortly after noon, as the president's message was being read to each house of Congress, the vice president left the rostrum and was seen by one and all as he walked over to a group of senators and held his nose with one hand, then turned down the thumb of his other hand. As Roosevelt's vice president, Garner had no choice but to give the proposal at least his nominal support. But his gesture was worth at least ten thousand words in expressing what he really thought about the idea.

Although Hatton Summers and Jack Garner each acted independently, the combined impact of their responses would have profound consequences. They had laid the groundwork for a rebellion that would rock the Roosevelt presidency and the New Deal to its foundations.

This uprising would take time to develop. Most of the early criticism on Capitol Hill was limited to hard-line conservative Republicans and a few Tory Democrats. But the press was more outspoken, and in the long run helped to arouse grassroots sentiment. The plan came under attack not only from conservative editorial writers but from relatively liberal and influential columnists such as Dorothy Thompson. "This is the beginning of pure personal government," she warned her readers in the *New York Herald Tribune* and sundry other papers, making a pointed comparison to the dictators holding power in Europe whose totalitarian authority seemed an increasing menace to many Americans. "Do you want it? Do you like it? Look around the world—there are plenty of examples—and make up your mind." Said the *New York Times*, which had usually supported the president: "Cleverness and adroitness in dealing with the Supreme Court are not qualities which sober-minded citizens will approve."

The press pounded the plan not only with the written word but with the sometimes even more potent weapon of cartoons. Under the caption "The Turnabout," the *Tampa Tribune* depicted a bearded justice confronting FDR with a manifesto signed by the "Supreme Court" reading: "Having decided the duties of the president are too arduous we hereby recommend two additional presidents."

"The newspapers are boiling over because of the president's message," Homer Cummings told his diary on February 8, three days after the plan's unveiling. But he did not seem overly troubled. "From all present appearance it would seem as if the proposition would go over successfully," he wrote, "although it is apt to be fought pretty bitterly in the Senate." This appraisal would turn out to be all too accurate, though greatly understated.

New Deal supporters tried to brush off signs of trouble. Ten days after the plan was announced, in a piece headlined "Roosevelt Will Win," the *Nation* reported "the tide has begun to run strongly in Roosevelt's favor. The flow of protest letters on embossed stationery has begun to peter out, and the folks who really elected the present Congress are beginning to be heard from." But this was a classic example of wishful thinking and sloppy reporting.

The mail pouring into congressional offices was running 9 to 1 against the plan and increasing in volume, not "petering out." To be sure, some of the protest was synthetic, inspired by right-wing publisher Frank E. Gannett's National Committee to Uphold Constitutional Government and other groups of that ilk. But a good part of it was spontaneous, coming from church groups and bar associations and middle-class citizens, many of whom had voted Democratic in 1936 but now denounced FDR as a power grabber and a threat to liberty and property.

"The protests reaching Washington from all sections have been overwhelming," Kansas Republican Senator Arthur Capper wrote. "We have seen nothing like it in years."

"To listen to the clamor, one would think that Moses from Mt. Sinai had declared that God himself had decreed that if and when there should be a Supreme Court of the United States, the number Nine was to be sacred," fumed Harold Ickes.

The angry public reaction reinforced conservative opposition to the president and also stirred uneasiness among some liberals worried that by tampering with the court FDR might undermine civil liberties. Still others were bothered not because the president had gone too far but because, acting out of political expediency, he had not gone far enough.

The drawback to Roosevelt's proposal, Nebraska's progressive Republican Senator George Norris wrote to a friend, was not that it was unconstitutional but rather because "it is not, in my judgment, fundamental, and will only be a temporary remedy."

Words did not suffice for Hatton Summers. He took action, lobbying members of his committee to oppose the measure. And within days of the bill's introduction he had gotten the House to approve his judicial retirement act, thus arguably eliminating the need for Roosevelt's plan. Meanwhile he had mustered a majority of five on his committee against the Court-packing bill.

FDR's bill already had a sponsor in the House in the person of Texas's Maury Maverick, a passionate liberal from San Antonio. No sooner had the clerk finished reading the bill on February 5 than Maverick picked up a copy, signed it boldly, and dropped it in the legislative hopper. For Maverick, who lived up to his surname by challenging the conservative hierarchy of his party in Congress, the president's thrust at the Court was a cause right after his own heart. Although only in his second term in the House, Maverick attracted attention and wielded a limited amount of influence as a leader of a group of thirty or so like-minded young Democrats who met regularly to promote a brand of populism that recalled William Jennings Bryan. But for all Maverick's energy and nerve, the White House knew that he and his band of liberal brothers were no match for the authority wielded by Summers, who would be able to keep the bill bottled up in his committee all summer.

The only strategy left to the administration was to gain approval in the Senate first, which could be then used as a lever to force House action. Although backers of the bill did not publicly acknowledge the fact, this was their first significant setback. And it created a dynamic that would assure more such reverses.

While the Democrats enjoyed large majorities in both houses, the White House lobbyists usually found it easier to bring pressure on the House members who, facing reelection every two years, were more dependent on presidential good graces than their Senate brethren. The Senate, whose individual members enjoyed much greater status and privilege, would be a tougher nut to crack. There the bill had the imprimatur of Judiciary Committee chairman Ashurst, who was so unfamiliar with its actual contents that he did not even put a title on it when he submitted it to his committee staff. The bill was known only as Senate Resolution 1392 until a clerk, in order to classify it, mundanely named it "A Bill to Reorganize the Judicial Branch of the Government," a title that stuck.

Ashurst was not the only Senate leader short of information about the proposal. On February 9, four days after its unveiling, Senate Majority Leader Robinson told reporters that the proposed increase in size in the Court would be temporary, for only as long as there were justices eligible for retirement. Eventually the number would revert to the original nine. When reporters asked FDR about this he was furious. "Read the bill," he snapped. Once they did they learned that the increase in number was intended to be permanent.

The apathy of the bill's supposed supporters helped clear a path for the counterassault by the opposition, whose ranks and militancy seemed to be growing every day. The more senators learned about the bill, the less they liked it, or so it appeared. After little more than a week had passed since its introduction, a few days after the UAW strikers celebrated their victory over GM in Flint, the *New York Times* reported that the plan was running into trouble "from the leadership down to the most junior member of the Senate." Around the same time, *Time*, which initially had foreseen easy sailing for the measure, now forecast that the bill faced a battle "more uncertain than that of any for which the New Deal had fought."

Piece by piece the elements of the opposition were staking out their positions and forming a coalition whose diversity enhanced its numerical strength, extending from the far right of the GOP to some on the Democratic party's left. Among the most fervid antagonists were the group of Southern senators who were hard-core opponents of the New Deal. No one was studying the bill more closely than these gentlemen from Dixie.

The more they thought about it, they saw it not only as a threat to the economic establishment, which supported them, but to something even more vital: the racial segregation that was the bulwark of their political and economic world. During his first term FDR had done little to threaten the barriers of racism. Indeed the South's Democratic oligarchs felt comfortable enough with Roosevelt that they had consented at the 1936 Democratic Convention to abolish the rule that required a nominee to win a two-thirds vote of all delegates. That rule had given the South an effective veto over selection of a nominee; agreeing to set it aside presumably assured continued support by the Democrats for the racist rules that governed politics and society in Dixie. But in 1936 when Negroes, responding to the economic relief brought by the New Deal, deserted the GOP en masse to vote for Roosevelt, Southern Democrats thought they saw the handwriting on the political wall.

Roosevelt "is determined to get the Negro vote, and I do not have to tell you what *this* means," North Carolina's Josiah Bailey, one of the New Deal's fiercest Senate foes, wrote to a friend following the announcement of the Court plan. Bailey, Carter Glass, and some of their confreres feared that the president would use his expanded appointive power to select justices who would overturn segregation and thus win more black votes for the New Deal, thus enhancing the influence of blacks in the Democratic party.

In their paranoia over how Roosevelt would use the Court against racism, Bailey and Glass were far ahead of their time, and far ahead of Roosevelt. Throughout his presidency Roosevelt would frustrate Negroes pushing for civil rights, refusing even to give any tangible support for a federal law against lynching. Civil rights was a cause he mainly left to First Lady Eleanor Roosevelt. It would take a Republican chief justice appointed by a Republican president to strike the Court's first great blow against segregation in the epochal *Brown* decision of 1954.

But of greater significance than the baseless fears that contributed to the predictable opposition of Dixie senators to the Court plan was the resistance of Democrats with moderate and even liberal leanings. This development owed much to the shrewdly calculated stance of forbearance adopted by the GOP.

From the first, leading Republicans saw FDR's move against the Court as a rich opportunity to reverse their fortunes. Alfred Landon, whose crushing defeat in 1936 had transformed him into a national joke, laid plans for a full-bore assault at the forthcoming Lincoln Day dinner of the New York Republican party. Herbert Hoover, the party's defeated 1932 standard-bearer whose once-honored name had been made ignominious by the depression, fired off an angry blast on the day the plan was announced. And the next day Hoover phoned Michigan Senator Arthur Vandenberg, one of the most ambitious members of the small GOP Senate contingent, to offer his services in what he assumed would be an all-out assault.

With this phone call the strategy that would prove the plan's undoing began to take active form. Although the voice on the phone was Hoover's, Vandenberg heard the rumble of destiny. Until that moment his career had been only a promise waiting to be fulfilled. The path that had taken him to the brink of opportunity had not been easy. After the 1893 depression ruined his father's harness-making business, his mother set up as a boardinghouse keeper and young Arthur kept himself going with odd jobs until he finished high school. Lacking the wherewithal to get his degree from the University of Michigan law school, at twenty-one he found a reporting job at the *Grand Rapids Herald*. He was only in his early thirties when he became editor and when his polemics against the League of Nations helped Henry Cabot Lodge kill the Treaty of Versailles in the Senate and break Woodrow Wilson's heart. That accomplishment earned him a stint as a speechwriter for Warren Harding, a promotion to publisher when he returned to Grand Rapids, and ultimately helped land him in the Senate in 1928.

There Vandenberg failed to live up to his advance billing. Seemingly uncertain of his own beliefs, he soon established himself as committed temporizer, veering from left to right, alternating between Hoover's stolid conservatism and Idaho Senator William Borah's Bull Moose iconoclasm. The columnist

Westbrook Pegler dismissed him as "a minor league publisher, up on his feet swishing his coattails and shooting his cuffs."

Yet the senator had his strengths. For one, he was quick-witted. He had a flair for rhetorical gimmicks, inventing the term "fiddle-faddle" and devising a new usage for "hitchhiking" in accusing the Democrats of seeking a free ride for one of their measures on a popular Republican bill. Once he chided an opponent for being "as consistent as a chameleon on plaid"—though some journalists thought the phrase suited Vandenberg as well as the other fellow.

Following the announcement of FDR's plan, Vandenberg quickly realized that opposition among Republicans was broad, including not only longtime conservative critics of the New Deal but progressives like Hiram Johnson of California and Idaho's William Borah, the ranking Republican on the Judiciary Committee. Vandenberg realized something else: here was the chance for him at last to live up to the high expectations for his career by giving direction to the opposition. Derailing the plan would require finesse and restraint, Vandenberg understood from the beginning. And this insight he shared with Borah and the Republican Senate leader Charles McNary of Oregon when they met in Borah's office on February 6, the day after Roosevelt revealed his plan.

Vandenberg passed on some advice he had gotten that very morning from a Democrat, Carl Hatch of New Mexico. "I am inclined to vote no," Hatch remarked. "But you Republicans, and particularly Mr. Hoover, must not make it too hard for me."

To the GOP leaders, the import of Hatch's message was clear; they had no trouble deciding what to do. "The general agreement," as Vandenberg later noted in his diary, "is that the Republicans shall stay in the background for a week or ten days and let the revolting Democrats make their own record."

Hoover at first rebelled. With the same stubborn narrowness of perspective that had demolished his reputation and put his party into political receivership, he demanded of Vandenberg: "Who is trying to muzzle me?" But eventually the Great Engineer agreed to go along, as did Landon and other party leaders. The GOP silence opened the way for the opposition among Democrats to expand beyond the ranks of the hard-core conservatives, who almost automatically opposed every New Deal initiative, to the moderates and liberals who had been willing, and sometimes eager, to back Roosevelt during his first term.

Probably the most colorful of this group of insurgent senators was Texas's Tom Connally, one of the most imposing figures in the Senate. Tall and powerfully built, he dressed in the style of William Jennings Bryan, with a white shirt and black string tie, and wore his hair long. He changed the color of the suits only for the seasons, wearing black in winter and white during Washington's torrid summer. The net effect impressed even his hardened colleagues, one of whom called Connally "the only man in the United States Senate who could wear a Roman Toga and not look like a fat man in a nightgown." Connally had stuck with Roosevelt even on such measures as the 1936 soak-the-rich tax proposal. But his ties to oil interests in his home state made him uneasy about what he regarded as departures from Democratic tradition, a category that to his mind clearly included the Court-packing scheme.

Another less flamboyant but equally significant moderate addition to the opposition was Bennett Champ Clark of Missouri, whose father James Beauchamp "Champ" Clark had been speaker of the House. The younger Clark had supported Roosevelt's currency policies and voted to establish Social Security. But he drew the line with Court-packing and, as with Connally, the simple announcement of his opposition gave a broader caste to the budding effort to block the plan.

By far the most important Democratic addition to the opposition was Senator Burton K. Wheeler, who would ultimately become the field marshal of the opposition forces. Among his

considerable assets were impeccable liberal credentials, stretching back to his start in politics as a legislator in his adopted state
of Montana. Wheeler labored so hard to curb the greed of Anaconda Copper, the corporate giant that controlled most of
Montana, that Anaconda did all it could to help defeat the
thirty-year-old Wheeler when he ran for state attorney general
in 1912.

Woodrow Wilson returned him to public life, making him
U.S. attorney for the state. But Wheeler balked at some of the
prosecutions his Justice Department higher-ups wanted to bring
under the repressive Espionage and Sedition Acts designed to
crush any breath of dissent against U.S. policies during the Great
War. During the infamous postwar Red Scare perpetrated by Wilson's attorney general, A. Mitchell Palmer, Wheeler's resistance
to the assault on civil liberties created so much indignation that
he resigned to avoid hurting the reelection chances of his friend
and ally from Montana, Senator Thomas Walsh.

He was not out of a job long. In 1922 his coalition of farmers
and rail workers trumped the economic might of Anaconda and
sent Wheeler to the U.S. Senate. He arrived just as the Teapot
Dome scandal was unfolding, which helped him quickly make a
name for himself. He raised such a storm about the failure of
Harry Daugherty, who Warren Harding had made attorney general to prosecute the culprits exposed in the great naval oil lease
scandal, that Daugherty was forced to resign. Wheeler's emer-
gence as a national figure was underlined in the 1924 presidential
campaign when he was chosen as running mate to Robert La Follette on the Progressive party ticket that won half as many votes
as the hapless Democratic party did that year.

Not only was Wheeler's liberalism beyond question, so was
his support for FDR. He was the first Democrat of note outside
New York to back Roosevelt for president. "If the Democratic
Party of New York will elect Franklin D. Roosevelt for governor,"
Wheeler declared early in Governor Roosevelt's 1930 campaign

for reelection, the West will demand his nomination for president and the whole country will elect him." And he helped steer FDR's bandwagon to victory at the 1932 convention where he first ran afoul of future Attorney General Homer Cummings because of Cummings's eagerness to push for repeal of the rule requiring two-thirds of the delegates for nomination. A suspicious man by nature, Wheeler came to conclude that Cummings figured his attack on the rule, which he eventually abandoned, would backfire and lead to the party nominating someone else, perhaps Homer Cummings. Although in this case his theory was probably far off base, in general Wheeler's instinctive wariness increased his effectiveness in political combat. Wheeler further bolstered his ties to FDR in 1935 when he led the fight for the Public Utility Holding Companies Act, the toughest challenge for the New Deal to that time.

Along with his record, Wheeler brought to the fray a dynamic and engaging personality. Born and raised in the East, he landed in Butte after losing his modest bankroll to local card sharks, and readily adapted to the rough-and-ready style of the West. With his rumpled suit, battered Stetson, and cigar clamped between his teeth, no one would ever mistake Burt Wheeler for a Roman senator. But his lack of pretention and a blunt manner made him seem more authentic than many of his colleagues. He combined affability and pugnacity in a way that many found disarming. "If I could smile like you while calling a man an SOB I'd give a million dollars," another Montana politician once told him.

Wheeler had known for some time that FDR wanted to do something to curb the Supreme Court's inroads on the New Deal. In 1936 Tom Corcoran, who had worked closely with Wheeler on the Utility Holding Company Bill, had urged the senator to introduce a bill adding three justices to the court. Wheeler told him that such a measure would assure the president's defeat in the forthcoming election. "The court was like a religion to the American people," he had warned Corcoran. Despite this caution, when he learned about FDR's court-reform "bombshell" from a newspaper story, he was "flabbergasted" at the boldness of the plan, which, as he said, "did not even have the virtue of being a constitutional amendment."

Wheeler had other grievances against FDR. For one thing, Roosevelt had turned federal patronage in Montana over to J. Bruce Kremer, a party leader and longtime foe of Wheeler's, an affront for which Wheeler blamed Homer Cummings, an ally of Kremer. For another, Wheeler felt jealous of Roosevelt, who as the new champion of liberalism got attention some of which used to go to Wheeler. "Who does Roosevelt think he is?" Wheeler demanded of a White House aide sent to soothe him. "He used to be just one of the barons," he added, using a figure of speech that revealed how Wheeler and other senators viewed their roles. I was the baron of the Northwest; Huey Long was baron of the South." Now, he complained, FDR had become "like a king, trying to reduce the barons."

Of course, separately or together these differences could not justify a serious quarrel with the president. But the Court-packing plan was something else. "Here was an unsubtle and anti-constitutional grab for power which would destroy the court as an institution," or so it seemed to Wheeler. And op-posing it offered him a chance to wage a grand-scale battle for principle but also in the process regain the spotlight—and not incidentally get his own back with Homer Cummings, the au-thor of the nefarious scheme. His determination to fight was bolstered by his wife, Lulu, who deeply mistrusted FDR and whom the president later branded as "the Lady Macbeth of the Court fight."

Denouncing the bill as an attempt to circumvent the Consti-tution, Wheeler swung into action with the same gusto he had fought against Anaconda back in Montana and for the Holding Company bill in Washington. Selected as leader of a group of opposing Democrats, including Champ Clark and Tom Connally, Wheeler assigned each man in the group to keep after certain senators who were either for the bill or uncommitted, and pressure them to come out against it. He used his clout as chairman of the Interstate Commerce Committee to line up radio broadcasts by other senators against the bill. And he coordinated overall strategy with newspaper magnate Frank Gannett and with the church and civic groups around the country that had joined the fight against Court-packing.

Not until February 14, nine days after the plan was announced, did the New Deal begin to fight back. Attorney General Cummings was the first to take on the challenge in a radio address. He sought to rebut the "insensate clamor" intended, he said, to divert attention from the merits of the president's proposal. But to make his case Cummings relied on the same disingenuous argument offered to justify FDR's scheme when it was first announced—that it was intended merely to speed the administration of justice. "He made a pretty good speech, but I don't think it was particularly telling," Harold Ickes observed afterward.

Cummings's talk did trigger a stinging retort from Virginia's Carter Glass. "The country is infinitely greater in need of an attorney general," Glass said, "than of judicial wet-nurses for six of the present members of the Court."

To stem the swelling opposition, Roosevelt decided to call upon his best weapon, himself, and to deliver two speeches. He began on March 4 with an address to a Democratic victory dinner in which he abandoned all pretense that his plan was merely an administrative reform. Instead he spoke of the country's desperate needs, harking back to the dramatic phrasing he had used in his inaugural address. "Here is one-third of a nation, ill-nourished, ill-clad, ill-housed, now!" he practically shouted for emphasis. And he reviewed the New Deal's efforts to meet those needs, adding, "You know who assumed the power to veto and did veto that program." With the cheers of his audience rising to a crescendo, the president added, "If we are to make democracy succeed, we must act now."

Reaction to the speech demonstrated again how the president's thrust at the Court had soured even some former admirers. "Mr. Roosevelt is not ambitious personally, but he has turned into an Eagle Scout whose passion for doing the country a good turn every day has at last got out of hand," groused E. B. White in the *New Yorker*. "His 'Now' remarks were a giveaway—the utterances of a petulant savior. America doesn't need to be saved today; it can wait till tomorrow."

The second speech, five days later, one of FDR's now legendary fireside chats, was less partisan and more reasoned but still charged with emotion. "We must take action to save the Constitution from the court and the court from itself," the president told the millions of Americans tuned in on their living room radios. Offering reassurance in his warm, vibrant voice Roosevelt said: "You who know me can have no fear that I would tolerate the destruction by any branch of the government of any part of our heritage of freedom. You who know me will accept my solemn assurance that in a world in which democracy is under attack I seek to make American democracy work."

Good as it sounded, it was no sale.

To be sure, the White House did receive the usual outpouring of approving letters and telegrams produced by almost any presidential speech. But only a trickle of protest reached the offices of lawmakers who opposed FDR's Court plan. No one who had been against the plan was converted to the president's side. Those who had been neutral stayed that way.

Roosevelt then reached for another weapon in his arsenal, the patronage of the presidency. Calling in all the chits owed him by farm and labor leaders, by officeholders from alderman to governor, and last but certainly not least by any wealthy Democrat who had ever made out a check to fund a campaign, he brought pressure on foes of his plan to change their minds. "We must hold up judicial appointments in states where the delegation is not going along," FDR urged his postmaster general and former campaign manager Jim Farley, who hardly needed instruction in this sort of thing. "We must make them promptly where they are with us."

Those on the receiving end of this treatment squirmed, but they did not budge, least of all their ringleader, Burt Wheeler. "Labor and farm leaders in Montana were 100 percent against me," Wheeler recalled. "They threatened me with political oblivion if I didn't switch and go along with the president."

But Wheeler stood firm. The Court plan was now more than a month old and growing more vulnerable each day. On March 10, the day after the president's eloquent but ultimately futile fireside chat, hearings on the bill opened in the U.S. Senate. The White House wished to speed the proceedings along. But the foes of the bill dragged their feet. The longer the hearings went on, they believed, the stronger the case against the bill. As the hearings got under way, Tom Corcoran asked Chairman Ashurst to get the committee to agree to a time limit.

But Ashurst turned him down. "You know how hard it is to get senators to agree to anything," Ashurst said. "Senators have their own minds. They like plenty of time to express themselves."

If James Madison could only have known, he would surely have been content. Ambition had been made to counteract ambition; the interests of political adversaries had been linked to the constitutional powers of their branch of government. It was all working according to plan.

But not according to President Roosevelt's plan. Not only was he losing control of the battle over the Court to his foes in Washington. On a broader front, his supporters in the labor movement, flushed with the success of the Flint sit-down, were stirring an embarrassing ruckus in factories, mines, and shops around the country.

6

National Pastime

On the first Sunday of Franklin Roosevelt's second term the *New York Times* served up to its readers an analysis of the New Year so grim that its impact went beyond sobering to downright depressing. Its author, Arthur Krock, was widely esteemed, not least of all by himself, as the paper's Washington correspondent. Krock's title somewhat understated his importance to the *Times* and his influence in the special world of the nation's capital. The *Times*, of course, employed numerous other correspondents in its Washington bureau. But Krock was officially dubbed *the* Washington correspondent, signaling that his eminence stood far above the rest.

For his first column of the year, Krock had taken as his theme the labor unrest roiling the nation. Although the sit-down strike in Flint had barely begun, he foresaw that there would be many more such disruptions during the course of the year. He acknowledged that numerous other problems confronted the new Congress and the president. "But every one of them," he contended, "is fundamentally affected by the causes and possible consequences of the strikes." Krock recalled the brief "era of good feeling" between business leaders and government that followed the election, when the heads of the giant corporations pledged their cooperation to the Roosevelt administration in speeding the work of economic recovery.

But that mood had vanished with the spread of strikes and the administration's apparent sympathy for the cause of organized labor. "Now," Krock wrote, "the seventy-fifth Congress is meeting in an atmosphere surcharged with peril—to recovery, to public and legislative order, and to equality of all population groups under the law. This is a depressing fact, but it is true."

This was a forecast that, at the time it was published, most in the New Deal would have judged far too Cassandra-like. But before the year was much older, events would make Krock seem like a journalist whose prescience had more than lived up to his lofty reputation.

While strikes in general increased markedly, it was the sit-down strikes that led the way. The UAW's success in Flint sparked workers in almost every trade to follow suit. Michigan, Detroit in particular, was where most of the trouble first erupted. In the final week of February, ten days after GM caved in to the UAW, some five thousand workers at more than a score of factories and other businesses around the Motor City went on strike, mostly the sit-down variety. On Monday three hundred autobody workers took over the Briggs Manufacturing plant in the Detroit enclave of Highland Park. The next day thirty liquor truck drivers for Star Transfer Lines sat down and won the gains they sought before the end of the day. On Wednesday three hundred workers, mostly women, at the Ferry Morse Seed Company sat down at their jobs and by the next day had gained a twenty-five-cent-an-hour raise and a forty-hour week.

The strike wave mounted as the week went on and reached a climax on Saturday in the midst of the weekend shopping rush. In the big Woolworth's Five and Ten in the heart of downtown Detroit, at the sound of a whistle blown by the organizer for the Waiters and Waitresses Union, some 150 women clerks halted work in unison. Then all of them, the lunch-counter brigade in their white short-sleeved uniforms and the others in their long fitted skirts and knitted tops, stepped back from their counters and folded their arms. "The jangle of cash registers stopped," reported the *Detroit News*, "and bewildered customers found themselves holding out nickels and dimes in vein."

Within the next few weeks similar scenes were repeated across the country as the sit-down surge swung into high gear. Shipyards and textile mills, college campuses, and even coffin factories all were hit in one town or another. The number of sit-downs, which had nearly doubled from 25 in January to 47 in February, made a quantum leap in March to 170, more than three times the total of all the prededing year, involving more than 160,000 workers. In Detroit, still the center of the storm, "Sitting down has replaced baseball as a national pastime," the *Detroit News* reported, "and sitter-downers clutter the landscape in every direction." The *New York Times*'s Rome correspondent traced the origins of the new American phenomenon to slowdowns staged by Italian metalworkers in 1920. But others pointed to an earlier example of European sit-downs by French workers building the Rouen Cathedral in the fifteenth century.

Democratic Senator Elbert Thomas of Utah contended the sit-downs had been inspired by the passive-resistance tactics of Mahatma Gandhi. But researchers discovered that American workers staged their first sit-down before Gandhi came to prominence. In 1884 brewery workers sat down in Cincinnati, barricading themselves behind beer kegs; attacking state troopers punctured the barrels, and the wine of the hops flowed into the Queen City's streets. In 1906 the IWW took command of General Electric's Schenectady plant for a sixty-five hour-siege, during which food was for the first time brought into a struck plant to feed the workers.

Whatever its origins, neither the United States nor any other country had seen such an epidemic of sit-downs as now engulfed the "heav'n rescued land." And they were by no means confined to the workplace. At penitentiaries in Pennsylvania and Illinois, inmates sat down to get better treatment but failed. In Zanesville, Ohio, housewives occupied the office of the director of public services, protesting against a dusty neighborhood street.

The spree had its lighter side. In the town of Neponset, Illinois, schoolchildren sat down in the local drugstore, demanding free candy until a generous resident resolved their grievance with a five-dollar check to the store owner. A divorced woman sat down in her ex-husband's apartment demanding he pay the back alimony he owed her. And in New York City's Madison Square Garden, the New York Rovers amateur hockey team kept fifteen thousand fans waiting for half an hour while they sat down in their dressing room because they had been denied the free tickets promised them.

But most strikes were in deadly earnest, sometimes accompanied by violence. In a metallurgy plant south of Waukegan, Illinois, more than one hundred sit-downers in a two-hour battle beat back a like number of police and deputy sheriffs who tried to drive them out of the plant. The officers laid siege to the plant, sent for reinforcements, and a few days later launched another attack. This time they forced the strikers to evacuate.

With public concern over such violence rising around the country, New Jersey Governor Harold Hoffman saw an opportunity to take a stand against the sit-downs—and not incidentally to repair his battered reputation. Not long before, Hoffman had been one of the few bright young stars in the GOP firmament. A small-town boy from South Amboy, he had served as a captain in the American Expeditionary Force in the Great War and came back to become secretary-treasurer of the South Amboy Trust Company. He then parlayed his military record into a political career, first as mayor of his hometown, then in 1926 moving up to Congress. While winning a second term in Congress, Hoffman managed also to get himself elected New Jersey motor vehicle commissioner.

At the time the move was widely attributed to Hoffman's hopes of building a political machine in the state which could help him reach the governorship. There was some truth to that; but Hoffman had another motive for taking over the state agency, which did not become apparent for many years, until after his death in 1954. Unbeknownst to the world, Hoffman's campaign for Congress had left him deeply in debt. Hoffman nevertheless continued to live in the style which he thought befitting to a congressman, hosting lavish parties and giving generous gifts to friends.

What no one knew at the time was that he financed this lifestyle by embezzling funds, eventually totaling $300,000, from the South Amboy Trust Company, where he was now president and principal stockholder. The benefit of taking over the state's motor vehicle department was that it gave him access to substantial funds collected in fees for license plates and drivers' permits. With forgeries, phony ledger statements, and fund transfers, Hoffman used these funds to help him cover his tracks at the bank.

Meanwhile Hoffman also exploited the political opportunities offered by his job. Standing only five foot seven but weighing more than two hundred pounds, with a perpetual grin, he fit everyone's favorite stereotype, the happy-go-lucky fat guy. He was a glib storyteller with a self-deprecating sense of humor. The Elks, Lions, Kiwanians, and other civic clubs around the state could not get enough of his jokes and his enthusiastic recitals of the free-enterprise principles underlying true Republicanism.

In 1934 Hoffman won the GOP gubernatorial nomination easily and trounced his Democratic opponent, a functionary of the notorious boss of Jersey City, Frank Hague. Given that the national political landscape everywhere resembled a cemetery for GOP prospects, Hoffman's victory in an important industrial state inevitably stirred talk about a place for him on the 1936 national ticket, at least as vice president. And he became much sought after as a speaker at Republican gatherings around the country.

But the glow soon faded. In 1935, his second year in office, Hoffman antagonized his own party by pushing through the legislature a highly unpopular sales tax. The next year he embarrassed himself and his supporters when he could not resist injecting himself into "the crime of the century," the kidnapping of the Lindbergh baby. The whole country was caught up by the seizure of Charles Lindbergh's young son from the family mansion in Hopewell, New Jersey, the discovery of the infant's s body two months later, and the arrest and conviction of Bruno Richard Hauptmann, a German immigrant carpenter. But Hoffman was not convinced of Hauptmann's guilt. Seeing an opportunity to make himself the hero of the case, he hired a New Jersey detective to find the "real killer." Sure enough, the detective got a Trenton man to confess to the crime. But when it was discovered that the admission was beaten out of him, the suspect was released, the detective was jailed, Hauptmann was ultimately electrocuted in April 1936, and the governor was left to look like a meddling fool.

In February 1937, catching wind of CIO plans to launch an organizing drive in New Jersey, Hoffman sought to redeem himself in the public eye by threatening to use force if need be to squelch sit-downs. Citing "the lawless methods and practices" of sit-down strikers in Michigan and elsewhere, the governor vowed he would not tolerate such activities in New Jersey. "A labor union has no more right to take possession of a factory than a band of gangsters has to take possession of a bank," he declared, adding, "There is no difference between the two, either in principle or in degree." Pledging to marshal all the resources of his state against the unions, Hoffman declared ominously, "The avoidance of the possibility of bloodshed is of course, desirable, but not at the expense of surrender to or compromise with or toleration of those guilty of such criminal acts."

When the New Jersey League of Women Voters questioned Hoffman's tough-guy stance, the governor replied in a letter in which he called the sit-down strike "a symbol of communism," and added, "The sit-down strike has as its basic principle a deliberate disregard for what we have always regarded as hallowed property rights and it is inevitably followed by contempt for honorable judicial procedures."

As it turned out, Hoffman's blast at the CIO, though it gained him national attention, did little to help his political career. But it did have the unintended consequence of helping to unite New Jersey's trade unions. An official of the state AFL, whose member unions had generally shunned sit-downs, said Hoffman's statements "must be construed as an attack upon all efforts to organize labor," adding, "We are not going to be divided by an issue of this kind."

A few days after Hoffman's diatribe, the organizers for the CIO's Steel Workers began courting workers at three big Trenton steel plants. Their major weapons were circulars bearing in bold type across the top the words: "The President wants you to join the union." That was more grist for Hoffman's mill. In a nationally broadcast radio address he labeled the CIO "a militant minority," which he denounced for "claiming governmental blessing as it seizes private property defies the law and denies the authority of the remaining 98 per cent of our people. To hold a factory for ransom by the process of a 'sit-down' strike is to refuse reason and law," he declared.

For good measure Hoffman also condemned FDR's Court-packing bill, one of the first politicians to speak of the two issues in the same breath. "It is a startling spectacle to see a president within a month after he has sworn to 'preserve, protect and defend the Constitution,'" he said, "calling upon Congress to give him by indirect methods that which the Constitution clearly denies him." Then, in a clear allusion to the sit-down strikes, he made a point that would trouble millions of other Americans in the weeks to come. "The president must set an example in keeping the faith," Hoffman declared. "Any indication that he is unwilling to do this lends assurance to those who seek to ignore lawful processes and who wish to forget the law."

Regardless of what Hoffman or anyone else had to say, FDR pushed ahead with his Court-packing scheme, and the pace of sit-downs quickened. In a single day, March 8, three hundred members of the United Electrical workers sat down at the Emerson Electric plant in St. Louis, where the union sought to organize two thousand workers. In Springfield, Ohio, three hundred workers at the Springfield Metallic Casket Company, members of the Casket Makers union, a CIO affiliate, sat down and stopped production. In Pittsburgh two hundred workers, members of the United Garment Workers of America, sat down at the American Trouser Company. The union said it was seeking a return to the 1929 wage scale of sixteen dollars a week for a forty-hour week and intended to organize all seven hundred pants makers in the city.

Later in the week 215 strikers sat down at four stores of the H. L. Green department store chain in New York City and presented the company with a 22-point program calling for union recognition, a 40-hour week, and a minimum weekly wage of $20. While negotiations with management went forward, the union's food distribution system provided workers at the largest of the stores, in downtown Manhattan, 85 pounds of veal, which they cheerfully made into goulash. At night a nearby Greek restaurant sent in dinner.

But the major battleground remained the starting point for the year's imbroglios, Michigan and the auto industry. This time the principal target of the United Auto Workers was the Chrysler Corporation, then the second-largest of the auto companies. And the struggle between the union and this manufacturer soon at least matched the bitterness of the battle in Flint.

The UAW's success at Flint had provided immediate dividends to the union and to GM workers. Suddenly Joseph Pagono, a long-frustrated organizer, said getting workers to join the union was no longer a problem. "I did not have to go out and seek members," he recalled. "They were seeking me." Moreover every day the union was winning concrete gains, bearing out the promise of the agreements reached with General Motors—pay raises, the rehiring of fired workers, the establishment of seniority lists, the settlement of petty but long-ignored grievances, the retiming of jobs to eliminate the speedup. "The inhuman high speed is no more," said Alfred H. Lockhart, a Fisher Body worker who had opposed the strike. "We now have a voice, and have slowed up the speed of the line, and are now treated as human beings, and not as part of the machinery."

Word of these betterments spread quickly among autoworkers in Detroit and helped to fuel the UAW drive against Chrysler. The leaders of the Chrysler strike had sent observers to Flint and had learned from the sit-down there. But so had Chrysler. When six thousand strikers took over eight Chrysler plants in the Detroit area, the company lost no time in obtaining an injunction. On March 15, while the union picketed his courtroom, a Wayne County Circuit Court judge issued a sweeping order giving the workers two days to evacuate.

The next day the strikers, arming themselves with clubs and wrenches, made plain they would defy the court. The company said the strike had idled 100,000 workers. But that was only part of Detroit's chaotic labor story. Sit-downs and lockouts closed the city's four leading hotels and crippled about 30 other industries. And new strikes were threatened by taxi and truck drivers, milkmen and store clerks.

Once again Governor Murphy was on the spot. On March 17, while the sit-downers at Chrysler defied the court order to evacuate and more than thirty thousand pickets cheered their disdain for the law, Murphy rushed to the scene to warn that his patience was running out. The strikes, he declared, in a statement that reflected both his liberal sensibilities and his instinct for political survival, had endangered democratic governance and paved the way for "the rule of mobs or dictators. Worst of all, labor movements and organizations are discredited, faith in liberal democratic government is permanently impaired and social progress is impaired." Until then, the governor pointed out, he had relied on negotiation and sought to avoid force. But, he added, "There is obviously a limit to this policy. No one should assume or infer that the government of this state will forsake its responsibility to maintain order and protect citizens in the full exercise of their legal rights."

Despite his harsh language, the governor was reluctant to bring force to bear against the strikers, and with good reason. Neither police nor sheriff's deputies were up to the job, and to call on the National Guard would result in a bloody battle. Instead Murphy set up a law-and-order committee made up of representatives of business, labor, church, and civic groups. UAW president Homer Martin, typically indulging his emotions, refused to meet with the committee because of Murphy's tough language and the tactics of Detroit police in ousting strikers from some of the city's other sit-downs. In fact Martin threatened to call a general strike in the city unless "the brutal evictions and ruthless clubbing of strikers was halted immediately."

Yet to the minds of some Americans and their leaders, a harder line was just what was needed to avoid the turbulence that threatened not only Detroit but other major cities. On the same day the Chrysler strikers defied the courts and challenged their governor, taxicab drivers battled strikebreakers and police in the heart of Chicago's Loop while thousands watched from office windows. A mounted policeman who rode into the mob was pulled from his horse and beaten while nearby another officer chased away strikers by leveling a shotgun at them. The strikers stopped cabs driven by scab drivers, threw passengers into the street, and in one case set the cab on fire.

In New York City a strike at five-and-ten-cent stores spread to Woolworth stores in downtown Manhattan and Brooklyn. Pickets climbed onto a second-story ledge above the store entrance, opened windows, and threw food, blankets, and other provisions to the strikers inside while private police tried in vain to stop them. The sit-downers sent a cablegram rebuking Barbara Hutton Haugwitiz Reventlow, the Woolworth heiress whose extravagant lifestyle had become an embarrassment to the company's executives. Babs, as the tabloids called her, had that very year bought $2 million in jewelry, two Rolls Royces, a 157-foot yacht, and a mansion in London. The strikers condemned her profligacy in the face of the hunger and poverty that prevailed in New York and elsewhere in the country.

In Clifton, New Jersey, Harold Hoffman's state, a sit-down strike by 150 employees of the Pacific Slipper Company, asking higher wages and cleaner toilets, went into its third day. But Hoffman, despite his previous bellicose stance, like Frank Murphy, was not eager to back up his words with actions. It was the job of local police to enforce the law, the governor said. If the police failed to act, the next move would be up to the courts. Should the local sheriff be unable to enforce the court's order, an appeal could be made to the governor. "At that time I will take such action as circumstances warrant," Hoffman said.

But in the U.S. Senate, whose members did not have to actually deal with the crises facing state and local officials, some decided that the time for dithering had passed. First to speak was one of the body's aging lions, Hiram Johnson of California. Although nominally a Republican, Johnson was better known for his willingness to defy the Republican establishment—and indeed the hierarchy of both parties—than he was for partisan loyalty. Florid-faced, short of stature, and wide of girth, at seventy he remained hard-driving, humorless, and often hamfisted in his approach to issues.

In charting his course Johnson tended more than most politicians to follow the dictates of his conscience and his principles. In 1912 he broke with the GOP to run as Theodore Roosevelt's vice-presidential candidate on the Bull Moose ticket, and even filled in for Roosevelt on the stump while TR recovered from an assassination attempt. After six reform-filled years as governor of California, he had won election to the Senate in 1916 and took his seat just as Woodrow Wilson was leading the country into the Great War. Johnson was a skeptic from the start. "When war comes, truth is the first casualty," he famously declared. Nevertheless he supported the war as a concession to what Wilson claimed was the national interest while he served his conscience by seeking to protect civil liberties against the excesses of Wilson's crackdown on alleged acts of espionage and sedition by the citizenry, and by fighting to raise taxes on war profiteers.

At war's end the Californian broke with Wilson completely over the League of Nations, which he charged was just a contrivance to preserve the "old dynastic empires of Britain, France, and Italy." Johnson got along no better with the White House during the Republican presidential hegemony of the 1920s. He supported farm measures opposed by the Republican high command and irritated GOP regulars even more, not to mention the utility industry, by sponsoring legislation that led to construction of Boulder Dam, the largest federal power installation of its day.

Johnson also caused consternation among business interests and their allies in the GOP in 1921 when he pushed through a resolution to investigate what he called a "state of civil war" between the coal industry and the mine workers' union in West Virginia. The ensuing hearings went on for three months, produced a thousand pages of testimony laying bare the extent to which the coal companies, owned by some of the nation's most powerful corporations, controlled the government of West Virginia, and gave the union rare reason for hope in its losing struggle.

With Roosevelt's election it appeared that the former Bull Mooser had at last found a president with whom he could get along. He saw in the New Yorker a kindred spirit of domestic reform who blessedly seemed, unlike Wilson and Hoover, to be free from the taint of internationalism. Accordingly, Johnson worked hard for passage of the New Deal economic reforms during the First Hundred Days. By the second half of Roosevelt's first term, however, Johnson, like many others in Congress, began to worry that the New Deal's leftward tide of reform had gone far enough, if not already too far. Refusing to campaign for FDR in 1936, the old reformer nevertheless voted for him, though as he later wrote a friend, "with many misgivings."

The unveiling of the president's plan for overhauling the Supreme Court lent substance to Johnson's doubts, and he denounced the proposal at the outset. The Republican strategy of allowing the Democrats to lead the assault on the Court plan constrained the senator from saying much more on that issue for the time being. But he felt no such inhibition about the sit-down strikes, which he viewed as another result of Roosevelt's reckless rule. If the president had not directly instigated these outbursts, at best he had appeared to encourage them by tolerating them.

Johnson was still not fully himself in the wake of a long illness. But now, he felt, was the time to speak out. On March 17, with sit-downs triggering violence and defiance of the law around the country, he rose in the Senate. "I desire to occupy just a minute," he said. Then, in an apparent allusion to his health problems he explained that he wanted "to issue a feeble warning as far as it lies within my power." What followed, the *New York Times* reported, was the briefest speech of Johnson's Senate career. "The most ominous thing in our national economic life today is the sit-down strike," he told the Senate. "It is bad for the government and in the long run it is worse for labor. If the sit-down strike is carried on with the connivance or the sympathy of the public authorities, then the warning signals are out, and down that road lies dictatorship."

That was all Johnson had to say. But his colleagues were just getting started. Rather than diminishing their impact, the brevity of Johnson's remarks seemed to add to their power. Enhancing their significance was the political profile of the speaker, a man noted for his independence of thought, his freedom from narrow partisanship, his support of New Deal policies, and his championship of working people.

First to respond was James Hamilton Lewis of Illinois, a Democrat whose party pedigree could not be questioned. He had arrived in Washington even before Johnson, in 1912, at the start of Woodrow Wilson's term, and had served as party whip, rounding up votes for Wilson's New Freedom proposals which anticipated the New Deal. Defeated for reelection in 1918 in the postwar Democratic collapse, he remained active in the party and regained his old seat in 1930. He was soon restored to his old position as whip, proving to be as loyal to FDR in that role as he had been to Roosevelt's old boss, Wilson. But the flood of disturbing news of labor unrest from Detroit and elsewhere, and Johnson's somber clarion, now stirred him to go against his grain and sharply challenge the leader whose interests he normally respected and served.

Lewis was born midway through the Civil War and carried himself in a nineteenth-century manner, affecting a billowing cravat, gloves, and walking stick, beribboned eyeglasses, and carefully parted chin whiskers. Unlike the often brusque Johnson, Lewis's oratory was replete with literary allusions and dignified, baroque phrases.

"May I propound a question to the Senator as a member of this official family?" he began. "Is the United States a government?" he demanded. "Is this government going to continue an apparently unobserving attitude throughout the country where indiscriminate paralysis of every form of business is being encouraged and every relation of commerce dismembered under the name of a controversy between employer and employee?"

Lewis linked the beginnings of Mussolini's rule in Italy and Hitler's in Germany to the decision by industrialists to support the dictators to defend themselves against the threat of Communist influence among the workers. "We sit silent here, indifferent to what all of this threatens us with," he said. "In every hour such as this there awaits another Hitler and there lurks in the shadows another Mussolini."

The attack on sit-downs was building into a barrage. No sooner had Lewis taken his seat than William H. King of Utah rose to pound away at the same theme. Like Lewis, King was also a Democrat, but a Democrat of a very different stripe, calling himself "a constitutional Democrat." A former Mormon missionary who was now in his fourth Senate term, he had little use for the New Deal from the start. Aligning himself with the hardest-shell conservatives of the Southern Democracy, he defended the rights of states against the encroachments of the federal government with the same vigor his colleagues from Dixie routinely displayed. Although his Utah was scarcely a hotbed of left wing politics, King was deemed so conservative by liberals in his state party that they defeated him in his bid to be a delegate to the 1936 national convention.

Now King told the Senate that the sit-down strike was "the chief weapon of the new labor movement," noting that its use was condemned by the likes of AFL president William Green. In Detroit, he said, a newspaper article had reported that "hundreds of armed men formed picket lines around the court rooms seeking to intimidate the decisions of the courts." A few years before, King reminded his colleagues, John L. Lewis had spoken out against an alleged Communist plot to take over his union, the United Mine Workers. "Revolutionary leaders in America are now making this large-scale attempt," he said, claiming "a sinister connection" existed between past Communist efforts to control the mine workers and the current tactics of the CIO and the sit-down strikers.

At this point Arkansas's Joseph Robinson, the majority leader of the Senate, could find no other way to silence the critics of the sit-down than to adjourn. Trying to calm things, he issued a statement conceding that the sit-down strikes were illegal but arguing there was little Congress could do about it. Instead he shifted responsibility to the Supreme Court, which had under consideration the Wagner Act whose protections for collective bargaining Robinson suggested might alleviate some of labor's grievances. Until the Court acted, Robinson said, "it is exceedingly difficult to make advancement."

But adjournment came too late to erase the impact of the anti-sit-down oratory. The next day's *New York Times* carried on its front page, along with headlines about the continued strike in Detroit, a streamer that declared "SIT-INS HOTLY DENOUNCED IN SENTATE," with even scarier subheads: "CHAOS IS FORESEEN" and "FASCISM HELD POSSIBLE."

Meanwhile Senate liberals sought to respond to the previous day's onslaught. Idaho's Borah came from the same Republican Progressive tradition as California's Johnson. But Borah took a broader view of the sit-downs than did his colleague from the Golden State. All would agree, Borah told the Senate, that obedience to the law is the foundation of free government. But, he added, pointedly, "my contention is that obedience from some and disobedience from others begets disobedience from all. I cannot disassociate this lawlessness from the lawlessness in the business world."

Another liberal, Hugo Black of Alabama, picking up the theme offered by Joe Robinson, sought to shift responsibility to the Supreme Court, which he cited as "an insuperable, impossible obstacle" to the enactment of laws that might deal with the underlying causes of the sit-downs. Black's like-minded colleague from Indiana, Senator Sherman Minton, could not resist a quip at the expense of the high court. Noting the justices seemed to have been taking their time reaching a decision on the Wagner Act, he remarked, ". . . Apparently there is a sit-down strike over there."

But the liberal counterattack was drowned out by the clamor of events. In Detroit on March 19, two days after Hiram Johnson fired the opening salvo against the sit-downers in the U.S. Senate, city police broke up sit-down strikes in seven downtown shoe stores, smashing the glass doors to gain entrance when the strikers refused to leave. Similar raids were staged against strikes in small cigar and meat-packing plants and other retail stores.

In the midst of this sound and fury, the Chrysler strike dragged on as the six thousand sit-downers refused to yield their positions in the plants despite the court order to abandon the factories. The strikers made plain that if an attempt were made to evict them, they would meet force with force. They barricaded some gates to the plant, locked others, and stationed pickets on guard both inside and out. On Friday, March 19, Governor Murphy bravely sounded a hopeful note. "The present status of the situation is encouraging," he claimed. "The authorities"—whom Murphy did not otherwise identify—"want exactly the right thing done and at the same time want a matter of this great magnitude settled in friendly and peaceful conference and in a spirit of reason and justice." But as the weekend came and went with no break in the strike, Murphy's optimism seemed increasingly detached from reality.

On Sunday, March 21, UAW president Homer Martin, in another outburst, again threatened a general strike—this time to protest the raids by police against sit-down strikers. He also called for a massive demonstration in Cadillac Square in the heart of Detroit to challenge the actions of city authorities in cracking down on the strikes.

On Capitol Hill some viewed these events as threats to the Republic. Others considered them protests against deep-rooted economic injustice. But in the House, Michigan Republican Clare E. Hoffman saw the strikes as a chance to berate FDR. The hard-line conservative probably expressed the outlook of millions of Americans weary of the sit-downs and skeptical of the president's handling of the strikes, when on March 22 he opened fire on Roosevelt. "If the president would tell his hired man in

Michigan, Governor Murphy, and this lady down here trying to run the Department of Labor," Hoffman said referring to Labor Secretary Perkins, "to have sit-downers get out, we would not have any trouble."

Martin Dies, Jr., of Texas saw something else in the sit-down strikes: an opportunity, which the thirty-six-year-old legislator moved quickly to exploit. Dies had followed in the footsteps of his father, into the House of Representatives where he had served Texas's Second District and his country for a decade. The son arrived in 1930, representing the same East Texas folks as his father, having just turned thirty, big, blond, and confidently sounding the chords of Bryan's old-time populist religion. He condemned "capitalistic tyranny" and the evils of monopoly, demanded lower tariffs, and urged cheaper currency to be achieved through a wider use of silver.

Like a number of other Southerners, including his state's junior senator, Tom Connally, Dies got along fine with Roosevelt at first, and then fell out of love, vehemently. He fought the administration on coal-industry regulation and minimum-wage legislation. And he became closer friends with fellow Texan John Nance Garner. Although Garner had made clear his lack of enthusiasm for the president's Court-packing plan, he was more troubled by the sit-down strikes than by the proposed change in the judiciary.

"No president can control the court," the vice president confided to a friend. "But let the sit-down strikes become established as an American custom and recognized in law and it will change our entire theory of property ownership and government."

Given Dies's closeness to Garner and the shared antipathy of both Texans to the sit-down strikes, it was no surprise that Dies decided the time had come to take action against this spreading menace. Thus it was that on March 23 Martin Dies rose in the House of Representatives to demand a full-scale House inquiry of this "epidemic of sit-down strikes" with a view toward developing remedial legislation. In the course of his thirty-minute speech, interrupted repeatedly by outbursts of applause, Dies branded the strikers as "lawless and un-American." And he called the strikes "an open challenge to law and order, and a bold threat to that stability without which no nation can ever survive." Dies's proposal was referred to the House Rules Committee, but few who sampled the temper of the House that afternoon doubted that if it had been put to a vote then and there, approval would have been overwhelming.

Two nights later, March 25, FDR called his sometime confidant, Harold Ickes. The president had heard Ickes had been suffering from the flu, and Roosevelt inquired into the state of his health.

Ickes was fine, he told the president.

But Roosevelt had some disturbing news for Ickes. Senate majority leader Joe Robinson of Arkansas and some of his cohorts "were jittery about the sit-down strike situation, fearing that it might have bad repercussions on the Court fight," Roosevelt confided.

Ickes himself did not disagree. Indeed it would have been hard to quarrel with Robinson's reasoning. All week long, as the president's allies sought to defend his Court reform plan, newspaper headlines trumpeted the ominous news of labor disruption, and sometimes violence, in Detroit and elsewhere in the country. And in an alarming indication of the extent of the problem, and the concern it was causing among the nation's leaders, the *New York Times* began listing each morning on its front page, under the heading "Day's Strike Developments," brief summaries of stories scattered throughout the paper about the sit-downs and other strikes. On March 24, for example, the day before Roosevelt called Ickes, these included, besides coverage of the seeming chaos in Detroit, reports of discord from Albany, New York, to Boston to Reading, Pennsylvania.

"There isn't any doubt that the opponents of the President on this issue are trying to use these labor disputes as an argument to their advantage," Ickes confided to his diary. Yet Ickes liked to think that the president's supporters had a potent counterargument. They could cite the strikes "as an example of what happens when we have "a Court that isn't up to date on social and economic questions." Noting that the Court had yet to rule on the Wagner Act, Ickes said the argument could be made that "the court is more responsible than the president for the present industrial unrest. As a matter of fact, unless the President is given powers by legislation which the Court will uphold, he cannot deal with this or with any other industrial situation."

But this contention was easier to make in the privacy of Ickes's diary than it was to argue convincingly in public. What the president might or might not be able to accomplish if only the Supreme Court would give him sway could only be guessed at, by Harold Ickes or anyone else. Far more tangible and threatening to the average citizen was the spectacle of militant workers taking control of their boss's property and holding it till they got their way. Here was a new source of power suddenly unleashed. And this disturbing image seemed to fit in all too well with the specter of a president so greedy for power he was trying to alter the shape of one of the country's fundamental institutions.

No one of course could predict the final impact of the sit-downs on the Court fight and the rest of the New Deal. But it was becoming increasingly clear to Ickes, Roosevelt, and everyone else concerned that even without the sit-downs the Court scheme was running into plenty of trouble.

7

The Baby Is Born

Encased in gleaming marble like a Grecian temple, separated by the broad expanse of Constitution Avenue from the din of Congress, the Supreme Court is among the most cloistered of Washington institutions. Before moving into this massive structure the Court had lived a nomadic existence for nearly a century and a half, shunting from one chamber in the Capitol to another. It took William Howard Taft, an ex-president who became chief justice, to convince Congress to give the Court a dwelling place of its own, and no small amount of symbolic significance was attached to its construction. In laying the cornerstone of the building in the fall of 1932, when the Republic and its citizens had fallen on terribly hard times, Charles Evans Hughes, Taft's successor as chief justice, declared with unmistakable emphasis: "The Republic endures, and this is the symbol of its faith."

This symbolism was made tangible by the sixteen marble columns supporting the portico over the main entrance, by the massive bronze doors, each weighing more than six tons, and by the interior great hall where the busts of all former chief justices looked out at new litigants from marble pedestals in their separate niches in the wall. For good measure the building also had, as the *New Yorker* wryly observed in 1935 when the justices first established residence, "fine big windows to throw the New Deal out of."

Such remarks aside, the dominant impression fostered by the building and ardently encouraged by the justices was of remoteness from the partisan concerns that animated the rest of the capital city. Thus on the morning of Monday, February 8, 1937, barely seventy-two hours after Franklin Roosevelt had stunned the nation by making public his plan for reorganizing the judicial branch of government, of which the Court was the most prominent and revered portion, a casual spectator might not have guessed that anything had happened to mar its splendid isolation. As the session opened the justices filed in, taking their customary places behind the lustrous mahogany bench, and the Court marshal sounded the traditional oyez: "God save the United States and this honorable court."

But closer observation might have suggested that something was amiss, something important enough to throw the Court off stride. Instead of all the nine justices making their entrance through the curtains behind the raised bench simultaneously, as was their invariable custom, Justice Brandeis appeared first, then realizing his mistake, turned to go back. Just then the rest of the Court, with the chief justice in the lead, came out as a group. Brandeis again reversed himself, made his entrance, and recovered his composure. Soon afterward the chief justice, usually the most precise of men, released the orders of the Court to the press thirty minutes late and in the wrong order. Anywhere else these would be minor matters, but in the context of the Court's normally seamless operation they were jarring enough to prompt the Court press officer to tell the journalist Raymond Clapper, "My God, the court is punch drunk."

If Brandeis and the chief justice seemed particularly discomfited, it was not hard to understand. To be sure, the rationale for reform laid out in the president's message—the contention that the justices could not handle their workload and the imputation that some were declining in mental and physical vigor—was a blow against all the nine justices. It called into question their professional reputations and their self-esteem. But because of who they were and what they represented, it was a thrust that stung Brandeis and Hughes more sharply than any of their brethren.

In Brandeis's case it was because he had devoted his life to battling for the very causes and elements in society that the New Deal claimed to represent, and now he found himself stigmatized by the mere fact that he had reached the age of eighty. Born in Louisville in 1856 to Jewish parents who had fled their prosperous life in Prague in the wake of the upheavals that shook Europe in 1848, young Brandeis entered Harvard Law at age eighteen without benefit of an undergraduate degree. Harvard had to make a special exception to give him the law diploma he earned because he had not yet reached twenty-one. He was only thirty-four when he and his law partner, Samuel D. Warren, published the "Right to Privacy," one of the most celebrated law review articles in the annals of American legal scholarship, which anticipated Supreme Court decisions in that area by many years. Brandeis and Warren asserted that the Constitution gave Americans "the right to be let alone" by their government, "the most comprehensive of rights and the right most valued by civilized men."

During the next few decades Brandeis established a thriving private practice, advising many important businesses. He also emerged as the preeminent legal champion of the rights of individuals and of human welfare against the encroachments of governmental ukase and corporate greed. He roamed around the nation to spearhead such causes as limiting the New Haven Railroad's control of New England's rail system and defending Oregon's wages-and-hours law. In politics he was an early backer of the progressive movement and became an enthusiastic supporter and then an influential adviser to Woodrow Wilson, helping shape many of Wilson's first-term New Freedom economic reforms. In 1916 Wilson and the U.S. Senate made him the first Jew to sit on the Supreme Court. For the privilege he had to endure an ugly confirmation battle during which his foes openly attacked his allegedly radical views while covertly spreading anti-Semitic claptrap. On the Court, Brandeis often teamed with Oliver Wendell Holmes, Jr., in dissenting against the majority's hard-line determination to place laissez-faire economic doctrine above social and economic reform legislation and in defending civil liberties.

By the time FDR gained the presidency he had been a long-time admirer of Brandeis. And the justice, though seventy-seven years old when Roosevelt entered the White House, and supposedly insulated from politics by his judicial robes, found ways to make his voice heard in the inner councils of the New Deal. Felix Frankfurter, who viewed Brandeis as a mentor and whom Brandeis considered "half-brother, half-son," eagerly served as a conduit for Brandeis's views, at the same time enhancing his own influence.

Brandeis had other channels too, provided by FDR's two young legislative lieutenants, Tom Corcoran, who had been Holmes's law clerk, and Ben Cohen, who had clerked for Brandeis himself. So it was that Brandeis had summoned Corcoran to the Court to explain his vote against the NRA in no uncertain terms. For while Roosevelt and his advisers took inspiration from Brandeis, the justice was not always pleased with the end result. He took as dim a view of centralization of power in government as he did of bigness in business, which led him to rule against NRA and to disapprove of other early Roosevelt efforts to deal with the economy.

Corcoran's most recent encounter with the justice was similarly unpleasant. On February 6 he had been dispatched by the president to the Court to give Brandeis advance notice of the Court-reform proposal. Getting this news was a painful experience for Brandeis. Setting aside his own personal feelings, he placed great store in the principle of judicial independence and revered the Court as an institution. He was disturbed by many of the same conservative rulings that troubled Roosevelt. Still, he viewed the protection of the Court's role as a separate branch more important than his substantive disagreements with opinions of the majority.

Brandeis listened to his young friend closely and asked him to thank the president for his courtesy. Then he told him firmly that he was dead set against the plan and warned that Roosevelt was making a serious mistake.

The early warning given Brandeis reflected the president's high regard for his intellect and the warmth generated by their mutual friendships. With Justice Hughes there were no such feelings, hence no such gesture was forthcoming from the White House. Indeed to some it seemed that Roosevelt had fashioned his plan to target the chief justice specifically. Among all the justices on the Court, the proviso that the plan took into account any justice who served ten years "continuously or otherwise" would affect only Hughes because of his previous tenure on the Court from 1910 to 1916.

In any event, Hughes had first learned of the proposal to make over the Supreme Court, which some people regarded as *his* court, at roughly the same time nearly everyone else did, soon after noon on Friday, February 5. As Hughes and his colleagues were listening to oral arguments on a relatively obscure issue, a clerk entered the chamber through the curtains behind the bench and laid out in front of each of the justices a mimeographed sheaf of papers. They were copies of the president's Court-reform proposal and related documents, which a Court attendant had brought from the Capitol just after they were presented to Congress.

It was probably not when and where Hughes would have chosen to be informed of this momentous development in his professional life. But from the point of practical politics—and

Hughes was both practical and political—the sooner he learned of Roosevelt's plan, the better.

Because he would need all the time he could find to plan a response. And no one who knew of the path Hughes had traveled to the Court doubted that the seventy-four-year-old chief justice would have as formidable a response as the man himself.

The only child of an itinerant evangelical minister, Hughes grew up in upstate New York, trained in the law at Columbia University, and passed the bar with an extraordinary score of 99.5, just short of the perfection he always sought. Indeed the pressure of the demands Hughes placed on himself took such a toll after his first few years in private practice that he had to take a sabbatical to restore his health.

But he never let up, on himself or on anyone else. It was said he grew the beard that became his hallmark to avoid taking the time to visit a barber. After making a name for himself as a reformer by leading a legislative probe into the widespread wrongdoings of New York's utilities industry, Hughes was elected governor of the state on the Republican ticket, narrowly edging out William Randolph Hearst. His frosty manner did not aid his political career; among the politicians he put off was Theodore Roosevelt, who called him "a bearded iceberg."

In 1910 he was glad to accept William Howard Taft's nomination to the Supreme Court. But in 1916, when the GOP and opportunity beckoned again, he left the Court to run for president against Woodrow Wilson. The campaign he waged mainly demonstrated again his unsuitability for elective politics. In a notably close election, his snubbing of California's senior Republican Hiram Johnson probably cost him the Golden State and the White House. In the wake of his loss, Hughes trimmed his beard, hoping to seem less remote, but it was too late to rescue his political career. Years later Hughes's son-in-law contended in an *ABA Journal* article that the outside world had failed to realize that the jurist had a human side, including a sense of humor. To prove the point he had to reach beyond Hughes's active career to an incident after the justice retired, when an elderly lady spotting him leaving an elevator in a Manhattan hotel told him in a hushed voice, "I thought you were dead."

Bowing, Hughes retorted, "Sorry to disappoint you."

His defeat by Wilson sent Hughes back to private practice where, except for a stint as Harding's secretary of state, he spent most of the next fifteen years rebuilding his fortune until Hoover chose him to replace the ailing Taft as chief justice in 1930. By some accounts Hoover actually intended to offer the job to his close friend Harlan Fiske Stone, who was already on the Court, but was advised that it would be bad form to pass over Hughes because of his distinguished record and service to the GOP. Hoover was assured that Hughes would turn the job down because accepting would mean that his son, Charles Evans Hughes, Jr., would have to resign his post as solicitor general. Hughes's acceptance jolted Hoover, who according to one published account remarked to an adviser: "Well I'll be damned. The old codger never thought of his son."

This story, first reported in the *New Yorker* and then amplified in a harsh book about the Court called *The Nine Old Men*, by Washington correspondents Drew Pearson and Robert S. Allen, caused Hughes considerable distress. He was so upset that he prevailed upon Hoover to provide him with a written denial of the unflattering tale. But a similar story also was given currency by Felix Frankfurter, who related it to his clerks at the Court and claimed to have heard it from a Hoover adviser with firsthand knowledge.

All that is known for sure is that Hughes did become chief justice, and his son did subsequently resign as solicitor general. The story that Hoover really preferred Stone, particularly the remarks attributed to Hoover by Pearson and Allen, may be largely apocryphal. But its persistence sheds light on how Hughes was viewed by some of his associates.

Regardless of how he came by the job, Hughes symbolized the Court much as Franklin Roosevelt had come to embody the presidency. Certainly with his imperious bearing and austere features, he looked the part of chief justice. When George S. Kaufman satirized Washington politics in *Of Thee I Sing*, he took care that all nine actors impersonating Supreme Court justices were made up to match Hughes's white-bearded visage.

Unfortunately for Hughes, as he sought to hold the Court together in this new storm while devising a response, the casting of the actual high tribunal was much less uniform. Hughes presided over a strong-willed and motley crew of jurists. Only one of his colleagues, Sutherland, wore a beard, and more important their approach to jurisprudence often varied sharply from Hughes's own beliefs. Starting from his right were the Four Horsemen of Reaction, as New Dealers dubbed them, with whom in recent years he seemed to side most often. James McReynolds, age seventy-four, Southern-born and -educated, had served as U.S. attorney general under Woodrow Wilson, when he was ferocious in attacking monopoly, from the Union Pacific to AT&T. Some thought him a radical, but he insisted that he was simply a consistent conservative who viewed competition as essential to the success of capitalism. Named by Wilson to the high court in 1914, he distinguished himself by his unremitting hostility to any federal or state regulation of business and by his virulent anti-Semitism, demonstrated by his open contempt for his two Jewish colleagues, Brandeis and Benjamin Cardozo. At dinner parties the chief justice had to divide the brethren into two groups so that McReynolds would be spared having to break bread with Jews.

Sharing McReynold's judicial philosophy, and to a degree his personal predilections, was seventy-year-old Pierce Butler, a Midwesterner who made his name and his fortune as a railroad lawyer. Butler was backed for the Court by Chief Justice Taft, who pointed out that he was a Democrat, at least nominally, while the Court already had seven Republicans. Butler was also a Catholic and a self-made man. Duly nominated by Harding, he was confirmed after bitter protests by unions and liberals who objected to his ties to big business. Justice Butler's performance matched expectations. He was, as Justice Holmes termed him, a "monolith" in his opposition to any regulation of business. When Hoover was considering the Cardozo appointment, Butler had joined McReynolds in urging Hoover "not to afflict the court with another Jew," but otherwise he kept his religious prejudice to himself. Nevertheless Hughes thought him the most difficult man on the Court to deal with. Tough-minded, tenacious, and authoritarian in discourse, Butler edged his arguments with harsh Irish humor.

The other two Horsemen, Willis Van Devanter and George Sutherland, were more congenial in spirit than the bigoted McReynolds and the overbearing Butler, though similarly dedicated to the sanctity of free-market economics. A man widely admired for his unfailing courtesy and consideration for others, Van Devanter was born before the Civil War and raised in the Midwest. But soon after graduating from Cincinnati Law School he set up practice in Cheyenne, and the ethos of the last frontier shaped his approach to the law. He believed in property rights, private enterprise, and the principle of the less government, the better. Van Devanter's work for the Wyoming Republican party earned him a slot in the Justice Department and then as a federal circuit court judge. In 1911 President Taft named him to the high court, where his subtle skills as a negotiator eased the path to conservative rulings and gained him the praise of Chief Justice Taft as "far and away the most valuable man in our court."

Born in England in 1862, Sutherland grew up in Utah where his family had immigrated, and took his law degree at the University of Michigan. Early on he came to believe that the U.S. Constitution was divinely inspired and that government power must be severely restricted to preserve individual liberty and economic expansion. As U.S. senator from Utah he modified his conservative instincts enough to back Theodore Roosevelt's economic reforms, but he opposed the constitutional amendment establishing the federal income tax. On the Court, to which his former colleague and good friend Harding nominated him in 1922, he was known for his temperate nature and tolerance of disagreement, and his dedication to conservatism. He fought the New Deal every step of the way, claiming that only "self-denial and painful effort" could solve the problems of the depression.

The trio of liberals on the Court included, besides Brandeis, the other Jewish justice, Cardozo, and Harlan Fiske Stone. One of the towering figures in American jurisprudence, the sixty-six-year-old Cardozo's presence on the Court was a political anomaly that reflected the respect in which he was held in the legal community. A liberal New York Jew, he had been nominated by a conservative Republican president, Herbert Hoover, at a time when the Court already had one Jew and two New Yorkers, Hughes and Stone. When this objection was raised, Idaho's Senator Borah told President Hoover that Cardozo belonged as much to Idaho as to New York, and Justice Stone offered to resign if need be to clear the way for his fellow New Yorker.

Cardozo had earned this recognition with a career dedicated to restoring the good name of his family after his father was forced to resign from the New York State Supreme Court when he became involved with the Tweed Ring and embroiled in public scandal. Practicing law himself in New York for twenty-three years, young Cardozo distinguished himself sufficiently so that the governor appointed him to the Court of Appeals, the state's highest tribunal, at the request of the other judges on the court. The international reputation he made there set him on course for the Supreme Court. A shy and sensitive man who remained a bachelor until his death, as a justice he nevertheless defended New Deal measures as vigorously as the Four Horsemen attacked them.

Stone, sixty-four, the least dependably liberal of the liberals, was a man more engaged by legal scholarship than by the actual practice of the law. Born and raised in New England, he quit his job as a high school teacher to enter Columbia Law School where he graduated and then taught, becoming dean of the school in 1906. Although a conventional thinker, his outlook was expanded by a largeness of spirit. In addition to legal discipline, he sought to instill in his students at Columbia a social conscience.

Selected by Coolidge in 1924 to rehabilitate the Department of Justice in the wake of the Teapot Dome scandal, Stone cleaned house and brought in new faces, among them twenty-nine-year-old J. Edgar Hoover as head of the FBI. Hoover, Stone said approvingly, "hasn't learned to be afraid of politicians." The next year Coolidge promoted Stone to the high court where he tempered his lifelong Republicanism with the recognition that twentieth-century conditions mandated a larger role for government in dealing with society's problems.

More or less in the center of the Court, along with the chief justice, was Justice Owen J. Roberts. With Hughes he shifted back and forth between the Four Horsemen of the right and the three liberals to establish the majority on any given case of importance. Just sixty years old when Roosevelt's Court-reform controversy erupted, Roberts was the Court's youngest member and the most ambiguous in ideological terms. Born and educated in Pennsylvania, like Stone he spent much of his early career teaching law, in his case at the University of Pennsylvania, taking time out to serve as a prosecutor in Philadelphia and for the federal government.

He first captured national attention in 1924 when Coolidge appointed him to investigate the Harding oil scandals, a probe that resulted in the voiding of some of the Teapot Dome naval oil leases. Roberts's performance there established his credibility as a potential Supreme Court nominee, and when Hoover nominated him in 1930, the Senate confirmed him without a dissenting vote. He cast his most controversial vote in 1936 in the infamous *More-*

head decision, overturning a New York state minimum-wage law and raising anger against the Court to new heights.

One thing all these different men had in common was their abhorrence of the president's proposal, an attitude for the most part they kept to themselves. Not that the media did not try to break through their silence. Radio was then still in its infancy as a news medium, but the broadcast networks had been used by both sides in the Court controversy as outlets for their views, and now they sought to air the views of the justices themselves for their listeners. In a telegram to Hughes, NBC offered its facilities to him or to any other member of the Court to discuss Roosevelt's plan. And an up-and-coming executive with CBS named Edward R. Murrow phoned Hughes's office to ask for a chance to persuade the chief justice to speak to the nation over his network. Hughes turned down both requests.

More aggressive was Pathe News, which along with the other newsreels in the pre-television era provided the only means for Americans to both see as well as hear major public figures in action. In its weekly release, distributed to movie theaters around the country, the Pathe narrator declared: "Roosevelt's plan to change the Supreme Court has become the greatest public issue since slavery," then introduced "this exclusive statement on the Supreme Court itself by Chief Justice Hughes." In point of fact Hughes's statement, taken from Pathe's files, had been given more than six months earlier at the unveiling of a statue, and had nothing to do with Court-packing.

This was of course irresponsible journalism, but not illegal. Nevertheless the outraged Hughes called Justice Stone's protégé, FBI chief Hoover—no great admirer of the rights of the press— who pressured Pathe into pulling the phony segment out of circulation and earned a warm note of appreciation from the chief justice.

Behind this façade of silence, Hughes's resentment of FDR's plan smoldered. But he waited to find his own time and place to vent his feelings. The resentment among his brethren spanned the ideological spectrum. On the left, Brandeis believed the president had acted too hastily. "He was convinced that with death and resignation the nature of the court would change," according to the veteran correspondent Marquis Childs, in whom he confided, and that the plan "was very wrong, that it threatened a very important institution." Brandeis's liberal colleague, Cardozo, also had a problem with the plan. He thought fifteen justices would be too many, he told a friend; indeed, he mused, sometimes nine seemed too many.

A similar point was made by Justice Stone in off-the-record conversations with Irving Brant, chief editorial writer of the *St. Louis Star-Times*. Stone feared, as he told Brant, that the increase Roosevelt proposed, rather than expedite the Court's work, would result in "a loss of efficiency" because the give-and-take between justices would lose its value if their number grew to fifteen from nine.

Among the Court's conservatives, Justice Sutherland also displayed a flair for expressing his views on the president's plan on the sly. After the inveterate New Deal foe Senator Josiah Bailey of North Carolina denounced the plan in a radio speech early in the fight, Sutherland wrote to Bailey cheering him on. "In my judgment there has never been a better speech," Sutherland said. Later on he wrote Texas's Tom Connally that the senator's argument against the New Deal's expansion of federal power "touches the most vital point in the whole controversy."

But such sub rosa tactics were not for Justice McReynolds. In mid-March, with the Senate Judiciary Committee's hearings on the controversial measure already under way, McReynolds abandoned all discretion in remarks to the annual reunion of his fraternity, Phi Delta Theta. "The evidence of good sportsmanship is that a man who has had a chance to present a fair case to a fair tribunal must be a good sport and accept the outcome," declared McReynolds. The justice did not mention Roosevelt as the exemplar of poor sportsmanship, but his Phi Delt brothers and everyone else knew whom he was talking about. Inevitably the more than one hundred or so guests in the Washington hotel ballroom where the justice spoke included a number of journalists, as McReynolds had every reason to realize.

Having breached the propriety of the Court, McReynolds went on to indulge his fondness for racial stereotypes. He himself, he claimed, in his years in the Court had done all he could to safeguard the interests of all Americans, from "the poorest darky in the Georgia backwoods as well as the man of wealth in a mansion on Fifth Avenue." This was a break for the president's supporters. McReynolds had unwittingly provided them with a rare bright moment in what had become an increasingly grim struggle. They pointed out that the talk of good sportsmanship ill became McReynolds, who was famed for his diatribes against those who disagreed with him on the bench. And the NAACP denounced him for using the racist pejorative "darky," pointing out that far from defending the rights of Negroes, McReynolds had dissented from the Court's landmark 1932 decision affirming the right to counsel of the railroaded Negro defendants in the *Scottsboro* case.

But McReynolds's blunder provided only short-lived relief to the president's supporters. They had hoped to use the hearings before the Senate Judiciary Committee to reverse the tide running against FDR. Instead the proceedings turned into a disaster for the Court plan.

The bill's backers got off to a weak start with the testimony of their first witness, Attorney General Cummings. Cummings had irritated other Roosevelt aides by his departure from Washington for an extended vacation immediately after his February 14 radio speech supporting the plan. He did not return until he appeared before the committee on March 10. Associate Attorney General Robert Jackson, whose own incisive testimony in favor of the bill evoked far greater praise than Cummings's presentation, later acknowledged that he "had some difficulty understanding how he

[Cummings] was willing to commit the prosperity of his brain-child to others." Cummings was not shy within the inner circles of the administration about claiming credit for the plan, Jackson wrote later, "yet while his plan was being torn asunder, he was vacationing in Florida—a vacation no doubt much needed, but unfortunately timed."

Now that he was back in the capital, Cummings seemed to revel in the spotlight of the hearings, swinging his swivel chair from side to side and salting his answers with wisecracks. To some he seemed flippant and even patronizing. He relied in the main on his original rationale for the plan as a managerial solution to the Court's inefficiency, an argument that even Roosevelt had discarded in his two major addresses. Referring to the huge volume of paperwork facing the Court, Cummings claimed that dealing with it in a timely fashion "would be like reading *Gone with the Wind* [the current thousand-page best-seller] before breakfast every morning."

But the attorney general was better at drawing laughs from the spectators than satisfying the doubts of the committee members. "Do you recognize that this does not afford a permanent remedy for the situation of which you complain?" Wyoming's O'Mahoney asked him.

"There is nothing permanent in this world, Senator," Cummings airily advised O'Mahoney, who presumably at fifty-two, after practicing law for more than thirty years and serving in the Senate for three, did not require such advice. "Those who dream of permanency are dreaming an idle dream."

Among those in Washington following the proceedings in the Senate, Charles Evans Hughes must have taken particular satisfaction from Cummings's performance. For by not broadening the case for Court revision, and instead sticking with the claim that the Court was underproductive and overworked, the attorney general had left the chief justice a target he was confident he could destroy.

Hughes decided that it was now time for him to have his say about FDR's Court plan. But much more calculation entered into his demarche than into Justice McReynolds's outburst. In making his plans, Hughes typically took full advantage of his assets, which included, besides his own prestige as chief, the unity among diverse members of the Court who opposed the president's plan.

On Saturday, March 20, ten days after Cummings's testimony before the Judiciary Committee, Alice Brandeis, wife of the justice, paid a call on an old family friend, Elizabeth Coleman, daughter of Senator Burt Wheeler, leader of the fight against Roosevelt's plan, in her suburban Virginia home. The ostensible reason for the visit was to see the Coleman's new baby. But when she left Alice Brandeis added a new dimension to her social call and helped turn the pages of history. "Tell your father I think he was right about the court bill," she said, a remark that Elizabeth Coleman lost no time in passing on to her father, the senator.

That was all Wheeler needed to hear. In two days he was scheduled to be the lead-off opposition witness at the Judiciary Committee's hearings on the Roosevelt plan, and he had been looking for a statement from a justice so as to start off with "a resounding bang." Now he was convinced he had his man in Justice Brandeis.

He was almost right. As Wheeler later recalled, Brandeis told him he had no intention of getting involved himself in the fight over the bill. But he had some useful advice for his old friend. "Call the chief justice," he said. "He will give you a letter."

Wheeler did as he was told, met with Hughes, and by mutual agreement came to the chief justice's home that Sunday afternoon, the day before he was scheduled to testify. When he arrived, Hughes handed him the promised letter and declared, "The baby is born."

When Wheeler showed up at the Senate hearings the next day, March 22, no one apart from those Court justices Hughes had informed of his letter knew of the explosive "baby" he carried in his briefcase. The senator took full advantage of the moment. At first he set an amiable tone, citing his early support, warm friendship, and continued high regard for the president. His manner became more serious as he spoke, more in sorrow than in anger, about the allegations made by the president and the attorney general that the Court was behind in its work and the implications of inefficiency made against the more elderly of the justices. To answer these grave charges, Wheeler declared he had a statement from someone who knew more about the Court than the president, the attorney general, or for that matter any of the senators in the hearing room—whereupon he reached inside his jacket pocket and with a flourish produced Hughes's letter.

The letter was only three pages long, but as Wheeler read it to a hushed hearing room it was clear that was all the chief justice needed to make short shrift of the administration's case. "The Supreme Court is fully abreast of its work," Hughes began. He ticked off a few relevant statistics about the current term's docket and added, "There is no congestion of cases upon our calendar." As to the appeals the Court had declined to hear, he pointed out that the question of granting review under federal statute was a matter of judicial discretion. In their seasoned judgment, the justices found that most petitions for review were "wholly without merit and ought never to have been made." It was the belief of members of the Court, he said, that if the Court erred in deciding what cases to review, "it is on the side of liberality." Increasing the number of justices, far from speeding the Court's work, Hughes contended, would have the very opposite effect. "There would be more judges to hear, more judges to confer, more judges to discuss, more judges to be convinced and to decide." Anyhow, Hughes contended, since the Constitution decreed only "one Supreme Court," the justices could not constitutionally divide up their business among its members, even if they wanted to.

To clinch his argument, Hughes said his statement had been approved by Justices Van Devanter and Brandeis. Time had not allowed him to talk to "the members of the court generally," but he was confident they agreed with his statement. He did not explain the basis of this confidence, and it would turn out to be misplaced. Some of the other justices, notably Stone, groused among themselves and expressed privately the complaint that Hughes had taken too much upon himself by professing to speak for the whole Court. But their objections to the inappropriateness of Hughes's conduct did not diminish the impact of the substance of his attack on the plan.

It was true that the chief justice's letter, with its suggestion that Roosevelt's plan violated the Constitution, seemed to violate the principle Hughes himself claimed to hold sacrosanct, that the Court should confine itself to deciding actual cases. And in a way, such behavior could leave the Court open to just the sort of demands for advice Hughes had rebuffed when offered by FDR. "It violates every tradition of our judicial process," fumed the *New Republic*. But such expressions about the niceties of judicial behavior were limited to legal scholars and journalistic defenders of FDR's proposal. They were drowned out by the thunderous impact of what Hughes had accomplished, placing the entire court in a general sense, and more specifically its two senior justices along with himself, on record against the president's proposal.

Hughes had struck, reported the *New York Times*, with "an authority and suddenness which took Administration forces by surprise and sent them scurrying." "The letter had a sensational effect," Wheeler later exulted, immodestly but accurately. "The newsreels photographed it, newspaper reporters clamored for copies and it was all I could do to keep it from being snatched from my hands when the session was recessed." Wheeler was amused to hear the president and his supporters were accusing Hughes of "playing politics." Harold Ickes was more candid in confiding to his diary. "It was good tactics," Ickes wrote of Hughes's gambit. And as Ickes noted, FDR had himself to blame for giving Hughes the opening. "This episode proves again the mistake in going to court with a weak case," he wrote.

Roosevelt had tried to veer from that early strategy in his March speeches, in which he depicted the Court's rulings as blocking him from the crucial task of meeting the needs of the disadvantaged "one-third of a nation." But the first impression given the public of his reasons for the plan—the overburdened Court and its congested docket—was hard to erase, particularly when that impression was reinforced by Cummings's testimony before the Judiciary Committee.

As for Cummings, whose advice had led the president into this ambush, he had little to say. On the day Hughes's letter was made public, he was reported to be preparing a statement in response. But nothing was forthcoming.

Meanwhile demands for his own resignation were now heard. After a particularly scathing editorial in the *Baltimore Sun*, Cummings sent a memo to FDR, calling the offending article "grossly libelous" and apparently hoping the president would speak out in his defense.

Roosevelt had other fish to fry. Bearing in mind what Senator Robinson had told him about public apprehension over the sit-down strikes, he sought to turn that issue against the Court and in his favor. On March 25, three days after Hughes's devastating attack on the Court plan, FDR dispatched Assistant Attorney General Robert Jackson and one of the New Deal's closest legislative allies, Wisconsin Senator Robert La Follette, to pin the blame for the sit-down strikes on the Court.

The sit-down strikes, La Follette told an American Labor party rally in New York's Carnegie Hall, were the answer of American workers to "the sit-down strike of a majority of members of the Supreme Court against the whole New Deal program of legislation. And now in the labor strife sweeping across the country we are reaping the whirlwind of violence and resentment against the lawlessness of employers who look to the Supreme Court to override the laws enacted by Congress."

For his part, Jackson, as befitting an officer of the court, was more restrained, though he offered a similar argument. "The greatest threat to the prosperity and good order of this Republic is the labor struggle," Jackson declared, adding that "a direct responsibility" for this danger "rests upon the Supreme Court of the United States." In particular Jackson targeted the Supreme Court's *Morehead* decision overturning a New York minimum-wage law. "The court has prohibited the states and the United States from exerting governmental power to provide ways to industrial peace," he said. After quoting from Justice Butler's majority opinion in *Morehead*, Jackson observed, "The effort of the state to solve labor grievances by deliberation is prohibited, and people wonder why industrial strife is persistent."

The effort to place the blame on the Supreme Court was an attempt to find a combined solution to the president's two most vexing problems—the opposition to his Court revision plan and the public distress over labor unrest. But this strategy had a major weakness. As the sit-down strikes proliferated, more and more Americans and their representatives in Congress had lost sympathy with labor. Most Americans did not know and many no longer greatly cared who was to blame for the wave of labor agitation that plagued the country. But they did know they wanted it stopped.

8

Law and Order

In the final week of March 1937, Franklin Roosevelt was like a fireman in danger of running out of hose as he sought to cope with the twin crises over the Supreme Court and the sit-down strikes. In addition to deploying La Follette and Jackson to New York to blame the Court for the sit-downs, he dispatched Jim Farley, his postmaster general and master political strategist, to Texas to rally support for the plan among state legislators. This was no easy task. These very same lawmakers had gone on record as opposing the president's scheme by overwhelming margins almost as soon as it had been unveiled, advising Texas's House and Senate members to do the same. It was hardly surprising therefore that though Farley got applause from the galleries, the legislators sat on their hands while he spoke. That same day a poll of small-town editors showed they were against what Roosevelt wanted to do about the Court by about 3 to 1. The negative verdict of the larger papers had already been registered, soon after the plan was introduced.

Even as FDR digested this latest disturbing news about the press, he sought to bring under control another conflagration on Capitol Hill, this time on the House side, where members were caught up with Congressman Dies's March 23 demand for an inquiry into the sit-downs. Caught off guard and out of town, in Warm Springs, Georgia, where he was on vacation, the president let it be known through his secretary, Marvin McIntyre, that he planned to consult with congressional leaders on the sit-down strikes as soon as he returned to Washington.

Meanwhile McIntyre advised the press that, as the *New York Times* reported, the White House was worried "that the issue of sit-down strikes in Detroit and throughout the nation might spread so generally and so rapidly" as to force a national "showdown" on the issue. The president wanted the country to know that he was taking all due steps to prepare for action if that became necessary, studying the response of the French and British governments to similar situations. Roosevelt's decision-making would be inevitably complicated, as the *Times* noted delicately, by the "claims of John L. Lewis that he and the CIO were entitled to reward for their services in the last campaign." No wonder then, as the *Times* reported, the administration was "moving cautiously."

Too cautiously to suit some people. On March 26, two days after the Warm Springs White House had passed the word to the press about the president's concerns over the sit-downs, a group of New England civic and business leaders, headed by Harvard University's president emeritus A. Lawrence Lowell, wired Vice President Garner demanding an end to what newspaper headlines were now calling the "sit-down revolt." "Armed insurrection—defiance of the law, order and duly elected authority is growing like wildfire," the statement declared. If such disregard of established authority and property rights continued, the distinguished signatories warned, "then freedom and liberty are at an end, government becomes a mockery, superseded by anarchy, mob rule and ruthless dictatorship."

In Garner, who promised he would present the statement to the Senate at its next session, the Lowell group could not have found a more enthusiastic messenger. Although typically he did not speak out publicly on issues, he made no secret of his views within the administration's inner councils. The sit-down strikes, he told Jim Farley, were "mass lawlessness" and "intolerable," and would lead to "great difficulty if not destruction." So frustrated was Garner about Roosevelt's failure to lambaste the sit-down strikers, as Garner thought he should, that during a cabinet meeting he stood behind Labor Secretary Perkins and berated her for being insufficiently rigorous in opposing such outbreaks until she began to cry.

Meanwhile the CIO and John L. Lewis were not deaf to the outcry against the sit-downs. Nor were they insensitive to the pressure being brought against their two most potent political allies, Michigan Governor Murphy and FDR. On March 23, even before Martin Dies issued his call for a sit-down probe, and before president emeritus Lowell's group had sounded the alarm about "armed insurrection" to Garner, Lewis had agreed at Murphy's behest to meet with Walter P. Chrysler, founder of the company that bore his name.

Along with the invitation to meet came an implied threat. As he drafted his invitation to Lewis, Murphy was well aware that at the rally in Cadillac Square a crowd of more than fifty thousand who responded to UAW president Homer Martin's call heard their leaders denounce public officials and the auto companies and threaten defiance of the courts unless their demands were met. The state government, Murphy warned in his message to Lewis, would use all means at its command to "protect property rights in the interests of the general public."

"Your message suggests that I confer under duress," Lewis responded. "Nevertheless I will come."

At the meeting, with characteristic realism, Lewis quickly accepted a deal proposed by Murphy, whose terms closely resembled the agreement that ended the Flint sit-down against GM.

The union would evacuate the plant. In return, the company would not resume production while collective bargaining continued. In these circumstances union and management reached a contract agreement in about two weeks. Chrysler granted recognition to the UAW as representing the workers who already were members. But most important for the union, Chrysler, as GM had done, agreed to give the UAW a clear field toward signing up its other workers and eventually achieving its goal of exclusive representation.

In advance of the eventual settlement, Lewis's order to end the strike provided a measure of welcome relief to the White House. FDR did not need the *New York Times* or anyone else to remind him of the political debt he owed the CIO and its president. And the end of the biggest and most troublesome of the post-GM sit-downs permitted him to fend off the wolves who were baying for Lewis's skin, at least for the moment.

On March 27, as bargaining sessions moved toward the anticipated resolution of the Chrysler strike, the president revealed through Senator Robinson, the Democratic Senate leader, that his heralded consultation with congressional leaders had persuaded him that there was no need for White House intervention. Labor Secretary Perkins, having brought the president up to speed on the Chrysler strike, predicted—correctly as it turned out—its early settlement and added hopefully, "When that is settled the whole movement in that area will be on the wane."

In Detroit itself, heart of the supposed revolution, the *Free Press*, responding to the alarms raised by Harvard's Lowell and others, advised: "Quit hiding under beds." The rally in Cadillac Square, which had been likened by some to the storming of the Bastille, was "far more orderly" than the celebration of the Detroit Tigers victory in the World Series two years earlier, the paper pointed out, "and only about one-tenth the size." Furthermore, the paper argued, the mundane reality that the greatest obstacle to street demonstrations was the lack of parking space for cars of the workers suggested that the proletariat were not quite ready to cast off their chains.

But the truth was that not everyone wished to calm down. The sit-down had made the CIO and industrial unionism a major force in the American economy almost overnight. But as a weapon it was a double-edged sword. Just as Lewis had used it to force management to make concessions almost undreamed of a few months earlier, the enemies of Lewis and the New Deal could use fear of the sit-downs to their own advantage. Those adversaries included not only the leaders of corporate America and the political leaders who made common cause with them but the one institution that stood to lose more from the sit-downs even than big business, the American Federation of Labor.

For months William Green, president of the Federation, had watched with increasing distress as the sit-down strikes helped the CIO score the most dramatic gains in American unionism since the halcyon days of the Great War. And this success was all the more painful for Green to contemplate because it came in the face of the AFL's abject failure to penetrate the nation's great mass-production industries, even when workers were in desperate straits. His attitude was no secret, but for the most part he had limited his disapproval to debates within the house of labor.

Now, with the sit-downs under attack from all quarters of national life, Green added his voice to the chorus of condemnations. On the heels of the White House announcement that FDR would take no action against the sit-downs, Green, propounding a verdict that the courts had not yet finally resolved, declared the sit-downs illegal. Not only that, he contended that despite the short-term gains they might win, they were in the long run damaging to labor's cause. "Public opinion will not support sit-down strikes," he said, meaning that labor would lose the backing it needed to succeed. Moreover, he warned, the spread of sit-downs would so rile the populace and the politicians that "re-pressive legislation" would result.

As if on cue, four days after Green's assault, during Senate de-bate on legislation regulating the coal industry, South Carolina Senator James F. Byrnes rose to offer an amendment broadly con-demning sit-down strikes as contrary to public policy. During the fifty-seven-year-old Byrnes's long career in Congress—fourteen years in the House followed by twelve in the Senate—his col-leagues had learned to pay attention when he spoke. "The art of legislating is the art of intelligent compromise," Byrnes liked to say. But some things Byrnes would not compromise, notably the Southern creed of white supremacy which he considered the backbone of Dixie and of the Democratic party. Moreover, no matter what "compromise" he helped to craft, he usually made certain that the net result granted him whatever he most wanted from whatever issue was under debate.

"When I see Jimmy Byrnes coming toward me," Republican leader Charles McNary declared, "I put one hand on my watch and one on my wallet and wish to goodness I knew how to pro-tect my conscience." A fellow Democrat, Congressman John Bankhead of Alabama, once told a New Deal official, "I would rather have any twelve other senators opposing me than Jimmy Byrnes opposing me. He's tireless, he's shrewd, and he's vindic-tive." A friend of FDR's since the Wilson administration, Byrnes had been a loyal and effective Roosevelt lieutenant during the president's first term and campaigned proudly as a New Dealer.

But after 1936, concerned that the New Deal was causing in-creasing irritation among South Carolina's business community and other conservatives, Byrnes began to look for ways to separate himself from the overly liberal White House. For this shift the sit-down strikes were made to order. But Byrnes had a more specific motive. A blow at the sit-downs and the CIO might help discour-age John L. Lewis from launching an organizing effort that had

Byrnes mightily worried, against the textile mills in his own South Carolina.

Although Byrnes's amendment, tailored to coal-regulating legislation, was aimed directly at that industry, he made clear that his purpose was to denounce sit-down strikes everywhere. Byrnes's strategy was shrewdly designed to create a dilemma for the president. If Byrnes's amendment was made part of the coal bill, the president would have to choose between vetoing the bill, which the CIO and Lewis wanted approved, or signing into law legislation that condemned the sit-down strikes.

For Byrnes the amendment served the purpose of distancing himself from the president and offsetting in his home state his earlier backing for the Supreme Court reform scheme. But now Republican senators, who were firm opponents of the Court proposal, jumped on the anti-sit-down bandwagon. Since they had agreed for the most part to hold their fire on the Court so that Democrats could take the lead, they were all the more eager to support a member of the president's party criticizing the sit-down strikes. And they sought also to pin the responsibility for this alarming phenomenon on FDR.

California's Hiram Johnson, who had been quick to denounce both the Court plan and the sit-down strikes, now focused on the latter evil, citing a federal law giving Washington the power to act against "insurrection" or "domestic violence" in any state. Although Johnson conceded that the statute required a request from state authorities for federal intervention, he contended that "this is a case where the president may act and it is his duty to act."

Then it was Michigan Senator Vandenberg's turn to complain of the administration's one-sided favorable treatment of labor, as against business. "Government agencies dealing with labor relations have been very vocal indeed about citing the obligations of employers" to their workers, he said, "but as silent as the tomb respecting the obligation to law and order and the maintenance of civil society."

Vandenberg's invocation of that potent phrase "law and order," which had become the watchword of the opposition to sit-down strikes, struck a responsive chord in the bosom of John Nance Garner. While the Senate watched in some bemusement, as soon as Vandenberg ended his remarks the Democratic vice president jumped down from the rostrum and rushed to embrace the Republican senator. "I want to congratulate you," he cried. "It was about time somebody said that." Following that extraordinary gesture, Garner huddled with Senate majority leader Robinson and suggested that by taking the lead in condemning the sit-down while Franklin Roosevelt preserved silence, the Senate would be doing the president a good turn.

As for Robinson, as the president's top man in the Senate he opposed Byrnes's amendment as expected. But reporters noted that the normally gruff senator seemed to carry on the battle with unusual geniality. Each time he asked for unanimous consent on a procedural tactic and North Carolina's Bailey boomed, "I object," Robinson responded with a grin.

When Robinson tried to get Byrnes to back off a bit, the South Carolinian, for all his talk about the value of compromise, refused to give an inch. But Robinson worked out a deal with some of Byrnes's supporters. Byrnes's resolution was put to a vote on April 5 and voted down by 48 to 36, with twenty-six Democrats voting for the resolution, including, in addition to the Deep South conservatives, such moderates as Harry Truman of Missouri. Two days later, under the arrangement Robinson had worked out, the Senate approved by a 75-to-3 vote a concurrent resolution which condemned the sit-downs as "illegal and contrary to sound public policy." For balance, the resolution also denounced the "industrial spy system," relied on by GM and other big corporations to fight unionism, as breeding suspicion and causing strikes and criticized companies that fostered company unions. Here was plenty of harsh rhetoric, but because it was just a resolution and not a law, no teeth.

Having put down an uprising in the Senate, the president and his allies the very next day faced another insurgency in the House, where Martin Dies's proposal for a congressional probe into the sit-downs and their causes came to the floor. It was voted down 286 to 149, with Democrats loyal to the administration opposing what they viewed as an effort by conservatives to place the blame for the sit-downs on the White House. But FDR's allies prevailed only after an uproarious debate. At one point Democrat John Bernard of Minnesota, demanding more time to speak against the resolution, thundered, "Is this a democratic body or is Hitler or Mussolini ruling here?"

In the babble that followed, one member shouted for order but another replied, "We don't want order!"

Moments later, as Michigan's Clare Hoffman, Republican foe of the New Deal, strode menacingly toward Michigan Democrat John Dingell, Republican Harold Knutson of Minnesota cried out, "If this were a police court we'd be held to be drunk and disorderly."

In the end it was the Democrats who had the last word. If the House wished to probe the causes of the sit-down strikes, Gerald Boileau of Wisconsin, one of the leaders of the New Deal forces, suggested—voicing a now familiar plaint for FDR supporters—members should cross the Capitol Plaza and ask why the Supreme Court was "sitting down" on the Wagner Act decision. "If the Supreme Court would only perform its duty and hand down the opinion in that case, the people of the country would know where they are," Boileau contended.

Boileau's theory about the Court and the sit-down strikes would be tested almost immediately. On April 12, five days after the Dies probe was squelched and Boileau had pleaded for the Court to rule on the Wagner Act, the justices handed down a surprising victory for unions and the New Deal, upholding the right to collective bargaining. The Wagner Act rulings were part of what would ultimately become clear as one of the most dramatic reversals in the Court's history.

The big change had begun on March 29, two weeks before the Wagner Act decisions were handed down, when the justices upheld a Washington state minimum-wage law not significantly different from the New York law it had held to be unconstitutional in the notorious *Morehead* ruling only nine months before. In the Washington case, *West Coast Hotel Co. v. Parish*, the new majority of 5 to 4 included Justice Roberts, who had voted the other in the *Morehead* case, but now voted with Hughes and the three liberals.

Roberts's momentous turnabout led to the coinage of the aphorism "A switch in time saves nine," a close paraphrase of a remark by future Supreme Court Justice Abe Fortas, then a Yale professor moonlighting as a lawyer for the Securities and Exchange Commission. Fortas's exact words to a Rutgers University forum, as reported by the *New York Times*, were "Mr. Justice Roberts's theory must be a switch in time serves nine." As union leaders in attendance applauded, Fortas added that the law must be viewed "as merely a guidepost, a set of ambiguous principles which can be adjusted to meet particular situations." Considering all this, Fortas said, the sit-down strike might come to be held as legal. The young lawyer's comments reflected the skeptical pragmatism that in later years would help make his fortune as a Washington lawyer, gain him the trust of President Lyndon Johnson, and earn him a seat on the Supreme Court under Chief Justice Earl Warren. The Warren Court was fully as much a political storm center as the tribunal led by Charles Evans Hughes. Indeed the political turbulence would contribute to Fortas being forced by the Nixon administration to become the first justice to quit under a cloud of scandal.

But these events were still sleeping three decades in the future. In the short term, Fortas's prediction about sit-downs turned out to be mistaken. In 1939 the Supreme Court held them to be illegal. But Fortas's quip about Justice Robert's switch achieved wide currency. It served to express the almost universally held belief that Roberts had made his change on the minimum wage in cahoots with Hughes, who as chief justice was well positioned to carry out such manipulation, in order to frustrate Roosevelt's plans for revision of the Court.

It turned out that Roberts had cast his crucial vote in December, before the release of FDR's Court-reform proposal. More important, his turnabout had come after Roosevelt's thunderous reelection victory, and when many believed some sort of presidential move against the Court was in the cards. The final vote was delayed until February when Justice Stone returned from his long illness. In a memorandum issued years later, Roberts attempted to rebut suspicions that he had acted out of political motivation, but the tortured legal reasoning he offered as an explanation failed to persuade many scholars or politicians.

For good measure, on the same day it reversed itself on the minimum wage the Court rejected a challenge to the Federal Farm Bankruptcy Act, an almost identical revision of a law it had held unconstitutional on "Black Monday" 1935. And it upheld an amendment to the Railway Labor Act promoting collective bargaining in interstate transportation. All these rulings were by 5 to 4, with Roberts's vote enabling the defeat of the Four Horsemen who remained intractable in their opposition to the New Deal and all its works.

As surprising as these results were, they were overshadowed by the Wagner Act rulings. These cases turned, as did much of the New Deal litigation before the Court, on the justices' interpretation of Section VIII, Clause III of the Constitution, known as the commerce clause. It gives Congress the power "to regulate commerce with foreign nations, *and with the several states.*" Those five words have probably been at the center of more intense and far-reaching debate among judges, scholars, and politicians than any other phrase in the nation's charter. The constitutional case for a good part of the New Deal's ambitious effort to guide the nation's economy depended on the judiciary granting a broad warrant for such intrusion based on the commerce clause. In drafting the Wagner Act, with its guarantees of labor's right to organize and its prohibition on employer interference with such efforts, the New Deal's legal architects buttressed the statute's link to interstate commerce by claiming that labor unrest, which the act sought to alleviate, contributed to economic disruption. On its face, in view of the sit-down strikes and the Memorial Day massacre, that argument seemed reasonable enough. But just the year before in overturning the Guffey Act, which attempted to regulate hours and wages in the coal industry, the Court had held that the government's reach far exceeded its constitutional grasp.

Understandably New Dealers had viewed the Wagner Act's fate before the Court with trepidation. Attorney General Cummings confided to his diary that he considered the act to be "of rather doubtful constitutionality." Tom Corcoran had been telling friends that the most he hoped for was to get two justices on his side.

In the event, by a 5 to 4 majority the Court delivered a stunning and for the administration a pleasing surprise. Hughes, who had concurred with the majority opinion in the *Carter* case, read the majority opinion in *NLRB v. Jones and Laughlin* and in four other cases testing the Wagner Act. Each time the Court based its decision on a remarkably generous view of the commerce clause, brushing aside the sort of distinctions which in the *Carter* case had led to the New Deal's defeat. "Although activities may be intrastate in character when separately considered," Hughes declared, if their control is necessary to prevent the obstruction of commerce, "Congress cannot be denied the power to exercise that control." The New Deal's attorneys could not have said it any better themselves.

Administration officials were astounded. Homer Cummings began the entry in his diary that evening: "Today, an amazing thing happened."

But for the president the Court's rulings were a mixed blessing.

On the one hand the Court's sudden acceptance of the New Deal doctrine of government authority undercut the claim that only the drastic remedy proposed by FDR could bring the Court to terms with twentieth-century economic realities. Indeed the Wagner Act decisions reinforced the belief that the underlying cause for the Court's turnabout was not some sudden enlightenment but rather an effort by Hughes, abetted by Roberts, to undermine support for the Court-packing scheme. FDR's friend and constitutional confidant, Felix Frankfurter, wrote to Brandeis that "the manner and circumstances of the over-ruling make last Monday one of the few real black days in my life." The decision, he explained, had robbed him of his faith "in the integrity of the Court's process." More succinctly, to FDR he wired: "After today I feel like finding some honest profession to enter."

On the other hand, whatever strategy Hughes might have in mind, the president could still take hope from the belief so often uttered by his supporters that by clearing the path for collective bargaining the Court would ease the underlying tensions provoking the sit-down strikes. Still, FDR and his labor allies were taking no chances. Who could tell how long the Court would cling to its new liberal outlook? The pro–New Deal decisions had all been rendered by 5-to-4 majorities that included the vote of Justice Roberts. And Roberts's consistency, as recent history had demonstrated, was a slender reed to lean on.

So the president drove on in his push for Court reform, enlisting in his cause the formidable voice and influence of John L. Lewis. In a nationally broadcast radio talk on May 14, Lewis thrust himself and his union to the forefront of the drive to change the Court. Lewis did not do such things halfway. A month after the Wagner Act decision, he condemned the Court as "a tyrannical and oligarchic tribunal which arrogates to itself even the power of defying the wishes of the people of the United States." But no longer would this be permitted, Lewis insisted. "The time of reckoning is at hand," he said. He was convinced that the president's plan for the Court had the support of "the overwhelming majority of Americans." Then he drove home his main point to trade union members: "The future of labor in America," Lewis declared, "is intimately connected with the future of the president's proposal."

Even as Lewis helped FDR make the case against the Court, he had grave troubles in his own bailiwick, specifically with the steel industry. It was steel that Lewis had initially had in mind to be the CIO's priority, until the desperate fervor of the sit-down strikers in Flint forced him to change his timetable. And it was with the steel industry, thanks to the stunning success of the sit-down strikes and the impression they made on Big Steel's Myron Taylor, that Lewis had scored his pathbreaking success in March, weeks before the Supreme Court had upheld the Wagner Act.

But while Lewis now hoped to take full advantage of that ruling, some of the masters of corporate America, particularly steel men, were determined to resist the new rules for labor management relations. Among the most intransigent and powerful were the chieftains of four major steel companies, Republic, Bethlehem, Youngstown Sheet and Tube, and Inland Steel. As a group they were dubbed "Little Steel," in contrast to U.S. Steel, or Big Steel, whose agreement to recognize the Steel Workers Organizing Committee, an arm of Lewis's CIO, had stunned and appalled them.

But it did not intimidate them. And, for that matter, neither did the Wagner Act. Although validated by the Supreme Court, that law, as the Little Steel manager obdurately interpreted it, required only that they bargain with their workers, not sign a contract with their union. And this they refused to do, particularly when the union was part of the CIO.

"I won't have a contract, verbal or written, with an irresponsible, racketeering, violent Communist body like the
CIO," declared Tom Girdler, the farm boy who had become
Little Steel's spokesman and the point man for unrelenting
corporate resistance to unionism. Born in rural Indiana in
1877, Girdler learned his three r's in a one-room country
schoolhouse. A wealthy aunt helped him get through Lehigh
University where he earned a degree in mechanical engineer-
ing. After a brief stint as a salesman, he found his natural home
in the steel mills. Starting as a foreman, he shifted from one
company to another, climbing a step on the managerial ladder
with each move.

Girdler hit his stride at Jones and Laughlin, where in 1920 he
became general superintendent of the company's plant at
Aliquippa, Pennsylvania. There he built a model town in which,
as he later boasted in his autobiography, he established "a benev-
olent dictatorship" with himself as "honorary caliph." Many of
his workers saw things differently. They called Girdler's domain
"Little Siberia," and federal investigators later described Girdler's
rule there as "systematic terror."

Girdler's own private militia, the J&L Police, kept all workers
under surveillance. Anyone who got out of line was fired. The
fortunate were simply chased out of town; others were beaten before they fled. Workers were segregated according to national ori-
gin and ethnic derivation, and management did what it could to
set them against one another.

But what counted for J&L stockholders was that the
Aliquippa plant helped to make them richer each year. As a reward, Girdler was named president of the company in 1928. Only
a year later, the restlessly ambitious Girdler left to form a new
company, Republic Steel, in partnership with Cleveland entre-
preneur Cyrus Eaton. Republic quickly became the third-largest
producer in the industry, but like the rest of American business
it was soon engulfed by the depression.

For a time Girdler viewed the New Deal as a lifesaver because of the NRA production codes, which he thought—by denying Big Steel some of the competitive advantages of its size—would prevent it from crushing Republic. But though he liked the production standards and was even willing to accept higher wages and shorter hours for his workers, he found the notion of having his workers represented by a union abhorrent. "We are not going to recognize any professional union," he told the American Iron and Steel Institute in 1934. Before he would deal with unions, Girdler vowed, he would shut down his plants and "raise apples and potatoes." One of his foremen told a militant local union leader, "When we get through starving you out, you won't want to strike."

Lewis branded Girdler a "heavily armed monomaniac with murderous tendencies." Many thought that description characteristically hyperbolic until it was disclosed that in readying his forces for the struggle against Lewis and the CIO, Girdler had invested nearly $50,000 to arm his company's own police department with an array of rifles, pistols, and gas grenades. He had also bought and distributed to his workers more than forty thousand copies of a pamphlet called "Join the CIO and Help Build a Soviet America."

On May 27, 1937, with the CIO's Steel Workers Organizing Committee under Phil Murray pushing its campaign against Little Steel, the American Iron and Trade Institute, controlled by Little Steel, elected Girdler its president. That same day Murray called a strike that would ultimately spread through the Midwest and involve 85,000 workers.

The stage was set for the bloodiest confrontation of this turbulent year, but it was not to come as a consequence of another of the much maligned sit-down strikes. Instead it resulted from a conventional strike at Republic's plant in South Chicago, just outside the limits of the Windy City but in the jurisdiction of Chicago police. Murray's strike call was aimed at three of the

Little Steel companies—Inland, Youngstown Sheet and Tube, and Republic. Both Inland and Youngstown Sheet and Tube closed their plants and prepared to wait out the strike. Given the meager union strike benefits, they knew that payless paydays would be hard for their workers to bear. Republic adopted a different strategy, closing some plants but continuing limited production at others, including the South Chicago operation, where half of the 2,200 workers had joined the strike.

The company kept the plant running by staging a sit-down strike in reverse. It kept nonstrikers inside the factory, where the company provided cots and food, thus making it unnecessary for them to face the ordeal of walking through a picket line of angry strikers. Chicago police helped out too. First they drove the union workers out of the plant, thus preventing a sit-down, and then pushed the picket line two blocks away from the plant, arresting a score of pickets who did not move fast enough. On the third day of the strike, May 28, some three hundred to four hundred strikers and women supporters set out to march to the plant gate to reinforce the token picket line of six to eight strikers that the police had permitted. Wielding their billy clubs, police bloodied a few heads and drove the marchers away.

The next day was quiet, but strike leaders called for a protest meeting on the following day, Memorial Day, May 30. A crowd of around fifteen hundred strikers and sympathizers gathered at Sam's Place, a dime-a-dance joint which had been taken over as strike headquarters, complete with soup kitchen and cots for pickets. They sang union songs—"The Ballad of Joe Hill," "Solidarity Forever," and, saddest of all, the lament of an IWW organizer, tortured into betrayal, who pleaded: "Comrades, slay me, for the coppers took my soul; close my eyes good comrades, for I played a traitor's role." They heard from union organizers who recounted the progress made by organized labor in general and the steel workers in particular. Franklin Roosevelt and John L. Lewis were lauded and the crowd cheered.

Then about a thousand backers of the union formed a parade behind two American flags and began marching to the Republic plant gate, about a third of a mile away, intending to demonstrate their support for the strike and for the pickets on duty. As they neared the plant they were confronted by about 250 blue-coated Chicago police who formed a human barricade about 300 yards from the gate. The march slowed but kept on toward the plant. The police, who had received a tip that the marchers were planning to invade the plant, closed ranks and stood their ground. With their revolvers in their holsters, they brandished their billy clubs. Some wielded extra-heavy clubs courtesy of Republic Steel; others had tear gas from Republic's stockpiles. The marchers stopped about three feet from the police lines and began shouting for the cops to let them pass. The police did not budge.

The impasse could last only so long. After a few minutes some marchers threw sticks and stones. The police responded with tear-gas bombs and then opened up with their revolvers, shooting point-blank into the mob and firing about two hundred shots. As the marchers fled the police followed, beating anyone in their path with billy clubs, including those who had fallen. They arrested everyone they could lay their hands on, herding as many as sixteen into paddy wagons built to hold eight prisoners, shoving the injured in with the rest, with no effort to treat or dress their wounds.

The death toll of the marchers would reach ten, six of them shot in the back, while more than fifty others were wounded by bullets or battered by billy clubs. The police counted sixteen injured, of whom three needed hospital treatment. Immediately afterward demonstrators clogged the business district in South Chicago to protest excessive violence by the police, and the Senate's La Follette Committee on Civil Liberties launched an investigation. Three days of hearings produced evidence, the most graphic of which was newsreel film taken by Paramount News, that the marchers did not attack the police and that instead those who were wounded were fleeing the police. The committee placed the blame for the bloodshed on the police, either because of "gross inefficiency" or "a deliberate effort to intimidate the strikers." If the police had permitted the marchers to reach the gate, the committee concluded, "the day would have passed without violence or disorder. We think it plain that the force employed by the police was far in excess of that which the occasion required."

But Paramount News, anxious to avoid controversy, did not release its film for more than a month, and even then its audience was limited because of local censorship. And the La Follette Committee did not make public its report until nearly two months after the Memorial Day clash. By this time the public had gained a very different impression of the events in Chicago, based on newspaper accounts and reinforced by the rhetoric of local politicians.

The *Chicago Tribune* described the attack as an invasion by "a trained military unit of a revolutionary body" and declared that the marchers were "lusting for blood." The *New York Times* headline declared "STEEL MOB HALTED," and a subhead asserted "Crowd Uses Guns and Rocks," though the ample photographic evidence of the confrontation provided by newspaper photographers and Paramount News showed no sign of weapons in the hands of the marchers. *Time* said the demonstrators "marched on the plant to seize and close it" and described the police as firing their weapons only after they had been assaulted by "the mob [which] began hurling rocks and steel bolts, using slingshots with severe accuracy." The *Washington Post* observed that "this ill advised resort to violence has the union in an even more indefensible position than that assumed by the company."

After a year marked by victories for organized labor, the Chicago Massacre, as union leaders called it, represented a dramatic setback. Refusing to concede defeat, Lewis and Phil Murray pushed ahead with the strike. But in South Chicago the workers were stunned and demoralized by the lethal punishment meted out on Memorial Day. And elsewhere Girdler and his Little Steel allies fought back by threatening to move their mills to other cities less hospitable to unions and by shouting to the rooftops about the menace of communism and the need to preserve law and order.

In June the CIO struck the Cambria Works of Bethlehem Steel, another member of the Little Steel group in Johnstown, Pennsylvania, whose blustery Mayor Daniel Shields held the distinction of being one of the few prohibition-era bootleggers to have been caught, convicted, and served time. Now proclaiming his determination that "law and order shall prevail in Johnstown," Shields wired FDR that the advent of the CIO "can only mean blood in our streets." He had been given to understand, the mayor added, that the CIO planned to blow up major bridges in addition to staging kidnappings and destroying the mayor and his family.

Roosevelt's only response was to suggest that His Honor tone down his language—"kind words instead of harsh words"—to serve "the best interests of law and order."

The president would not involve himself on either side. Even before he brushed off Shields's plea to stem the Red tide, the White House had turned down an appeal from Phil Murray of the Steel Workers for help. Local steel unions flooded the White House with telegrams, pleading with the president to force their companies to sign contracts. But beyond a mild observation on what the Wagner Act really meant, that it was "just plain common sense" to put a wage agreement in writing, which the companies refused to do, Roosevelt neither did or said anything to back up the unions.

With the strike on its last legs, on June 25 Murray once again asked for help from Roosevelt. He got his answer in stunning fashion at Roosevelt's June 29 press conference. Reaching back to

Romeo and Juliet to express his disdain, FDR told reporters that the country as a whole was saying of the strikes, "a plague on both your houses." And to underline his statement he allowed himself to be quoted directly, making an exception to the rule that barred direct quotes of the president. Roosevelt refused to elaborate on his remark. But he did not need to. John L. Lewis got the drift. The CIO leader was seated on the edge of a desk when a reporter told him of the comment. He said nothing. But his heels beat against the panels of the desk until it seemed, a reporter thought, that he would smash the wood to splinters. Little more than six weeks earlier, Lewis had placed his own prestige and that of his union at the service of the president's chief priority, the revamping of the Supreme Court. The Court plan was still uppermost in Roosevelt's mind. But it had been running into rough seas. In the past few weeks the tide had turned against Lewis and his CIO too. Roosevelt was not prepared to help.

On July 3, three days after FDR's Shakespearean dismissal of the union cause, FDR's labor secretary returned to the issue of the legality of sit-down strikes. In January Frances Perkins had declared that to be an unsettled question. But now she announced that, contrary to general belief, the Department of Labor had never viewed the sit-down strike as "either lawful, desirable, or appropriate."

Once FDR had believed he needed Lewis's help to rescue his foundering plan to reform the Supreme Court. Now he had concluded that the best way to save that ship was to throw Lewis overboard. But the question remained whether even that would do the job.

9

With the Bark Off

Ever the perfect host, coatless and tieless, his soft shirt opened at the neck, the big jovial man sat under an aged locust tree with a whitewashed trunk, greeting his guests by first name, his booming laugh echoing across the waters of Chesapeake Bay. Just like the tree, the thirty-second President of the United States stayed rooted to his post at stage center for nearly every daylight moment of what everyone in attendance agreed was certainly the grandest stag party Washington had seen in many a day.

Those favored by his hospitality, nearly all of the 407 Democratic members of the House and Senate, had been ferried over by retired navy subchasers from the mainland in relays to the Jefferson Island Club, a former bootleggers' hideout that was now a Democratic fish and game club. For three days, on this last weekend of June 1937, the lawmakers swam in the nude, shot clay pigeons, fished, played pinochle, and gorged on crabs, potato salad, cold cuts, and apple pie washed down with cold beer and mint juleps.

When it was over the *New York Times* reported that everyone involved in this splendid splurge agreed that the president had done himself and his plan for Supreme Court overhaul "a world of good." But what everyone also recognized was that the president needed every ounce of goodwill he could squeeze out of this or any other occasion. Because in the weeks preceding the Jefferson Island bash the prospects for the Court plan had endured one punishing hammer blow after another.

Following the earlier setbacks in March and April, Chief Justice Hughes's letter demolishing the claim that the Court was overworked, and the minimum-wage and Wagner Act decisions suggesting that the Court might not be so hopelessly conservative after all, some Democrats had urged the president to compromise on his plan. The argument pressed upon Roosevelt was that since the Court appeared headed in the direction he wanted to go, he should accept some modification of his proposal and declare victory.

But the president made clear to his supporters that he wanted more than a 5-to-4 majority, which was how the minimum-wage and Wagner Act rulings had been decided. "It is not a wholesome situation when an administration under a mandate to carry out a progressive program must have a court of nine, with four votes lost to it in advance," Homer Cummings dutifully argued in a statement issued after the Wagner Act ruling. "The margin is too narrow and the risk is too great."

Roosevelt himself offered a grander version of his rationale to Wyoming Senator Joseph O'Mahoney and economics professor William Zebina Ripley, who were among those who called on him to make the case for compromise. Not only did he want more votes on his side, he explained, outlining a view of constitutional structure that was far afield from the understanding of his visitors, but he wanted a Court that would "cooperate" with him. Offering the same vision he had unsuccessfully proposed to Chief Justice Hughes four years before, the president said he hoped for justices with whom he, as chief executive, could work out their differences in advance of legislative policy. This, he contended, would be much preferable to having to wait in uncertainty for the Court to make up its mind about actions already taken. And this state of affairs he hoped to achieve by appointing six justices whom he could readily approach and consult on the great problems of the day. His visitors were so startled by what they had heard that after they left the White House they compared notes to make certain they had not been mistaken.

While keeping this novel concept of the proper role of the Supreme Court mostly to himself, Roosevelt was sufficiently confident of prospects for his Court plan to leave April 28 for a fishing trip in the Gulf of Mexico off the Texas shore. He returned May 14, still in no mood for compromise.

Three springs previous, Roosevelt had come back to Washington from a similar excursion in the friendly Gulf waters to face a reputedly rebellious Congress. Despite this friction, thirty senators and two hundred representatives had gathered at the station and even brought with them a band, all to make a happy homecoming. Responding to their welcome, the president had delivered a tough message, albeit cloaked in humor. "I have come back with all sorts of new lessons which I learned from barracuda and sharks," he remarked. His auditors got the point, and within a few days the revolt withered away and the lawmakers set to work pushing through a list of the president's legislative priorities.

But three years later the discontent on Capitol Hill, fostered by the Supreme Court fight and the sit-down strikes, was much deeper and could not be swept away by a few artfully chosen words. For this spring's homecoming there were no lawmakers on hand in Union Station to greet him, and no speeches, and no band. Instead the president hurried back to the White House where he soon made his resolve clear to the Democratic congressional leadership who called on him. "The battle will go on," Senate Majority Leader Robinson told reporters afterward. "I see no prospect at this stage of any adjustment or agreement."

Did no "adjustment" also mean no "compromise"? he was asked.

It did.

Did "at this stage" mean the president might compromise later?

"Strike out 'at this stage,'" Robinson snapped.

But this tough talk began to take on a hollow ring with the events of the next few days.

On May 18, three months after Roosevelt's plan for judicial reform had been submitted with such bright hopes, the Senate Judiciary Committee voted 10 to 8 to reject it. To make the vote even more damaging, seven members of the president's own party were among the nay votes.

A second blow, delivered that same day, was even more hurtful. This was the announcement of the retirement of seventy-seven-year-old Justice Van Devanter, the timing of which was no accident. Van Devanter had contemplated leaving the bench for some time, since Hattie Summers had pushed through his bill guaranteeing him the same salary and tax benefits he received on the bench. But at the suggestion of two leaders of the opposition to the Court plan, Senators Borah and Wheeler, he made the announcement to coincide with the Judiciary Committee vote against the president's proposal, thus enhancing its symbolic impact.

There was a time when the resignation of Justice Van Devanter would have been a cause for rejoicing in the White House. But not now. The departure of one of the Four Horsemen would make it that much harder to demonstrate the need to overhaul the Court. It also forced the president to face the issue of selecting a replacement, a matter in which he would not have an entirely free hand. It was widely understood in Washington, particularly in the Senate, that this opening had already been promised to Senator Joe Robinson, as a reward for his many services to the New Deal. A hulking figure of man possessed of little subtlety but great energy and force, Robinson was many praiseworthy things: a stalwart of the Democratic party, an able parliamentary technician, a trustworthy ally, and a formidable foe. But, as he himself would be quick to admit, he was no liberal, at least not the sort of intellectual firebrand left-winger that the New Dealers fancied.

Born sixty-five years earlier in a log cabin in rural Arkansas to a country preacher and his part-Indian wife, Robinson was a backcountry schoolteacher until he earned his law degree. He served five terms in Congress, mostly taking the side of the farmer against the railroads, came back home to win the governorship, and in 1913 convinced the state legislature to send him to the U.S. Senate. There he supported Woodrow Wilson in war and peace, became his party's leader in 1920, then fought tooth and nail against the high tariffs and pro-big-business slant of the Republican administrations.

In 1928 he accepted the thankless challenge of serving as Al Smith's vice-presidential running mate in a campaign foredoomed by bigotry and reinforced by social arrogance. Through all the muck aimed by Republicans at his Catholic running mate from the sidewalks of New York, Robinson remained steadfast and resourceful. He took it upon himself to squelch the stories spread by Republicans about Smith's alleged weakness for hard liquor. In a campaign speech in Dallas he declared, "The statement has been made that he is a drunkard," and paused for effect. Then he shouted at the top of his lungs: "THERE'S NOT ONE WORD OF TRUTH IN IT!" The shout did not silence the gossip, but it helped earn Robinson an even stronger position in his party.

But if Robinson's allegiance to his party was hard to question, so was his conservatism, which naturally flowed from his rural Southern roots. During the 1920s he had fought against government development of the proposed electric power project at Muscle Shoals in Alabama, which became a stellar New Deal achievement. All across the line Roosevelt's drive for economic and political reform created divisive conflicts with Robinson's core beliefs. The senator had been troubled by the NRA codes, fearful they would put Southern industry at a disadvantage. And he worried even more about the deficit spending that became a New Deal hallmark, concerned, as he wrote a friend, that it would "bankrupt the country and tend to centralize all power in the national government."

On top of all this, his relationship with FDR was barren of personal links. Roosevelt's blithe ambiguities inevitably made the stolid, blunt Robinson uneasy while the senator lacked the polish and intellectual flair that engaged Roosevelt. Roosevelt's own predilections aside, many New Dealers saw the senator as one who served the cause out of duty and party loyalty but in his heart and mind was not really one of them.

"A Supreme Court Justice is not responsible to the president who appoints him," the *Nation* pointed out in an article whose negativism reflected the unequivocal judgment of its title: "Robinson Will Not Do." Once confirmed on the Court, the magazine warned, Robinson would be free to vote his own convictions, and those beliefs placed him on the side of the haves versus the have-nots. "Senator Robinson is a conservative Southern rural Democrat," the *Nation* continued. "That a man who so thoroughly represents the ruling class in Arkansas would be elevated to the Supreme Court at this juncture is ironical and dangerous."

Roosevelt seemed to share some of these reservations. While Robinson's friends and colleagues in the Senate rushed to shake his hand and pat his back in anticipation of his appointment to the Court, the president sat on his hands.

The passage of time only made this situation increasingly uncomfortable and obvious. Trying to make a joke of the tension, a reporter asked FDR if he was going to "confirm" the Senate's "nomination" for the Supreme Court. His answer was a glare and the statement that all reports of whom he would nominate should be labeled "Surmise No. 23." When Senators Byrnes and Harrison went to the White House to put in a good word for their

Arkansas colleague, the president, convinced that Robinson had inspired the visit, politely sent them packing.

To those who urged him to act on Robinson and thus pave the way for a compromise on his Court plan in the Senate, the president turned a deaf ear. As he told his treasury secretary, Henry Morgenthau, he had no intention of appointing a conservative to the court, even a loyal Democrat such as Joe Robinson, until he could name some liberal justices to take their seats alongside him. And that would take approval of his Court plan, which Roosevelt still professed to believe Congress would ultimately enact.

With the president locked into his position, his aides in the White House were reduced to a strategy based on perverse hopes. The Court still had before it one hugely important issue for the New Deal, the constitutionality of the infant Social Security plan. In their hearts New Dealers wanted a green light for Social Security, perhaps the one Roosevelt proposal more than any other that was imbued with the philosophy of protecting the collective welfare as opposed to the advancement of individual ambition. But in their heads they calculated that a negative verdict against Social Security would provide a basis for arguing that the justices really had not changed their spots, that they were just as adamantly committed to their paleolithic view of government's role in society, and that only the strong medicine prescribed in Roosevelt's original plan would cure the nation of this affliction.

But most strategies based on winning by losing are inherently flawed, and this was no exception. The big drawback was that the Supreme Court would not go along with the scenario envisioned by the die-hard backers of the president's bill. Instead, by the same 5-to-4 majority that had upheld minimum-wage laws and the Wagner Act, the Court gave its approval both to the unemployment compensation provision of the Social Security Act and to the old-age pensions that were the heart of the law, thus establishing a broad constituency of beneficiaries who would become

Roosevelt's most enduring political legacy. Moreover in the latter ruling the Court repudiated its prior dictum that the general welfare clause of the Constitution applies only to subjects specifically cited in the Constitution. Instead it held that the crucial language amounted to a broad grant of authority to the federal government to act in the general welfare.

The Social Security rulings were only the latest in the series of events that undermined the arguments for the president's plan and all but sealed its doom. But unpleasant realities often take a while to sink in, at the White House as elsewhere. When Jim Farley met with him a week or so after the Social Security rulings, the president "still refused to regard the situation as desperate, which it was." To help the bill's prospects, Farley urged the nomination of Robinson, which would win support for Court reform from the Senate leader's many friends in that body. The suggestion was seconded by Homer Cummings who joined the discussion, and Roosevelt agreed. Next day Farley phoned Robinson, greeted him as "Mr. Justice," and told him the good news.

Even so, it was not until June 3, ten days after the Social Security decisions were announced, that the president took the only course left to him. He summoned Joe Robinson to the White House to ask him his view of the lay of the land. Robinson told him the plan for a fifteen-justice Court was dead. Better take a compromise, if one could be had, he advised. If the president wanted him to do so, he, Robinson would do his best to work something out.

FDR agreed to put Robinson in charge. And to give him incentive for the task he told him drily, "if there was to be a bride, there must also be bridesmaids—at least four of them." In other words, Robinson's chances of getting the seat on the Court that was his heart's desire depended on FDR getting authority to appoint at least four other new justices in addition to Robinson.

Ten days after Robinson took command of the Court bill, no compromise had emerged. Instead the president had to deal with another item of disturbing news. John Nance Garner, his vice president and one of FDR's chief behind-the-scenes wire-pullers, was leaving for six weeks' vacation in his home state. In Washington, where the behavior patterns of the prominent and the powerful are closely watched and recorded, this news caused a tremor of sizable proportions. Never before while Congress was in session had Jack Garner allowed himself to be more than a cab ride away from the Capitol dome.

Before he became Franklin Roosevelt's vice president, John Nance Garner of Texas had spent thirty years in the House of Representatives mastering the art of backroom deals. But none of the various bargains he had made on Capitol Hill could rival for importance the deal struck at the 1932 Democratic Convention in Chicago when he traded the delegate support for his presidential candidacy to FDR in return for a place on the national ticket. Not that Garner wanted to be vice president, or president either. He was chiefly interested in the Democrats selecting a ticket that would assure their control of the national government.

Once in office Garner became famous for his frank denigration of the vice presidency, which he regarded as a demotion from his role as speaker of the House of Representatives. He dismissed the vice presidency as "the spare tire on the automobile of government" and more earthily as "not worth a pitcher of warm piss." Consistent with this attitude was his aversion to publicity, astounding in national political leaders even in that pre-television age. He declined most speaking invitations and requests for interviews, describing himself as "only a junior member of the firm." And he also refused Secret Service protection, contending "there is nobody crazy enough to shoot a vice president."

Yet Garner's own performance on the job belied his reticence. Making the most of his long experience and close relationships on Capitol Hill, he became FDR's field general in building support for the historic legislation that created the New Deal. Throughout his first term Garner sought to maintain discipline among Democrats made anxious by what they viewed as the excesses of reform, arguing that the national crisis demanded innovations and preaching party loyalty. "It doesn't matter what kind of fool you think he is," he scolded one skeptical Democrat. "He's your fool just as long as he's president."

Now Garner had attracted maximum attention to himself by the simple expedient of disappearing from the scene. Although he uttered not a word in public critical of the president, his absence spoke volumes, none of it favorable to FDR. Many speculated that his abrupt departure signaled his distaste for the Court plan, but Garner himself indicated to intimates that his leave-taking had more to do with FDR's failure to deal more aggressively with the sit-down strikes. In a letter to Jim Farley he expressed his irritation at Roosevelt's tolerance of these disruptions of the usual order of the business world. "I am not only unalterably opposed to mass violation of the law, but any kind of tolerance of violation of the law, regardless of class," he wrote.

Yet his return to Texas in mid-session was taken as another sign of disenchantment with the Court plan among the leaders of the president's own party, a point well understood by Roosevelt. "Why in hell did Jack have to leave at this time for?" he complained to Farley, who functioned as FDR's unofficial ambassador to other Democrats. "This is a fine time to jump ship."

But Garner's unexpected exit was but a pinprick compared to the bludgeoning the president's cherished idea suffered two days later at the hands of the Senate Judiciary Committee when it released its report on his plan, a thunderous sequel to its earlier vote of disapproval. The twenty-four-page report did not merely reject the president's plan, it demolished it. Before they even got around to assaulting the substance of the plan, the senators lashed out at the disingenuousness of the president's approach to the problem. His plan, the report said, revealed "the futility and absurdity of the devious." If Mr. Roosevelt wished to trick the country about his purposes, he had not fooled the Judiciary Committee. The report branded the plan, with all its pretensions to reform, as nothing more or less than an effort "to punish the justices" whose opinions had been resented by FDR. And by doing so, what the president proposed amounted to "an invasion of judicial power such as has never before been attempted in this country" and which, if enacted, would create a "vicious precedent which must necessarily undermine our system."

Undercutting the independence of the judiciary, an inevitable consequence of the measure, would subject the government and its citizens to autocratic dominance, "the very thing against which the American Colonies revolted, and to prevent which the Constitution was in every particular framed."

All these jabs were preparation for the final haymakers. "We recommend the rejection of this bill as a needless, futile, and utterly dangerous abandonment of constitutional principle." Then came the concluding sentence, which few journalists could resist quoting: "It is a measure which should be so emphatically rejected that its parallel will never again be presented to the free representatives of the free people of America."

Authors or actors punished by such a review probably would be discouraged from returning to their muse, at least for a while. But Franklin Roosevelt practiced a different form of art, and it was not in his nature to allow his spirit to be dampened. Two days after this castigation of his brainchild, when Senator Robinson had proposed that the president might profitably spend a weekend parleying with party leaders, Roosevelt not only agreed but inflated Robinson's idea into the extravaganza on Jefferson Island. To Robinson's suggestion that he meet with the party's "leaders," Roosevelt responded that he considered all 407 Democratic members of the House and Senate to be leaders, and so directed that all be invited.

Well, not quite all. The Democratic contingent to the House of Representatives included three women: Nan Honeyman from Oregon, Virginia Jenckes from Indiana, and Carolyn O'Day from

New York. But since the Jefferson Island Club was, as *Time* magazine described it, "a sanctum of male Democratic leisure," these ladies were not invited, just as Labor Secretary Perkins's name was omitted from the guest list which included her nine male colleagues in the cabinet. There were also absentees who *had* been invited, among them senators—such as Virginia's Carter Glass and Nebraska's Edward Burke—so estranged from the New Deal that they saw no need to waste a weekend pretending otherwise.

But if their absence was noted, it in no way diminished the enjoyment of those in attendance. For his part the president was determined to let nothing stand in the way of his intensive fence-mending. Among those on hand were "Cotton" Ed Smith of South Carolina, who had fought the New Deal every step of the way, and was famous even among Southern Democrats for his enthusiastic racism. When a Negro minister was called upon to pray at the 1936 Democratic Convention, Smith abruptly departed, exclaiming as he went, "By God, he's as black as melted midnight." But when Smith regaled the company with his "darky" yarns, in heavy dialect, FDR guffawed along with the rest.

He laughed also when Martin Dies of Texas, who only three months before had denounced the sit-down strikers, as the self-declared president of the "House Demagogues Club" inducted the president into that apocryphal organization. As part of his initiation Roosevelt was asked to pledge support for all appropriation bills and oppose all taxation bills, and not submit controversial legislation to Congress.

Word of this good fellowship went forth across the broad Atlantic to officials at Whitehall, to whom His Majesty's ambassador to the United States reported: "The meeting of the Democratic Congressmen on Jefferson Island had rather surprising results, for the Roosevelt charm was turned onto them as through a hose pipe and they have returned to the Capital in a far more malleable spirit." According to Sir Ronald Lindsay's informants, the feelings that inspired seven Democratic senators to sign the Judiciary Committee's damning report "are no longer in fashion."

But that opinion was subject to dispute. Others, like Republican Senator Charles McNary of Oregon, sarcastically dismissed the performance as a "weekend charm school." One thing was clear, whatever the bonhomie generated on Jefferson Island: none of the signers of the Judiciary Committee report was issuing a retraction. It soon became clear that at most the president's hospitality had bought a bit more time for Joe Robinson to make his case for a compromise.

Meanwhile, though, there were plenty of people arguing for the other side. For the foes of FDR's now greatly diminished plan the Judiciary Committee report was a bonanza beyond their fondest dreams, and they sought to take full advantage of it. Frank Gannett's Committee to Uphold Constitutional Government had been busy all spring mailing out rhetorical broadsides issued by the likes of Virginia Senator Carter Glass, who warned against the consequences of the president's plan in biblical prose: "He shall break his judges if they cross his word. . . . We shall take our station, dirt beneath his feet, while his hired captains jeer us on the street."

Now Gannett's group got enough copies of the committee report to mail to every newspaper in the country. Unfriendly congressmen ordered another seventy thousand copies for their constituents, and Methodists hostile to the plan sent the report to more than a hundred thousand clergymen.

FDR's allies pointed out that the president had easily overcome the opposition of many of the same forces in his victorious reelection campaign. But these groups were much more united in opposition to the Court plan than they had ever been in support of Alf Landon, who many regarded as insufficiently staunch in his conservative convictions. Moreover in the spring of 1937 the foes of the Court plan had a powerful new weapon. This was the mounting public resentment of the perceived excesses of union labor, and of FDR's seeming tolerance, if not outright approval, of these outbreaks.

True, the number of sit-downs had declined from their high of 170 in March, when the Chrysler strike dominated the headlines, to 58 in April, when the Court upheld the Wagner Act; and numbers continued to fall for the rest of the year. But the seizure of the auto plants by their workers would remain with the public as a disturbing memory for some time to come. Press coverage of the Memorial Day bloodshed at Republic Steel reinforced the public's anxieties about the threat to good and welfare from the aggressive tactics of the newly aroused labor movement.

In July, well after the sit-downs had passed their peak, a Gallup poll showed that two-thirds of the public thought the states should make sit-downs illegal, and a similar majority favored state and local governments using force to eject the strikers. More than eight of ten Americans favored a law regulating the conduct of strikes. And in June about two-thirds of the public said they thought more favorably of AFL President William Green, who had denounced the sit-downs, than of John L. Lewis, whose CIO had spearheaded their use.

This negativism toward labor had prompted Roosevelt to back away by declaring a "plague on both your houses," scorning his old allies in organized labor as well as the leaders of business in his press conference at the end of June. In midsummer, as the Senate debated Roosevelt's Court-reform proposal, the *Boston Traveler* ran a telling advertisement advising vacationing New Englanders to "come on down to Cape Cod for a real vacation where the CIO is unknown and over 90 percent are Republicans who respect the Supreme Court."

But it was too late for the president to avoid the damage caused by labor unrest to the coalition that had swept him to victory in 1936 and that he had counted on for support in the fight for his Court plan. Farmers had been a key element in the Roosevelt alliance. And Roosevelt had counted on their all-out backing for his Court plan, particularly because of their anger at the Supreme Court's invalidation of such New Deal efforts to aid the farmer as the AAA and the Farm Bankruptcy Act. But just as the farmers resented the Supreme Court decisions against their interests, they also felt threatened by the surge of lawless unrest among big-city factory workers. And many had heard the words of Carter Glass of Virginia in his nationally broadcast warning against this plan to pack the nation's highest court with "judicial marionettes to speak the ventriloquisms of the White House," and urging "men and women of America who value liberties" to "protest to Congress against this attempt to replace representative government with autocracy." One after another the three major farm organizations—the Farm Bureau Federation, the Grange, and even the relatively radical Farmers Union—refused to give the plan the backing Roosevelt wanted. Indeed their leaders signaled that if pushed too hard, their members might decide to take a stand against the plan.

Organized labor was the cohort in the coalition that Roosevelt counted on most heavily. He had expected the backing of both the AFL and the CIO. But here again the sit-downs played havoc with his hopes. The trouble started first at the AFL, where Bill Hutcheson, president of the Carpenters Union, Lewis's old foe, was unwilling to lift a finger to do anything that might aid a scheme of FDR's, whom he viewed as a patron of Lewis and the CIO. Unable to prevent the AFL from giving the Court bill its official endorsement, he nonetheless wielded enough influence to keep the Federation's lobbyists from making the all-out effort the Court bill needed. "The AFL lobbyists put in a good word for the bill when they found time, but the heat was never really turned on," veteran Washington journalists Joseph Alsop and Turner Catledge reported.

Add to this the tension between Roosevelt and John L. Lewis generated by the sit-downs. To be sure, when the Court bill was announced, Lewis gave it his official backing, and in mid-May he went on the radio to speak in support of the plan. Yet he did not deploy his lobbyists in a full-scale effort on Capitol Hill. Before doing so, he wanted more backing from FDR in his dealings with the steel industry. But Roosevelt, wary of labor because of the outcry in Congress against the sit-downs, was unwilling to do more than sit on the fence. FDR himself killed any hope of real help from Lewis with his "plague on both your houses" malediction, just as the debate over the Court reorganization plan headed into its most critical phase on Capitol Hill.

That left Joe Robinson pretty much on his own, except for the assistance of a few trusted colleagues. They included two men who would some day sit on the Supreme Court themselves— Hugo Black of Alabama, one of the most ardent New Dealers in the South, and Sherman Minton, another FDR stalwart, from Indiana. Also helping out were Wisconsin's La Follette, who could be counted on to support nearly every liberal cause, and Alben Barkley of Kentucky, who like Robinson had an extra incentive to have the Court plan succeed. Just as Robinson yearned for the Supreme Court seat that had been promised if only he could arrange for some "bridesmaids," Barkley hankered for the Senate leader's position that would open up if Robinson got his just deserts.

As June marched into its closing days, Robinson and his lieutenants canvassed the Senate, seeking men whose minds were truly open, at least open enough to listen to Robinson's talk of compromise. Nearly every morning they would corral one or two or three and send them on to Robinson's office. There the leader would try cajolery, flattery, browbeating, or whatever other tactic seemed most promising to get a pledged vote for a compromise on FDR's plan.

But of course nothing definitive could be accomplished until the compromise itself had become something more than some hazy phrases outlined in Robinson's sales pitch. Finally, on

July 1, Robinson was ready to unveil his plan. Instead of providing for the appointment of an additional justice for each member of the Supreme Court over seventy years, as FDR had originally sought, Robinson's trimmed-down proposal granted the president one extra nomination for each member over seventy-five. This reduced the possible number of additional justices from six to four. The president would not be permitted to appoint more than one additional justice in any calendar year. Thus all four additional justices could not be seated before 1940, and if some elder justices retired before that time all four might never be appointed.

Still, Roosevelt would come out of this arrangement quite well. By the beginning of January 1938—only six months away— he would be able to nominate three new justices to the Court: one for the 1937 calendar year, one for the 1938 calendar year, and one to fill Van Devanter's seat.

With the plan now articulated, Robertson stepped up pressure on his colleagues. But the going was difficult. For one thing, public sentiment was running against Robinson and the president. Indeed, according to opinion polls, Court-packing had always been a tough sell. The first Gallup poll on the issue, back in February, showed the public opposed to FDR's proposal by a margin of 53 to 47 percent. By May the picture grew worse— 59 percent said that Congress should defeat the plan. And by mid-July, after Robinson had introduced his compromise, the percentage against approval rose to 62 percent.

Facing a rigorous battle, on July 6 Robinson formally opened debate on the president's bill as amended. Heralded as one of the more dramatic confrontations in the long, controversy-ridden history of the Senate, the showdown drew long lines of curious citizens, four abreast and stretching far down the corridors, waiting outside every glass-paneled door leading into the Senate gallery.

Although he had collaborators in his defense of the bill, as commander of the president's troops Robinson would bear the brunt of the battle. This was no small burden for a man in his mid-sixties whose energy had already been drained by the tension and exertions of the previous weeks of intense haggling. Yet Robinson held nothing back as he launched into his opening speech. One arm on his desk to support his bulky frame, the other pounding the air with emphatic gestures, his florid face growing steadily redder, he showed no signs of weakening as he bellowed his challenge at his foes. "I am given to understand that those who oppose this bill will try to filibuster; let them try," he cried. "I warn them now that ways will be found to meet their obstruction. It will not be tolerated." With his arms flailing and his feet stamping the floor, Robinson reminded one correspondent of an enraged bull at the plaza de toros, while his opponents, like banderilleros, pecked away at him with sharp questions.

As time went on Robinson's ruddy face became even more florid, his husky voice hoarser, his sweeping gestures wilder. At one point Senator Royal Copeland of New York, a physician as well as a politician, saw reason for concern and crossed the well of the chamber to whisper to his leader: "Joe, the cause you're fighting for isn't worth your life. For God's sake, slow down."

But the real cause Robinson was fighting for was not the president's Court bill. Rather it was his own prospective place on the Court and in history, and he crankily shrugged off his friend. As the afternoon wore on and his foes continued to beleaguer him with questions, Robinson seemed to lose track of where he was and what he was doing. Reaching into his pocket he took out a cigar and struck a match, a flagrant violation of Senate rituals. Catching himself in time, he hastily threw down the match. "I am through!" he roared. "No more questions today. Good-by!" and he rushed for the cloakroom. But he was back at his post the next day, and the day after that, and so on.

Anticipating a two- to three-week debate, the Senate had extended its work week into the weekend to run through Saturday.

On Sunday, July 11, Robinson finally had a chance to catch his breath and escape the tension in the Senate for a few hours. Even with the time off, he had trouble relaxing. He was depressed by the uncertain progress of the struggle and by the disturbing messages he received from White House aides warning him that defeat for the bill would mean the end of his hopes for a Court seat. On top of all that, Washington was suffering through one of its customary midsummer heat waves. Thousands of residents who could get away from their normal tasks had fled to the relative comfort of higher land in Virginia and Maryland. Two senators had been forced to enter Bethesda Naval Hospital for treatment of heat stroke.

On Monday, July 12, Robinson resumed the battle, but one did not need a medical degree to notice that his physical and mental exhaustion now verged on life-threatening. After a few hours of debate he sent for Sherman Minton and asked him to have Barkley take over. "I've got a terrible pain here," he said, pressing his chest. "I've got to go to my room."

On Tuesday, July 13, Robinson came to the Senate as usual, to keep an appointment, but soon he went home to the tiny apartment he kept across the plaza from the Capitol. His wife was away in Arkansas, so he was left to brood alone in the heat. Sometime that night after he had gone to sleep, he got out of bed to go to the bathroom when his heart gave out. The maid found the old warrior the next morning, in his pajamas, sprawled next to his bed, a copy of the *Congressional Record* by his right hand.

With Robinson's death on July 14, the long battle over Court reform began to grind toward its inevitable conclusion. Even had he lived, the chances of success for the truncated version of FDR's play were dubious. Opposition in the Senate showed no sign of melting away. And even if Robinson could prevent a filibuster and gain a majority, a hostile reception awaited the measure in the House, where Hatton Summers would lead the welcoming committee.

And so the saga played out to its conclusion, with plenty of melodrama left, the most extreme instance of which was provided by Senator Wheeler, the leader of the opposition. All through his career Wheeler had been a shrewd exploiter of emotions, and given Robinson's death he rose—or as some would have said, sunk—to the occasion. "Joe Robinson was a political and personal friend of mine," Senator Wheeler declared on the morning Robinson's body was discovered. "Had it not been for the court bill he would be alive today. I beseech the president to drop the fight lest he appear to fight against God."

If Wheeler was trying to get the president's attention, he succeeded. Roosevelt responded immediately in a letter to Senator Barkley as acting majority leader of the Senate, which came to be known in the history of the Senate as the "Dear Alben" letter. FDR first lamented—in an unstated but clear allusion to Wheeler's "fight against God" comment—that his foes had sought to take political advantage "of what in all decency should be a period of mourning" following Robinson's death. Then, proceeding to do exactly what he had accused his opponents of doing, Roosevelt restated the objectives of his plan and demanded that Congress meet its responsibility by enacting his proposal into law.

Whatever benefit this letter may have accomplished for FDR's cause by rallying his troops was probably offset by the widespread resentment it provoked among Senate Democrats. Many of them viewed the letter to Barkley as amounting to intervening on behalf of the Kentucky senator in the hotly contested competition to succeed Robinson. Roosevelt also did himself no good by his decision, made after Robinson's state funeral in the Senate chamber, not to attend his burial in Little Rock, Arkansas. Overruling his advisers, he claimed as an excuse the tension in the Far East where Japan had just gone to war against China. And that anyway it would set a bad precedent—this from a president who delighted in breaking precedents. In any event, Roosevelt's absence served further to estrange him from his friends in Congress and give new ammunition to his foes.

One politician who did not miss the funeral was Vice President Garner, who ended his vacation in Texas to pay his respects in Little Rock—and not incidentally to engage in intensive political palaver with the two score senators on board the funeral train that carried Joe Robinson home for the last time. By the time the train returned to Washington on July 19, many stories about Robinson had been told, some even true, much bourbon had been consumed, and Garner had become convinced that whatever chance the president's plan had for approval had gone a-glimmering with Robinson's death. Robinson may once have had the votes he needed, or been close to that total. But many of those who had agreed to go along considered their pledges to be personal, made to Robinson, not to the bill. Once Robinson was gone, so was the basis for their votes.

True, Garner's conclusion about the dim prospects for overhauling the Supreme Court jibed with his own well-advertised aversion for the project. But with Robinson departed, there was no one else on the scene whom Roosevelt trusted enough to challenge Garner's judgment. On July 20 Garner was back in Washington and ready to report to the president on the state of the Court fight.

"Do you want it with the bark on or the bark off?" he asked FDR. To the puzzled president, Garner explained that back in Texas "with the bark off" meant the unadorned truth. That was the way he wanted it, said the president.

"All right," Garner said. "You are beat. You haven't got the votes."

Roosevelt asked Garner to go back to the Senate and get the best deal possible. From Roosevelt's point of view, the vice president did not begin very auspiciously. First he called on Wheeler and told him, "Burt, you can write your own ticket." When

Wheeler asked what that meant in specific terms, Garner added, "I meant just what I said. But for God's sake and the sake of the party, be reasonable."

No wonder, then, that all Garner could wring from the opposition were two face-saving concessions for the funeral of Court-packing. The words "Supreme Court" would not be uttered while the corpse was being interred, and the bill would be sent back to the committee with instructions for redrafting to permit "judicial reform." And there would be no roll call to embarrass the president and his followers.

But neither promise would be kept when the Senate, after nearly six months of wrangling and scheming, finally dealt with FDR's plan to overhaul the Supreme Court. First, on the decisive vote to recommit the bill to the Judiciary Committee, previous assurances notwithstanding, Republican leader McNary demanded and got a roll call vote. And before the vote could even be recorded, Hiram Johnson rose to demand an explanation of the phrase "judicial reform."

"Does it refer to the Supreme Court or the inferior courts?" Johnson insisted on knowing.

Democratic Senator Marvel Logan of Kentucky, presiding over the Senate at the time, explained that there had been an agreement in the Judiciary Committee that the phrase "did not refer to the Supreme Court. That was not to be considered at all, I may say."

But Johnson persisted: "The Supreme Court is out of the way?" he asked.

Logan gave up. "The Supreme Court is out of the way," he said.

Raising his arms to the skies, Johnson shouted the epitaph for Court-packing. "Glory be to God," he cried, and the galleries burst into applause.

Next came the anti-climactic but embarrassingly one-sided roll call on which seventy senators voted for recommittal and only twenty senators in the Congress once thought to be owned by Franklin Roosevelt voted with the president.

So much for saving face.

In mid-August both houses of Congress passed the new judicial reform bill. It offered the president some minor concessions. The new law gave the federal government the right to protect its interests in private lawsuits raising constitutional issues, and to appeal directly to the Supreme Court in cases involving constitutional questions. It also banned a single federal judge from enjoining enforcement of a federal law on grounds that it was unconstitutional. But any hint of Roosevelt's bold attempt to revamp the Supreme Court was obliterated. "A meager performance," Cummings told the president. Nevertheless on August 26, 1937, with as little fanfare as possible, the president signed it into law.

Franklin Roosevelt had suffered the first major defeat of his presidency. The Court fight had ended, but the underpinnings of the New Deal had only just begun to crumble.

10

On the Ropes

All summer long John L. Lewis had been patient. Ever since Roosevelt's dismissive press conference rejoinder of late June, lumping both labor and business together as public nuisances, the country had been waiting for Lewis to hit back in kind. But the CIO leader had held his tongue, even when he was given further cause for anger. On July 3, three days after FDR's Shakespearean affront to the union cause, FDR's Labor Secretary Frances Perkins returned to the issue of the legality of sit-down strikes. Once Perkins had held that to be an unsettled question. But now she declared that, contrary to general belief, the Labor Department had never viewed the sit-down strike as "either lawful, desirable, or appropriate."

Still Lewis remained silent, watching while Roosevelt suffered a double humiliation at the hands of the Senate dominated by his own party. First came the rejection of the president's Court plan by a landslide roll call vote in late July. Then in late August, in order to maintain the appearance of his purported interest in reform, FDR had been obliged to sign the only court reform Congress offered him, a shrunken and bloodless version of his own proposal.

Whatever mixed emotions he felt on watching Franklin Roosevelt suffer defeat in a cause that Lewis had once made his own, the labor leader kept those feelings to himself. He had graver concerns, closer to home. And on the eve of Labor Day weekend, September 3, 1937, Lewis unburdened himself about the condition of the labor movement. The goals of organized labor were not political in a narrow partisan sense, Lewis insisted in a radio address, and labor should not be dovetailed with any political party. Yet if it should happen that a political party asked labor's support and made promises in return—as Lewis did not need to explain that the Democratic party had done—that party "must in equity and good conscience, keep that faith and redeem those promises."

But the Democrats had broken that faith, as Lewis was quick to argue, seizing upon Congress's failure to enact the Wages and Hours bill. Intended to establish a minimum pay scale and a maximum workday, the bill had become snarled in the legislative logjam created by the controversy over Court-packing. After disposing of the Court issue the Senate had passed Wages and Hours in July. But a hostile Rules Committee stalled the measure in the House, which failed to act by the time Congress recessed for the summer. Lewis lamented "the spectacle of august and dignified members of Congress, servants of the people and agents of the Republic, skulking in hallways" to prevent a quorum from acting upon a labor measure. Behavior of this sort "emphasizes the perfidy of politics and blasts the confidence of labor's millions in politicians' promises." Such hypocrisy would not go unpunished, Lewis made clear. "Those who chant their praises of democracy but who lose no chance to drive their knives into labor's defenseless back," he declared, "must feel the weight of labor's woe even as its open adversaries must ever feel the thrust of labor's power."

Then, finally, Lewis got something off his chest, a resentment that had gnawed at him since he had sat drumming his heels against a desk when he first learned of the president's reproof.

"Labor, like Israel, has many sorrows," Lewis intoned. "Its women weep for their fallen, and they lament for the future of the children of the race," he continued, building a brooding, somber mood. Then he lashed out. "It ill behooves one who has supped at Labor's table and who has been sheltered in Labor's house to curse with equal fervor and fine impartiality both Labor and its adversaries when they become locked in deadly embrace." He named no names, but no one had any doubt about to whom he was referring.

As for Roosevelt, unwilling to be goaded into a direct answer, he treated Lewis's reproof with the disdain of a statesman who has more important concerns than the complaints of a labor leader. Asked at his subsequent press conference what his response had been to Lewis's remarks, Roosevelt replied cuttingly, "There wasn't any."

Immediately after this exchange, FDR's aides, trying to heal the breach, persuaded the president to invite Lewis to the White House for a brief visit later that month. Afterward Lewis and Roosevelt collaborated briefly on particular issues when they found common goals. But in the wake of the sit-down strikes and the Court fight, such occasions were fewer and farther between.

The tensions between Roosevelt and Lewis reflected the strains that had always colored the uneasy partnership between the New Deal and organized labor, and now seemed more intense. It was not hard to understand why FDR would try to distance himself from the labor movement, but even for a politician as skilled as Roosevelt it was a neat trick. Roosevelt and his New Dealers were tied to the trade unions, both in perception and reality. They benefited from labor's successes but suffered from what the public considered to be its excesses. This was the general impression of politicians. And it was backed up by a recently developed kind of statistical evidence—polling data.

George Gallup, head of the Institute of Public Opinion, founded only two years before, reported that the majority of the public had been sympathetic to labor unions at the start of the year. But, Gallup said, labor had since lost popular support because of the sit-down strikes, which his latest survey showed were opposed by 70 percent of the public. Among the groups now most opposed to labor, that mainstay of Roosevelt's 1936 coalition, Gallup reported, was another key component of that alliance, farmers. It was an ill omen for the coming midterm elections. So was another Gallup statistic: more than 40 percent of those who had voted for Roosevelt considered themselves conservatives and were opposed to one or more of his policies.

But Roosevelt faced an even more urgent problem than labor's loss of public favor. By the time of Lewis's Labor Day rebuke, the economy, whose apparent revival had been the New Deal's proudest achievement, was collapsing around the president. In part Roosevelt himself was to blame. Although nearly nine million workers were still jobless—an unemployment rate of 14 percent—Roosevelt, with the same confidence that had assumed victory for his Court-packing scheme, concluded that prosperity was on its way back, if not already arrived. He had begun to worry more about inflation than the continuing depression, and had reduced federal spending accordingly.

By September 1937 the Works Progress Administration, the New Deal's most effective jobs program, had cut its rolls nearly in half, from 2.5 million to 1.45 million. Meanwhile the Federal Reserve Board, caught up in the same misguided optimism, had tightened credit, making it harder for businesses to maintain their payrolls, never mind adding new workers. In August 1937 the stock market plummeted, the Dow Jones average dropping from 190 to 115 by October. Even worse, unemployment soared. It would reach 20 percent by the end of that grim winter.

As if this was not trouble enough for the president, the Supreme Court came back to haunt him. In August Roosevelt decided to fill the vacancy left by the retirement of Justice Van Devanter, the slot that had been promised to Joe Robinson, by nominating Senator Hugo Black of Alabama. As the president acknowledged to Ickes, he did not consider Black an "outstanding lawyer." But, more important to FDR, Black was a proven liberal who might have a hard job winning reelection in Alabama because of his steadfast loyalty to the New Deal.

At first things seemed to go smoothly. Rumors were aired that the senator had once been a member of the Ku Klux Klan, but Black evaded the issue and the Senate did not look into it seriously on its way to confirming his nomination. Soon after, hard evidence surfaced that Black had indeed been a Klansman. A great uproar developed, which Roosevelt did little to help by letting it be known that he had not been aware of this aspect of Black's past. Then the president headed off on a trip through the Western states to rebuild goodwill. Black, who had been in Europe when the story broke, returned home. In a poignant radio address to the nation he admitted his earlier Klan membership but disavowed any of the bigotry that inspired the white-sheeted night riders who had once spread terror and hate through the South. In time Black's ties to the Klan were all but forgotten as the justice went on to become one of the high court's great champions of civil liberties. But in the summer of 1937 the episode served to add insult to the damage FDR and the New Deal had suffered over the Court.

That injury, along with the loss of public confidence as a result of the sit-down strikes, weakened FDR's ability to deal with the new economic crisis. Where once he had acted boldly, he now seemed to dither. At a cabinet meeting early in October, his anxiety and irritation were both evident to Jim Farley. The president "leaped down the throat" of his commerce secretary Dan Roper for uttering panglossian pronouncements about the condition of the economy, Farley noted. "You have just got to stop issuing those Hooverish statements all the time," Roosevelt told him bluntly. But then Roosevelt himself went on to talk in terms reminiscent of his unfortunate Republican predecessor. He had been all around the country, he assured his cabinet, and he knew conditions were good. "Crops are good. Farmers are getting good prices. Industry is busy and is bound to keep busy if crops and prices are good." The apparent economic difficulties he blamed on a "concerted effort" by the economic royalists to drive the market down and make him look bad. In sum, the president expressed confidence that the problem was only temporary and superficial. "Everything will work out all right if we just sit tight and keep quiet."

This hardly sounded like the chief executive who in his second inaugural earlier that same fateful year had offered a vision of his government as a transforming political force. The New Deal, he had then vowed, would establish "practical controls over blind economic forces and blindly selfish men." In addition, it would "create those moral controls over the services of science . . . necessary to make science a useful servant instead of a ruthless master of mankind."

But the hard truth was that if FDR had any plans to implement those bold promises, he was in a poor position to act. To Harold Ickes it was clear from looking at the president that he had "paid a heavy toll" for his tenure in the White House. His face was "heavily lined" and "gaunt," and he seemed "distinctly more nervous" than he had been when he first took office. "He is punch drunk from the punishment that he has suffered recently," Ickes noted.

His legislative program lay in ruins on Capitol Hill, a victim of the backlash against his Court-packing scheme and the sit-down strikes. Roosevelt had at first placed the Court plan at the top of his 1937 legislative agenda, reasoning that once it was approved it would strengthen his hand in dealing with Congress. By late spring, when Roosevelt at last realized that his Court measure faced heavy going, he decided to reverse the order and the strategy, assuming that the approval of what he believed to be popular measures to meet the nation's economic distress would build momentum for his Court plan.

Fat chance. With conservative opponents stronger than they had been since the booming 1920s, those popular measures were no longer so popular. By the time the seventy-fifth Congress adjourned it had done only one thing for which it would be remembered, and that was to defeat the president's Court-reform plan.

On the ropes, but refusing to admit defeat, the president decided to call Congress back into special session in November to concentrate on an ambitious legislative agenda he submitted to the country in a fireside chat. The main items he docketed were a farm bill to reduce crop surpluses, wages-and-hours legislation, and, dearest to the president's heart, a plan for a major reorganization of the federal government, to bring order to what he called the "higgledy-piggledy patchwork of duplicate responsibilities and overlapping powers."

But the president's bold blueprint turned to dust. Congress was no longer in the obeisant mood that had prevailed during most of FDR's first term. And the president's popularity was no longer the force it had been. By the time the session concluded after thirty-seven days, *Time* listed its major achievements as appropriating $225,000 to pay members' traveling expenses to and from the extra session, lending four of the Capitol's gallery of portraits of signers of the Declaration of Independence to the Corcoran Gallery of Art for a belated sesquicentennial exhibition, and approving an extension of the time limit for a bridge to be built over the Tennessee River at Sheffield, Alabama.

When Congress returned for its regular session in 1938, FDR fared little better. Indeed he suffered a defeat second in its importance for the New Deal only to the crushing of his Court-reform effort. That the occasion for this setback was FDR's plan for executive reorganization, an idea originally regarded as an innocuous exercise in management technocracy, illustrated the decline of the president's prestige and the increased vigor of his foes. In fact there was more to Roosevelt's proposal than most people realized. By making the government more efficient and increasing the control of the chief executive over the executive branch, it was intended to strengthen the presidency and enhance the potential for expansion of the liberal activism that the New Deal had brought to Washington.

But that chance had faded away. The proposal had met mostly apathy when Roosevelt first put it forward in 1937. When a more modest version was introduced in the Senate in March 1938, *Time* reported, "the instantaneous reaction of Congress and a large section of the U.S. press and public was a horrified suspicion that Franklin Roosevelt wanted to make himself a dictator." The reason for this apparent paradox, as the magazine explained, "was, of course, that the Court Plan, brought up and beaten since the Reorganization Bill's inception, looked enough like a grab for power to make anything remotely resembling another power grab doubly alarming and doubly vulnerable."

About all the bill proposed to do, besides allowing the president to reshuffle any of the hundred-odd agencies under the executive branch, was to establish a single civil service administrator instead of a three-man commission and empower the president to hire six administrative assistants. But the New Deal's foes seized upon some of its provisions as evidence that totalitarianism was knocking at the door. With Hitler on the march in Europe, many in Congress—though unwilling to act to block the threat abroad—were eager to warn against danger from within. "It is not too much to say that what we are now here considering today is the question of plunging a dagger into the very heart of democracy!" Massachusetts Democrat David Walsh, archenemy of the New Deal, told the Senate.

In an attempt to rebut the attacks, Roosevelt took the extraordinary step of publicly disavowing dictatorial ambitions. "I have none of the qualifications which would make me a successful dictator," Roosevelt wrote. "I have too much historical background and too much knowledge of existing dictatorships to make me desire any form of dictatorship for a democracy like the United States." This gesture, smacking of desperation, helped the bill squeak by in the Senate. But in the House the Democratic ranks would not hold, and the bill went down to defeat.

Soon the president encountered yet another legislative disappointment. Congress finally adopted the long-sought Wages and Hours Act, but only after the conservatives had severely watered it down. Southern pressure forced the exemption of much of the farm workforce. And many businesses were allowed to postpone for years payments of what labor deemed "a living wage." The bill had been so riddled with compromises and exceptions that the House's leading smart aleck, Martin Dies, offered a facetious amendment requiring the secretary of labor to report to Congress "whether anyone is subject to this bill."

Frustrated by the growing strength of his opposition, Roosevelt decided to take back the initiative with a bold maneuver, to strike at the bulwarks of conservatism in his own party. Initially the president hoped to use party primary elections to eliminate nine Democratic senators up for reelection who had opposed his Supreme Court bill. He narrowed the list to five only after Jim Farley persuaded him that the others were too strong to challenge.

Even so, in taking on Walter George of Georgia, "Cotton" Ed Smith of South Carolina, Millard Tydings of Maryland, Guy Gillette of Iowa, and Frederick Van Nuys of Indiana he faced a formidable task. Roosevelt laid down the gauntlet in a fireside chat on June 24, 1938. After denying, somewhat unconvincingly, that he was actually taking part in Democratic primaries, he proceeded to provide a rationale for just such participation. Since he considered himself responsible, he explained, for implementing the "definitely liberal declaration of principles" made by the Democrats in their 1936 platform, he felt justified in speaking out "where there may be a clear-cut issue between candidates for a Democratic nomination involving those principles." His attempted "purge," as it came to be known, defied the traditions of American politics. Roosevelt was insisting that voters make party allegiance and ideological consistency the chief criteria for their ballot choices. But these factors mattered far less to most Americans than personal loyalties and local concerns.

Even before he issued his public manifesto, FDR had helped to recruit and encourage candidates to challenge the incumbents he had marked for defeat. But his intended victims fought back, and all five prevailed. As Roosevelt's futile drive was nearing an end, Jim Farley offered a succinct verdict to reporters: "It's a bust."

New Dealers had more reason to brood about the results than even Farley realized. Not only had the president lost all the Senate races he seriously contested; his abortive purge spurred development of the alliance between Republicans and conservative Democrats that emerged as a potent force in the Court fight and would become a real-life nightmare for liberal Democrats for many years to come. In July, Republican National Chairman John Hamilton journeyed to Mobile, Alabama, to urge that Republicans make common cause with "Jeffersonian Democrats." And in Georgia a local GOP official urged members of his party to back Walter George in his primary fight against FDR's challenger.

The only meaningful success achieved by Roosevelt's intraparty struggle came in the House of Representatives. In Manhattan, Roosevelt aides conspired to upend a Tammany Hall stalwart, John J. O'Connor, who had used his position as chairman of the House Rules Committee to bottle up New Deal legislation, in favor of an all-out Roosevelt man. But no one in Roosevelt's political household pretended that this single triumph offset the damage to presidential prestige and to party harmony incurred by the purge.

Just as the president's offensive against conservatism was ending in failure, he found himself thrown on the defensive by a new assault led by a familiar adversary, Martin Dies of Texas. Dies's bid to investigate the sit-down strikes in the spring of 1937 had yielded plenty of headlines, even if Congress had turned down his proposed probe. In the spring of 1938, with the help of his mentor, Vice President Garner, Dies proposed yet another investigation, this one aimed at "un-American activities." This notion, which was to have consequences that extended far beyond the careers of Garner and Dies, was rooted in the nativism common to both men and agitated Dies in particular.

Straying far from his early New Deal beliefs, Dies became persuaded that immigrants, by taking jobs from American-born workers, had helped prolong the depression. It was an easy step from that conclusion to the judgment that the foreign-born, combined with radical forces to which they were supposedly particularly susceptible, posed a growing threat to the American way of life. Dies's proposal to use a congressional committee to expose "un-Americanism" won wide backing, even the support of liberals who naively believed Dies would investigate fascist organizations springing up in the country, inspired in part by the rise of the Nazis in Germany. But Dies, who chaired and dominated the committee, soon made clear he had little interest in exposing any threat except from the left. In that campaign year he zeroed in on a favorite target from the year before, Michigan Governor Frank Murphy. It was an open secret that Communist organizers had played a key role in the sit-down strikes. There was no evidence that they had done anything more insidious than energetically pursue the objectives of the strikes. But to angry conservatives their very presence was proof that the sit-downs were part of a Kremlin-hatched conspiracy—and Dies was most vociferous in making these charges.

In October, only a few weeks before election day, Dies's committee in four days of hearings aired sensational though markedly unsubstantiated charges against Murphy, claiming in effect that the patience he had exhibited toward the sit-downs demonstrated that he was a pawn, if not a willing instrument, of the Red conspiracy. Witnesses included the former city manager of Flint, John Barringer, fired by the city council for recruiting vigilantes as strikebreakers, who condemned the "treasonable attitude of Governor Murphy" for allowing civil order to break down.

Asked about the charges, in a question planted at his press conference, Roosevelt first said that any extemporaneous remarks on the subject he would make might not be printable, then issued a written statement calling the hearings "a flagrantly unfair and un-American attempt to influence an election." After dismissing the "lurid charges" against Murphy, FDR praised him for helping bring an end to the strike without bloodshed. "For that act, a few petty politicians accuse him of treason: for that act, every peace-loving American should praise him." Roosevelt dispatched Harold Ickes and Solicitor General Robert Jackson to Michigan to campaign for Murphy, and in a nationwide radio address on the weekend before the election Roosevelt once again endorsed Murphy's "democratic wisdom" in handling a strike "that had frightened a whole nation."

But none of this was enough to save Murphy. He lost by nearly 100,000 votes, a result that Ickes called "the most serious defeat" suffered by the New Deal forces on election night. The sorry truth was that Murphy had plenty of company among his fellow Democrats. The Republicans gained 81 seats in the House, 8 in the Senate, 11 governorships, and almost defeated Democratic Governor Herbert Lehman of New York. It was an even bigger victory than the Democrats had carried off in 1930 when they won 55 new seats in Congress preparatory to turning out Herbert Hoover two years later. Not one of 103 incumbent Republicans seeking reelection in 1938 failed to regain his seat. Of 25 former Republican incumbents who tried to come back, 14 succeeded. Democratic House losses included the defeat of

14 so-called Young Turks out of a total of 38 members reckoned as the most ardent New Dealers. Among the losers: Maury Maverick, who had rushed to be the first to sponsor the Court bill. In the Senate Roosevelt could hardly take comfort in the fact that the returning Democratic incumbents included all 5 he had tried to purge.

The Democrats still maintained control of both houses of Congress by substantial majorities, on paper. But in reality their dominance had been greatly reduced; as Roosevelt and his liberal supporters recognized, a right-wing coalition of conservative Republicans and Southern Democrats now ruled the roost. If this anti–New Deal alliance could not force Roosevelt to retreat, it could prevent most attempts at new advances. "The hookworm Democrats will be more savage than ever after the attempted purge," Kenneth Crawford predicted mournfully in the *Nation*, in a derisive allusion to the party's emboldened Southern contingent. "Dependable New Dealers will be definitely reduced to minority status in both branches. It is not a pretty prospect."

The election returns served mainly to underline a political reality that had become apparent the year before in the wake of the Court fight and the sit-down strikes. As the presidential historian Alonzo Hamby observed in his illuminating study of 1930s political turmoil, "The New Deal was effectively dead."

To be sure, the agencies created in Roosevelt's first term would not be dismantled. The bureaucrats appointed by the New Deal would remain in charge of the government. And here and there Democrats would patch together additions and improvements to the existing framework of government, as they did with the Wages and Hours law. Moreover the New Deal coalition, the diverse amalgam of racial, ethnic, and economic interests that FDR had assembled, would remain a potent force in American politics for at least another generation.

This was the enduring bequest of Roosevelt's program. But the New Deal was far more than a set of departments, statutes, and interest groups. It was a dynamic for change that offered millions of Americans of all races, creeds, and economic strata the promise of fairer treatment and greater opportunity under the system that controlled their lives. When the New Deal could no longer move forward, its promise faded and its followers drifted apart.

In the fall of 1938, even before the midterm election rout, the historian Walter Millis delivered a somber verdict on the New Deal. It had been, he wrote, "reduced to a movement with no program, with no effective political organization, with no vast popular party strength behind it, and with no candidate."

As for Roosevelt himself, he seemed nothing more than a lame duck politician who had lost his grip, facing the dead end of his career. In the spring of 1939 a *Fortune* magazine survey showed that only a little more than one-third of the electorate would support the president if he ran again. The war, of course, would save FDR's political skin and allow him to embellish his place in history. But it did not bring the New Deal back to life.

In fact it was Roosevelt himself who made the death of the New Deal official, though he waited until much after the fact, midway through World War II. "Old Dr. New Deal," he said, "has been replaced." There was a new doctor in the house— "Dr. Win the War."

But this was just an epitaph, not an explanation. The killing of the New Deal was one of the great collapses in the history of American politics. How did it happen? The most common answer is that Roosevelt blundered with his Court-packing plan. "Seldom in American history has a simple instance of one man's muddleheadedness had greater social impact," contended the esteemed Roosevelt biographer Kenneth S. Davis in a typical verdict. FDR's mistakes, it has been widely asserted, took the political community, including his allies, by surprise in trying to disguise his real purpose. Critics also claim that FDR's behavior was totally out of character, the president's normally acute strategic instincts having been clouded by the extent of his landslide victory in 1936.

But this analysis is far too simplistic and trivializes the importance of the episode. First, it ignores the impact of the sit-down strikes, which Roosevelt could not have reasonably foreseen. They greatly hindered his effort to overhaul the Court and heightened the consequences of his defeat in the Court fight. Still another flaw in the conventional judgments is that they treat as an aberration behavior that was part and parcel of FDR's modus operandi. The dissembling that Roosevelt undertook in presenting his Court-packing proposal was much the same approach he used all his political life, culminating in the way he led the nation into war.

In 1940 FDR sent fifty overage U.S. destroyers to embattled Great Britain, thus locking the nation on a course that led into World War II. He presented the deal as a boost to U.S. defenses, citing the naval bases in the West Indies that Prime Minister Churchill traded for the destroyers; but its real purpose was to save Britain from defeat by committing the United States to its assistance. On that occasion Roosevelt sidestepped Congress, carrying off the momentous trade by executive order, flouting the statute books and the Constitution in the process.

Franklin Roosevelt was the most successful politician in our history, and his operating style reflected his intuitive grasp of the system and his ability to tailor his actions and utterances to the political obstacle course that is the American system of government. The structure of the Constitution has created what amounts to a gap between politics and government. In simplest terms, politics defines what people want; government decides what they get. For democracy to work, government must respond to politics. This is where political parties come in. They are the best means available for connecting politics and government, and for holding government accountable to the electorate. But under the Constitution the parties were born to fail and government destined to flounder. By curbing the authority of parties in government, the Constitution in effect institutionalizes the gap between politics and government.

Franklin Roosevelt had accepted this gap and adjusted to it. Recognizing the hindrances of the Constitution, he abjured explicit promises to carry out policies because he knew he could not count on party discipline to help him keep his promises. Instead he asked voters to focus on his own personality, as he did in both of his first two presidential campaigns. Roosevelt has been criticized for avoiding public debate on the Court. But substantive public debate was not part of his leadership profile. Thus in the 1934 campaign he sought to preserve his base of popular support while keeping his finger to the political winds.

"No one who voted for him did it because he presented himself as learned or competent in all the matters he talked about," Rex Tugwell, a charter member of the Brain Trust later pointed out. "They voted for the big easy smiling man who had no fear of failing at anything, who seemed capable even of saving sinners from themselves."

Given his penchant for ad hoc solutions, it's no wonder FDR rejected advice that he lay out his grievances with the Court during his reelection campaign. Such a move would have stirred opposition from defenders of the Court and shifted the focus of his candidacy away from where FDR wanted it to be—on his own personal leadership qualities.

Moreover, if he had triggered a campaign debate on the Court, Roosevelt would have been obliged to announce a plan for dealing with the problem, which is the last thing he wanted to do. After the election, when he finally was ready to develop his plan, Roosevelt knew that whatever he proposed would face tough sledding. The more substantive his plan, the more complex would be the argument over it. By that reasoning it made some sort of sense to do what Roosevelt did: duck the complexities by

treating the Court as a managerial problem, a question of wasted
time and motion. Wary of being depicted as a radical ideologue,
Roosevelt cast himself as an efficiency expert.

His critics would charge him with deviousness, he knew. But
given the other things being said about him as he once recounted
them—"that I was driving the nation into bankruptcy, that
I breakfasted every morning on a dish of 'grilled millionaire'"—
deviousness was a relatively innocuous fault.

Perhaps the most important question about the Court plan to
be asked is whether it was in fact a mistake. Roosevelt did not
think so, or at least would not admit it. Citing the dramatic
changes in the Court's attitude toward the New Deal, the president later described his Court-packing proposal as not only "one
of the most significant events of my administration"—but more
than that, a "turning point in our modern history." In a com-
mentary written four years after the event, FDR attributed the rejection of his proposal in Congress to the dramatic change in the
Court's attitude toward the New Deal in the spring of 1937, while
the Senate was still debating his plan. "The Court yielded," Roosevelt wrote. "The Court changed. The Court began to interpret
the Constitution instead of torturing it." He was convinced, he
added, "that the change would never have come unless this
frontal attack had been made upon the philosophy of the majority of the Court."

To be sure, Roosevelt's move against the Court also contributed to far-reaching negative consequences which he did
not anticipate and certainly did not want. But any judgment of
Roosevelt's actions in 1937 and their impact requires a realistic
appreciation of the president and of the system in which he operated. Despite the grandness of his reelection victory, the truth
was that FDR's tenuous hold on the loyalty of congressional
Democrats, and the high esteem in which the public held the
Court as an institution, left the president no easy answer to his
problems with the justices. Any move he made was bound to set

off a firestorm of opposition. Much of the criticism of the course the president did choose relies heavily on hindsight. Some say he should have ignored the issue and waited for time to take its toll of the elderly conservative justices and for the Court as a whole to pay heed to Roosevelt's election triumph. But FDR had no way of knowing when or whether this would happen. As Roosevelt himself later wrote: "The reactionary members of the Court had apparently determined to remain on the bench as long as life continued—for the sole purpose of blocking any program of reform."

The Court had paid little attention to the 1934 mid-term election returns in its rulings during the next two years. And on the eve of 1937 the justices were about to rule on key legislation, notably the Wagner Act and Social Security. If the majority had stuck to its recent ideological line, the loss of those measures could have led to the near destruction of the New Deal. Could Roosevelt afford to take the risk that the justices might suddenly change their minds?

Roosevelt is accused of not compromising soon enough once his plan ran into trouble. The president himself later claimed that he was open to a compromise that would achieve his objective. "I received, however," he wrote, "no reasonable guarantee or assurance that some other definite method would obtain Congressional approval."

This contention may be somewhat disingenuous. But criticism of his alleged refusal to bargain on the Court issue overlooks the attitude of the president's strongest supporters, who would have viewed any giving of ground as a betrayal. The Court controversy, claimed the *Nation*, reflecting the view of many New Dealers, "is the key to the whole Administration program of Mr. Roosevelt's second term." Once the president's opponents "have forced Mr. Roosevelt to retreat on the Court bill, they will harry the Administration forces until they have surrendered all along the line."

In the end, Roosevelt did compromise. And he wound up losing the bill and losing face too.

Of course, Roosevelt made mistakes in dealing with the Court and with the sit-down strikers, as in other matters. He himself later claimed that he had erred in his initial presentation of the Court-reform play by not stressing "the real mischief," the decisions that the Court had been handing down, hamstringing the New Deal, instead of resting his case on the need for increased efficiency. But as he pointed out, he soon shifted his strategy and made his argument on substantive grounds in two major speeches in March 1937, the month after his proposal had been introduced. Yet this new strategy failed to help his case.

One glaring mistake FDR did make was in selecting Attorney General Cummings as the chief designer of his Court scheme. Cummings let his own ego interfere with his lawyerly judgment. His careless draftsmanship, particularly overstating the extent to which the Court was bogged down by its caseload, gave Chief Justice Hughes and Senator Wheeler the opportunity to undercut the president's case.

Some critics claim that Roosevelt was so steeped in hubris that he did not take the challenge to the Court plan seriously enough. But this charge ignores the concerns he expressed privately. "Even if you do not agree, suspend final judgment," he wrote to Felix Frankfurter a couple of weeks before the plan was made public. Almost on the eve of the announcement, Missy Lehand asked Sam Rosenman to spend the night at the White House because "the president is terribly nervous." This does not sound like a man blithely complacent about the outcome. Rather it sounds like a politician having made a choice about a problem which he realizes offers nothing but difficult choices.

Roosevelt's fundamental problem was that the New Deal was an idea whose time was rapidly running out. The longer it went on, the greater was its conflict with the ethos of middle-class America—its reverence for individualism and property rights, and its mistrust of government. In the battle to change the Court, one Democratic senator after another who had stood with Roosevelt through his first term turned against him. The gravamen of their complaint was that the New Deal had gone far enough, and perhaps too far already. Now was the time to draw the line. That attitude was already building in Congress and in the country when the sit-down strikes shook the nation, intensifying and spreading the anxieties of the middle class. The aggressiveness of the striking workers in overriding the hitherto sacrosanct rights of property owners came to represent to many a nightmarish view of what America's future would become if FDR and his allies had their way with the country. Thus James Byrnes of South Carolina, who supported Court-packing, took his stand on the floor of the Senate against the sit-down strikes. And John Nance Garner, who literally held his nose over Court reform, condemned the sit-downs as an even greater evil. The Court fight and the sit-down strikes were two great political dramas that played out simultaneously on the national stage in the winter, spring, and early summer of 1937 and transformed the balance of power in the country. Taken together, the two controversies became a whole far greater, and more devastating to the New Deal, than the sum of its parts.

Roosevelt and the New Deal demonstrated the potential, even in the face of constitutional obstacles and middle-class anxieties, for using government to serve the needs of the citizenry. His experience in 1937 with Court reform and the sit-down strikes demonstrates the limits of that potential. But by pushing the system to its limits, he left an enduring legacy.

Three decades would pass before any president would attempt change on the sort of massive scale FDR sought. That was Lyndon Baines Johnson. After serving as a Capitol Hill aide, Johnson won his own seat in Congress in a special election held in the midst of the battle over Court-packing, having given his hearty endorsement to FDR's Court-reform plan and all his other works. He arrived in Washington in time to see the bitter end of FDR's battle, and it made an impression that shaped his presidency. "I have watched the Congress from either the inside or the outside, man and boy, for more than forty years," Johnson told the administration's lobbyists assembled in the White House only a few weeks after his landslide 1964 victory which rivaled in scope FDR's triumph in 1936. "And I've never seen a Congress that didn't eventually take the measure of the president it was dealing with."

Obsessed with the fleeting nature of his popularity, Johnson drove the Congress with its huge Democratic majorities into adopting a multitude of Great Society proposals. His achievements were long-lasting, notably landmark civil rights laws and Medicare. But in other areas on his agenda, Johnson moved in such haste that he allowed little time to build public understanding and support for his programs, just as FDR neglected to develop backing for his Court plan. Moreover, just as FDR while leading the Court fight had to reckon with the sit-down strikes, Johnson while his heart was set on the Great Society could not get the Vietnam War out of his mind. Worried that failure to stop the supposed Communist menace in Southeast Asia would threaten his domestic programs, Johnson escalated the war by stealth, stirring such a backlash that it destroyed his presidency — though, as with Roosevelt and the New Deal, his Great Society's impact remains.

In the ensuing years, resistance to significant reform has stiffened, and the will of leaders of the Democratic party to challenge the system has notably lessened. The two Democratic presidents since Johnson, Jimmy Carter and Bill Clinton, were both distinguished by the minimalist scale of their ambitions.

"Government can't solve our problems," Carter told Americans after his first year in the White House had tarnished the radiant promise of his post-Watergate candidacy.

"The era of big government is over," Clinton declared as he sought to recover from the historic defeat his party had suffered in the 1994 midterm elections.

Instead of proposing bold new initiatives, both men sought to neutralize the leaders of backlash by borrowing their rhetoric and accepting their values. In this way they hoped to avoid disappointment and defeat. But in the process they ignored pervasive injustice and inequity. Not only did they forfeit the chance to match the accomplishments of FDR and LBJ, they surrendered the political initiative to the backlash. The result of this Democratic default has been a Republican counterrevolution, first led by Ronald Reagan, and then more aggressively by George W. Bush.

The events of 1937 make up a cautionary tale, demonstrating the difficulty of political change in the United States. But the four previous years of Franklin Roosevelt's first term, and Lyndon Johnson's first two years in the White House, tell a different story, illustrating the possibilities for progress given effective leadership. Those who now dominate the Democratic party tend to attribute the achievements of FDR and LBJ to extraordinary circumstances. The Great Depression cleared the path for FDR, it is said, just as the assassination of John Kennedy generated psychological momentum for Lyndon Johnson.

True enough. But this argument ignores the fact that circumstances also gave Presidents Carter and Clinton rich opportunities, had they been willing or able to take advantage of them.

Entering the White House in the wake of the Watergate scandal and the ordeal of Vietnam, a white man from the Deep South who had been elected with the votes of African Americans, a born-again Christian who had helped bring conservative Christians back into the political system, Jimmy Carter came to the presidency with seemingly unlimited opportunities for leadership. The journalist James Fallows, then a Carter speechwriter, remembered that the last state governor to win the presidency had been Franklin Roosevelt. He believed Carter "had at least the same potential to leave the government forever changed by his presence."

Like Roosevelt and Carter, Bill Clinton had also been a state governor, and like them he also had a great act to follow. His predecessor, George Herbert Walker Bush, had been forced out of the White House by an economic recession that had probably caused more devastation to middle-class Americans than any slump since the Great Depression. Perhaps even more important a benefit was the fact that Clinton was the first Democratic president since Roosevelt who did not have to contend with the life-or-death tensions of the Cold War and with the burden of having to prove to his fellow citizens that he could be as tough on Communists as any Republican. And not only would he have a peace dividend from cutbacks in defense spending, the election gave him a clear mandate to spend it on what many, even Republicans, regarded as one government program for which the public clamored—national health insurance.

No one can tell when a Democrat will win the White House again. But whenever that happens, and whoever he or she happens to be, history suggests the opening will be there for great achievement. The tougher question to answer is whether that next Democratic chief executive will have the wisdom and fortitude to redeem that opportunity.

Notes

Please refer to the Bibliography for full citations of the references used in the Notes.

1. THE PRESIDENT

page
3 The presidential flag: Burns, p. 451.
3 The celebrating began: McKean, p. 80.
4 Allies like Farley: Schlesinger, III, 642.
4 Strangest of bedfellows: Swanberg, pp. 515–519.
5 Kansan's name disappeared: Ward, October 31, 1936.
5 Softening the reception: Ickes, I, 704.
5 Hearst praises FDR: Swanberg, p. 569.
6 Panoply of triumph: Alsop and Catledge, p. 22.
7 Nine minion jobless: McElvaine, p. 297.
8 An approving roar: Burns, p. 274.
8 No "small minority": Weir.
8 "I am not criticizing": "Going Places."
8 By one analysis: Schlesinger, III, 633.
9 "Psychoanalyzed by God": Leuchtenburg, "The First Modern President."
9 "A second-class intellect": Burns, p. 157,
10 "Mind does not follow": Stimson, December 18, 1940.
10 "Franklin was accused": Tugwell, p. 247.
10 "There is one issue": Moley, p. 342.
10 "Like a football team": Hurd, p. 164.
11 "Up against your belly" : Ickes, II, 659.

11 "Frictionless command": Freidel, p. 66.
11 Recast their marriage: Maney, p. 22.
11 "Apparatus of defense": Tugwell, p. 66.
12 "Delightful relations": Roosevelt, *Personal Letters*, pp. 307–308.
12 A consultative relationship: Alsop and Catledge, p. 16.
12 "An independent branch": Wheeler, p. 330.
12 "In complete control": *NYT*, October 6, 1932.
12 Republicans pounced: *NYT*, October 10, 1932.
13 "What I said is true": Byrnes, p. 65.
13 "Were much offended": Swindler, p. 15.
13 Partisan allegiance: Leuchtenburg, "Origins," citing Homer Cummings to
     FDR, November 8, 1933, FDRL, office file 41, box 114.
14 The ice company case: *New State Ice Co. v. Liebmann*, 285 U.S. 262 (1932);
     Swindler, pp. 8–9, 23.
14 "More power than any man": Ibid., p. 24.
14 "Our Constitution is so simple": *PPA*, 1933, pp. 14–15.
15 "To expose and resist": *NYT*, October 2, 1934.
15 The midterm results: Campbell, p. 7.
15 First skirmishes inconclusive: Swindler, pp. 33–39.
16 Significant for symbolism: *Humphrey's Executor v. United States*, 295 U.S.
     602 (1935); Swindler, pp. 43–44.
17 A law to help farmers: *Louisville Joint Stock Land Bank v. Radford*, 295 U.S.
     555 (1935); Swindler, p. 43.
17 The NRA decision: *Schechter Poultry Corp. v. United States*, 294 U.S. 495
     (1935); Schlesinger, III, 281–283.
17 Newspapers hailed decision: McKenna, p. 105.
18 FDR's reaction: Alsop and Catledge, pp. 17–20; Baker, pp. 115–118.
18 Brandeis's reaction: Schlesinger, III, 280.
19 The country was with him: Alsop and Catledge, p. 17.
19 "Since the Dred Scott case" *NYT*, June 1, 1935.
20 Vandenberg's comment: *Washington Post*, June 1, 1935.
20 Early planning on court: Swisher, p. 147.
20 Roosevelt hinted: Creel, *Rebel*.
21 "Fire that": Ibid.
21 Poll results: Cantril, p. 148.
21 "Marching farmers": Leuchtenburg, "Origins."
21 "Might be a revolution": Schlesinger, III, 453.
21 Overturning the AAA: *U.S. v. Butler*, 297 U.S. 1 (1936).
22 Poll on AAA: Cantril, p. 135.
22 Back to square one: Ickes, I, 529–530.
23 Norris's complaint: Leuchtenburg, "Origins."
23 Marshall's precedent: Foner and Garraty, p. 681.

23 Undercutting the SEC: *Jones v. SEC*, 298 U.S. 1 (1936); Swindler, pp. 50–51.
23 Overturning the Guffey Act: *Carter v. Carter Coal Co.*, 298 U.S. 328 (1936); McKenna, p. 206.
23 Muncipal bankruptcies ruling: *Ashton v. Cameron County District*, 298 U.S. 513 (1936); Swindler, p. 432.
24 The minimum-wage decision: *Morehead v. New York ex rel. Tipaldo*, 298 U.S. 587 (1936); Swindler, p. 94.
24 Hoover joins in: *NYT*, June 7, 1936.
25 "The turning point": *New York Herald Tribune*, June 2, 1936.
25 Frankfurter to FDR: McKenna, p. 216, citing FDRL, president's personal file, 1440, June 9, 1936.
25 "A no-man's land": *NYT*, June 3, 1936.
25 Landon's telegram: *NYT*, June 10, 1936.
25 At Roosevelt's insistence: Moley, pp. 346–347.
26 Democratic platform: *NYT*, June 26, 1936.
26 Barkley's speech: *NYT*, June 25, 1936.
26 GOP campaign limerick: Lorant, p. 613.
27 "Over the next few years": Ickes, I, 602.
27 "Another happy day": *NYT*, November 7, 1936.
27 Cabinet discussion: Ickes, I, 705.
28 Orders for Cummings: Alsop and Catledge, pp. 31–34; McKenna, p. 245.

2. CAPTAIN OF A MIGHTY HOST

30 Lewis's work ethic: Zieger, *John L. Lewis*, p. 14.
30 Lewis's background: *American Biography.*
31 Uncle Sol's story: Cummings, p. 89.
31 "Our ship made port": Zieger, *John L. Lewis*, p. 19.
31 Without ever standing: Dubofsky and Van Tine, p. 38.
32 Unprecedented walkouts: Dubofsky, pp. 76–77.
32 Lewis's 1920 victory: "President Lewis."
32 Coal companies reneged: Zieger, pp. 29–33.
33 A landslide into the gutter: Mooney, p. 127.
33 Lewis grew stronger: Zieger, pp. 37–43.
33 Bryan and Jeffries: "President Lewis."
33 A theatrical flair: Dubofsky and Van Tine, p. 18.
34 "A mighty host": Labor Hall of Fame, dol.gov/laborhalloffame.
34 "They can't eat percentages": "President Lewis."
34 *Time* hailed him: "President Lewis."
34 Labor and capital: Zieger, p. 31.
35 "Wall Street lays an egg": *Variety*, October 30, 1929.

35   The stock market crash: Galbraith, p. 146.

35   Massive bank failures: Shannon, p. 72; McElvaine, pp. 137–142.

36   Thirteen million jobless and farm discontent: Schlesinger, I, 3.

36   Russian jobs: *Business Week*, October 7, 1931.

36   Plight of workers and farmers and starvation deaths: Bird, pp. 27–35.

37   Lewis argued eloquently: Zieger, pp. 62–63.

37   Pious platitudes: Dubofsky and Van Tine, p. 182, citing *United Mine Workers' Journal*, March 1, 1933, pp. 3–4.

37   "Suits our purposes": Lauck to Lewis, May 5, 1933, Lauck Papers, Box 39.

37   "Since emancipation": Dubofsky and Van Tine, p. 184.

38   "Beer and sauerkraut": Wechsler, p. 72.

38   West Virginia ballad: Korson, pp. 301–305.

38   Labor's problems: Dubofsky and Van Tine, p. 205.

39   Hutcheson's background: Levinson.

40   Lewis vs. Hutcheson: Zieger, p. 82; Dubofsky and Van Tine, pp. 219–220; Levinson, pp. 99–117; Bernstein, pp. 96–97; De Caux, p. 316.

40   "Sock him again": NYT, October 20, 1935.

41   "Sold down the river": Alsop and Catledge, p. 169.

41   Non-Partisan League: Dubofsky and Van Tine, pp. 248–250.

41   "We cannot forecast": NYT, August 9, 1936.

41   Backing FDR: Dubofsky and Van Tine, citing *United Mine Workers' Journal*, July 15, 1936.

41   Roosevelt pledged help: Jett Lauck diary, June 22, 1936; NYT, June 23, 1936.

42   "Boiled in a bathtub": NYT, October 28, 1936.

42   Union campaign spending: Dubofsky and Van Tine, p. 252.

42   "Hold the light": NYT, November 5, 1936.

42   Demand on Congress: NYT, November 21, 1936.

43   Top priority was steel: Bernstein, p. 435.

43   Pinkerton activities: Fine, pp. 37–41; Auerbach, pp. 99, 207.

43   Union members disgusted: Linder.

44   Early union strategy: Dubofsky and Van Tine, p. 256.

44   Union delegate a Pinkerton: Kempton.

44   "Worked like fiends": Linder.

44   Gene Richards's ordeal: Kraus, p. 44.

44   Martin wires GM: Fine, "A Re-examination."

45   As early as 1906: Linder.

46   "The Leaping Parson": "Automobile Armageddon."

46   Martin's failings: Fine, p. 78; Bernstein, 508; *American Biography*.

46   Mortimer's influence: Bernstein, p. 520.

46   Not Communist plotting: Fine, p. 223.

47   Sit-down strike ballad: Bernstein, p. 501.

48   The Cleveland sit–down: Fine, pp. 141–142; Linder, p. 11.

48   "Laid out situation": Linder, p. 12.

49 Fisher strike song: Linder, citing *United Auto Worker*, January 22, 1937.
49 Lewis demands FDR's help: Dubofsky and Van Tine, p. 253.
50 The spreading strike: Bernstein, p. 525.
50 Three-fourths of GM production: Fine, "Re-Examination."
50 Judge Black's stock: *NYT*, February 8, 1937.
51 Attack on Fisher No. 2: Fine, pp. 1–6.
51 Victor Reuther's warning: Kraus, p. 214.
52 Ballad of the Running Bulls: Fine, p. 8.
52 A man of many parts: Fine, pp. 150ff; Bernstein, pp. 531ff.
53 The ruling spirit: *American Biography*.
54 Preferred to be AG: Moley, p. 124.
54 "Lap of oneman": Fine, "Lewis Discusses."
55 Opinion polls on unions: Cantril, pp. 871, 816.
56 "Arm of the governor": Kraus, p. 141.
56 Walking a tightrope: "Alarums & Excursions."
56 Martin's turnabout: Kraus, pp. 162, 167.
57 Perkins as a proxy: Fine, pp. 254ff; Dubofsky and Van Tine pp. 262ff; Bernstein, pp. 535ff.
57 Perkins's background: *American Biography*.
57 "Only when climbing trees": Bernstein, p. 13.
58 Green's adverse reaction: "Truce at a Crisis."
58 Lewis's doubts: Bernstein, p. 535.
58 Lewis's press conference: *NYT*, January 22, 1937.
60 "intellectual inferiority": Fine, p. 257; *NYT*, January 23, 1937.
61 More pressure from Perkins: *NYT*, January 31, 1937; "Washington v. Detroit."
61 " A better position now": Fine, p. 259.

3. ANSWER TO A MAIDEN'S PRAYER

62 Cummings's background: *American Biography*.
63 Remembered long after: McKean, p. 87.
63 Father Dahme murder trial: www.symes.tv/Schubin.
64 Tall, stooping figure: Schlesinger, III, 261.
64 The 1924 convention: Murray, pp. 91, 157–164.
65 Did not forget: Acheson, p. 62.
66 All four ballots: *Guide to U.S. Elections*, p. 198.
66 Cooler heads prevailed: Baker, p. 27.
67 "Perfectly idiotic": Cummings diary, December 8–11, 1935, p. 65.
67 Walsh's record: *American Biography*.
68 "A chew of tobacco": *New York Sun*, March 1, 1933.
68 He hedged the decision: McKenna, p. 9.
69 "Tell me how I can do it": Schlesinger, III, 229.

70   Pondering the same issue: Moley, p. 145.
70   "I am ready now": Moley, p. 146fn.
71   Frankfurter turns it down: Freedman, pp. 111–112.
71   Cummings's revenge: Acheson, pp. 159–161.
72   Second rater's: Schlesinger, III, 261.
72   "The president understands": Ickes, I, 24.
72   "Take the next 15 minutes": Schlesinger, III, 261.
73   Prodded by Cummings: McKenna, p. 18.
74   "I would prefer it from you": Acheson, p. 181.
75   Negative view: Moley, p. 358; Jackson, p. 51.
75   Coining the term "Brain Trust": Rosenman, p. 81.
75   No intellectual: Schlesinger, II, 524.
76   "The governing principle": Tugwell, "On the verge of the presidency."
76   "And I will tell you why": Tully, p. 172.
77   The enemy camp: Alsop and Catledge, p. 33.
78   "A good deal of criticism": Cummings diary, December 26, 1937, p. 190.
78   The genius of Cummings's plan: Ibid.
78   "Unduly terrified": Ibid.
79   "Answer to a maiden's prayer": Alsop and Catledge, p. 36.
79   In the dark: Ibid.
81   The cheering Democrats: NYT, January 7, 1937.
81   "The problems are still with us": PPA, 1936, pp. 635–642.
81   Limiting the court: Ickes, II, 32.
82   Hatton Summers background: Moley and Jedel.
83   "Black letter learning": Patterson, p. 90.
83   Resignation talk: Alsop and Catledge, pp. 40–41.
84   Court plans of senators: Alsop and Catledge, p. 41; NYT, January 10, 1937.
84   "Peace without victory": "The Shape of Things."
85   "An awful shock": Freedman, p. 377.
86   "Yes, but": Rosenman, p. 144.
86   "One-third of a nation": PPA, 1937, pp. 1–5.
87   Corcoran's dislike for Cummings: Moley, p. 358.
87   FDR confides in Lewis: Cummings diary, January 24, 1937.
87   A working lunch: McKenna, p. 274; Rosenman, pp. 146ff.
90   Dinner for the Court: Rosenman, p. 153; "All at One Table."
90   FDR at ease: Davis: p. 62.
90   "Like a conspirator": Rosenman, p. 154.
91   A line from Tennyson: NYT, February 3, 1937.

4. SOLIDARITY FOREVER

93   Perkins's admonition: NYT , January 27, 1937.
93   Barricade of Buicks: "The 1936–37 Flint, Michigan, sit-down strike."
94   Sloan's response: Ibid., January 28, 1937.

94 Backing up its rhetoric: Ibid.
94 "You ought to be ashamed": Woodford.
95 Fluctuations in strength: Sears.
95 Plans to go home: "Sit-Down Strike Journal."
96 A long ordeal: Linder.
96 A "reception committee": Bliven.
97 "Control and discipline": Walker.
97 Wives to the windows: Levinson, "Detroit Digs In."
98 "This is your fight!": Linder.
98 "Form a line": Kraus, p. 234.
98 No Joan of Arc among them: Vorse.
99 Anti-strike violence: "Washington v. Detroit."
100 Create a diversion: Linder; Kraus, pp. 201–217.
101 The least damaging: Fine, p. 274.
101 "I'd leave office first": *NYT*, February 3, 1937.
102 "Law of the jungle": Fine, p. 281.
102 "A dangerous weapon": *NYT*, February 6, 1937.
103 Signs of wear and tear: "Deadlock at Detroit."
103 Murphy would plead: Fine, "Lewis discusses."
104 Major stumbling block: Bernstein, pp. 542ff.
105 That idea would not do: Fine, p. 288, citing Murphy Papers, strike chronology, February 5, 1937.
105 Lengthened to six months: Bernstein, p. 544.
105 "Or we are done": Fine, p. 291.
106 Vowed to "do something": Fine, p. 298.
106 Different accounts: Fine, pp. 299–300; Bernstein, pp. 545–547.
106 Letter to Lewis: Howard.
107 Even more colorful: Alinsky, pp. 144–146.
109 Agent on the prowl: *Detroit News*, February 8 and 9, 1937.
109 "Some lousy Pinkerton?": Fine, "Lewis Discusses."
110 Lewis glared at Smith: De Caux, pp. 248–249.
111 Mortimer read terms: "Peace and Automobiles"; Kraus, pp. 289–291.
111 "Defeat is complete": "Peace and Automobiles."
111 Fruits of success: Bernstein: p. 551.
112 Impressed by determination: Dubofsky and Van Tine, pp. 276–277; Bernstein, p. 467.
112 The deal with Big Steel: Zieger, *CIO*, p. 58.
112 Praise from Garner: *NYT*, February 12, 1937.
112 A jaunty prediction: "Peace and Automobiles:

5. IF MEN WERE ANGELS

113 "Highly confidential": Ickes, II, 65.
113 Grinding out copies: Alsop and Catledge, pp. 64–65.

114   Deliberations in Philadelphia: Bowen, pp. 3, 23–24.
114   The framers' dilemmas: Burns, *Deadlock*, pp. 16–20.
114   "If men were angels": Fairfield, p. 160.
114   An unlikely figure: Morris, *Witness at the Creation*, p. 96.
115   Congress had become "unhinged": Burns, *Deadlock*, p. 43.
116   Holding companies act: Leuchtenburg, pp. 154–156.
117   Loyalty test: NYT, June 12, 1935.
117   Nothing to prepare: NYT, June 8, 1935.
118   "He'll have kittens": Moley, p. 310.
118   Claim of victory, Patterson, p. 69.
119   "A breathing spell": Moley, pp. 317–318.
119   The cabinet session: Ickes, II, 65–68.
120   The president's message: NYT, February 6, 1937.
121   "Cash in my chips": Alsop and Catledge, p. 67.
122   "Pure personal government": *New York Herald Tribune*, February 11, 1937.
122   "Cleverness and adroitness": NYT, February 6, 1937.
122   "The Turnabout": *Tampa Tribune*, February 15, 1937.
122   "Newspapers boiling over": Cummings diary, February 8, 1937.
122   "Roosevelt Will Win": Ward, February 20, 1937.
123   Nine to one against: Alsop and Catledge, pp. 72–73.
123   "Have been overwhelming": Capper to William Allen White, February 25, 1937, White papers.
123   "Moses from Mt. Sinai": Ickes to William Allen White, February 25, 1937, White papers.
123   "Only a temporary remedy": Patterson, p. 89.
124   A majority against: Alsop and Catledge, p. 88.
124   Maverick's background: Caro, p. 545.
124   Maverick's sponsorship: NYT, February 6, 1937.
125   "Read the bill!": NYT, February 10, 1937; "Visibility Poor."
125   Running into trouble: NYT, February 14, 1937; "Batter Up."
126   "To get the Negro vote": Patterson, p. 98.
127   Hoover's blast: NYT, February 6, 1937.
127   Hoover calls Vandenberg: Cole, p. 212.
127   Vandenberg's early years: Patterson, pp. 101–102.
127   Vandenberg's career: Meijer.
128   "The general agreement": Patterson, p. 109.
128   "Who is muzzling me?": Alsop and Catledge, p. 98.
129   Connally's imposing figure: *American Biography*.
129   Champ Clark's background: Ibid.
129   Wheeler background: Wheeler, pp. vi–ix, 37–97.
130   Wheeler's resignation: Ibid., pp. 158–164.
131   "Like a religion": Ibid., p. 320.
132   Blamed Cummings: Schlesinger, III, pp. 138–139.

132   "Like a king": Burns, p. 341.
132   Lady Macbeth: Cole, p. 215.
133   Cummings's talk: NYT, February 15, 1937.
133   "Not particularly telling": Ickes, II, 75.
133   "Judicial wet-nurses": "Visibility Poor."
133   "We must act now": NYT, March 5, 1937; PPA, 1937, pp. 113–121.
134   "An Eagle Scout," New Yorker, March 15, 1937, cited I "Quiet Crisis."
134   "To make democracy work": PPA, 1937, pp. 122–133.
134   No sale: Alsop and Catledge: p. 113.
134   FDR brought pressure: Farley, p. 74.
135   "100 percent against me": Wheeler, p. 327.
135   "How hard it is": Alsop and Catledge, p. 122.

6. NATIONAL PASTIME

136   Krock's gloomy view: NYT, January 2, 1937.
136   Krock's self-esteem: Krock's good opinion of himself, though arguably justified by his professional accomplishments, at times nettled other journalists of distinction. James B. "Scotty" Reston, who succeeded Krock as chief of the Times's Washington Bureau, wrote that Krock "did not run the bureau, he presided over it." Reston also noted that when Dean Rusk became President Kennedy's secretary of state, Krock wrote him a note promising that if Rusk wished to call on him, he would be welcome. John F. Stacks, Scotty: James B. Reston and the Rise and Fall of American Journalism (Boston: Little Brown, 2003), pp. 93–94.
137   Detroit strikes: Zinn, et al., pp.75ff.
138   "Folded arms": Ibid., p. 61.
138   Even coffin factories: Howard, pp. 115–116.
138   A quantum leap: "Number of Sit-Down Strikes in 1937"; Levinson, pp. 173–174; Fine, p. 331.
138   "Replaced baseball": Detroit News, March 14, 1937.
138   European sit-downs: Fine, p. 122.
138   Gandhi's tactics: NYT, February 18, 1937.
139   Penitentiary sit-downs: NYT, January 25, March 4, 1937.
139   Drug store candy and back alimony: Ibid., February 17, March 7, 1937.
139   Rovers' protest: Ibid., February 15, 1937.
139   Waukegan strike: Ibid., February 20 and 28, 1937.
139   Hoffman background: Blackwell; "Joker's Heritage"; Time, June 28, 1954.
141   A preemptive strike: NYT, February 16, 1936.
142   "A symbol of communism": Coleman.
142   AFL reaction: NYT, February 16, 1936.
142   Steel workers' drive: Ibid., February 21, 1937.
142   "A startling spectacle": Ibid., February 23, 1937.

143   One single day: Ibid., March 9, 1937.
143   Chain store strike: Ibid., March 17, 1937.
143   Immediate dividends: Fine, pp. 327–328.
144   Two days to evacuate: *NYT*, March 16, 1937.
144   Chaotic labor story: Ibid., March 17 and 18, 1937.
145   Chicago, New York, and Clifton, N.J., strikes: Ibid., March 18, 1937.
146   Hiram Johnson background: *American Biography*, www.sacbee.3com/
        static/archive.
147   "State of civil war": *NYT*, May 25, 1921, West Virginia Coal Fields Hear-
        ings, p. 304.
148   Senate debate on sit-downs: *NYT*, March 18, 1937.
149   James Hamilton Lewis's background: *American Biography*.
150   King's background: *Utah History Encyclopedia*, www.media.utah.edu.
151   Senate liberals respond: *CR*, March 18, 1937, pp. 2478, 2483.
152   Police raids in Detroit: *NYT*, March 20, 1937.
152   Murphy's hopeful note: Ibid.
152   Martin warns of general strike: Ibid., March 22, 1937.
152   "His hired man": Ibid., March 23, 1937.
153   Dies's background: *American Biography*.
153   "It will change our entire theory": Timmons, pp. 215–219.
153   A full-scale inquiry: *NYT*, March 24, 1937.
154   Sit-down jitters: Ickes, II, 102.
154   "Day's strike developments": *NYT*, March, 24, 1937.

7. THE BABY IS BORN

156   "The Republic endures": *The Supreme Court in American Life*.
157   "Fine big windows": Brubaker.
157   "The court is punch drunk": Leuchtenburg, "The Nine Justices," citing
        Raymond Clapper diary, February 8, 1937.
157   Brandeis background: *American Biography*.
159   "Half-brother, half-son": Lash, p. 37.
160   Brandeis warned: Sherwood, p. 90; McKean, p. 89.
160   Bought from Capitol: Alsop and Catledge, p. 135.
161   Hughes's background: *American Biography*.
161   Trimmed his beard: Gosset.
162   "I'll be damned": Buchanan, Pringle, Person, and Allen, pp. 74–75.
163   McReynolds's background: *American Biography*.
163   Dividing the brethren: Baker, p. 120.
163   Butler's background: Danielski, pp. 3–20; *American Biography*.
164   "Afflict the court": Baker, p. 121.
164   Van Devanter background: *American Biography*.
164   Sutherland background: Ibid.

165   Cardozo background: Ibid.
166   Stone background: Ibid.; Mason, pp. 77–85.
166   Roberts background: Ibid.
167   Media queries: Baker, p. 36.
168   Brandeis believed: Leuchtenburg, "The Nine Justices," citing Marquis Childs, Columbia Oral History collection, pp. 68–69.
168   Cardozo's concern: Baker, p. 165.
168   Stone feared: Leuchtenburg, "The Nine Justices"; Baker, p. 172.
168   Sutherland's two letters: Leuchtenburg, "The Nine Justices," citing Sutherland to Bailey, February 22, 1937; Sutherland to Connally, June 5, 1937; Sutherland MSS, Library of Congress, Box 6.
168   McReynolds's outburst: *Washington Post*, March 17, 1937.
169   Cummings irritated other New Dealers: Jackson, p. 41.
169   Cummings testimony: *Reorganization Hearings*, I, 4–12; "Quiet Crisis," *Time*, March 22, 1937; *NYT*, March 11, 1937.
170   Hughes enters the fray: Wheeler, pp. 327–329.
172   Hughes's letter: *NYT*, March 23, 1937; *Reorganization Hearings*, I, 488–490.
173   Some justices groused: Leuchtenburg, "The Nine Justices."
173   "Violates every tradition": "The Chief Justice's Letter."
173   "Sent them scurrying": *NYT*, March 23, 1937.
173   "A sensational effect": Wheeler, p. 333.
174   "It was good tactics": Ickes, II, 103.
174   "A scathing editorial": *Baltimore Sun*, March 28, 1937; McKenna, p. 388, citing Cummings to FDR, April 3, 1937, president's personal file, FDRL.
174   Blaming sit-downs on the Court:. *NYT*, March 25, 1937.

8. LAW AND ORDER

176   Farley to Texas: *NYT*, March 25, 1937.
177   McIntyre advised the press: Ibid.
177   "The "sit-down revolt"": Ibid., March 27, 1937.
178   "Mass lawlessness": Farley, p. 85.
178   Perkins began to cry: Patterson, p. 136, citing Raymond Clapper's diary, December 28, 1937.
178   Murphy's warning: *NYT*, March 23, 1937.
178   Lewis accepts deal: *NYT*, March 25, 1937; Bernstein, p. 554.
179   No need for intervention: *NYT*, March 28, 1937.
179   "Quit hiding under beds": *Detroit Free Press*, April 1, 1937.
180   Green condemns sit-downs: *NYT*, March 29, 1937.
181   Byrnes's background: *American Biography*.
182   Putting stop to sit-downs: "Rip Tide."
183   Garner embraces Vandenberg: Patterson, p. 137.
183   For balance: *NYT*, April 8, 1937.

184　An "uproarious" debate: Ibid., April 9, 1937.

185　Washington state ruling: *West Coast Hotel Co. v. Parish*, 300 U.S. 379 (1937).

185　Fortas's quip: *NYT*, June 15, 1937.

185　Fortas's rise and fall: see Robert Shogan, *A Question of Judgment: The Fortas Case and the Struggle for the Supreme Court* (Indianapolis: Bobbs Merrill, 1972).

186　Sit-downs held illegal: Bernstein, pp. 678–680; *NLRB v. Fansteel Metallurgical Corp.*, 306 U.S. 240 (1939).

186　Roberts's memo: Roberts.

186　Wagner Act rulings: *NLRB v. Jones & Laughlin Steel*, 301 U.S. 1 (1937).

187　Overturning Guffey Act: *Carter v. Carter Coal Co.*, 298 U.S. 238 (1936); McKenna, pp. 205–206.

187　Corcoran had been telling friends: *Detroit News*, April 14, 1937.

187　"Doubtful constitutionality:" Cummings diary, June 20, 1935.

188　"An amazing thing": Cummings diary, April 12, 1937.

188　"Real black day": Leuchtenburg, "The Nine Justices," citing Frankfurter to Brandeis, March 31, 1937.

188　"Some honest profession": Freedman, p. 397.

189　"A tyrannical tribunal": *NYT*, May 15, 1937.

190　"I won't have a contract": *NYT*, June 25, 1937.

190　Girdler's background: *American Biography*.

190　"Girdler's "systematic terror": Bernstein, pp. 475, 483, 495.

190　Strike at Republic: Bork.

191　Memorial Day march: Fast.

193　Police response: Sofchalk.

193　Senate committee probe: Auerbach, pp. 123–125.

193　Paramount delayed release: Sofchalk.

194　"Revolutionary body": *Chicago Tribune*, May 31, 1937; June 6, 1937.

194　"Steel mob halted": *NYT*, May 31, 1937.

194　Provoked by the mob: "Strikes of the Week."

194　"Ill-advised violence": *Washington Post*, June 1, 1937.

195　CIO a threat to blow up bridges: Bernstein, p. 493.

195　Turned down Murray's appeal: *NYT*, June 16, 1937.

196　Heels beat against the desk: "Washington Notes," September 8, 1937.

9. WITH THE BARK OFF

197　The grandest stag party: *Washington Post*, June 27, 1937; *NYT*, June 26, 1937; Leuchtenburg, "Second Life"; "Visiting Week."

197　"A world of good": *NYT*, June 28, 1937.

198　Argument for compromise: Alsop and Catledge, p. 155.

198　"The margin too narrow": Swisher, p. 161.

198 His visitors were startled: Alsop and Catledge, p. 155.

199 No mood for compromise: Ibid., pp. 201–205.

199 Three springs previous: Farley, p. 82.

199 The battle goes on: "Fighting Clothes."

200 Van Devanter's retirement: Alsop and Catledge, p. 206; "The Time Has Arrived . . ."

200 Expectations for Robinson: Alsop and Catledge, p. 64.

201 Robinson's background: *American Biography.*

201 "Not one word of truth": "Three Whispers."

202 Made Robinson uneasy: Patterson, p. 64.

202 The *Nation's* warning: "Robinsion Will Not Do."

202 "Surmise No. 23.": "The Time Has Arrived . . ."

203 Social Security ruling: *Helvering v. Davis*, 301 U.S. 619 (upheld the old-age benefits provision of the statute); Swindler, p. 434.

204 Refused to accept situation: Farley, p. 86.

204 "There must be bridesmaids": Ickes, II, 153.

205 Garner's background: Hatfield, pp. 385–393; Timmons.

206 "Unalterably opposed": Farley, p. 85.

206 "Futility and absurdity": *Reorganizaton Report*, pp. 11–15 and passim; *NYT*, June 15, 1937.

207 "Needless, futile and dangerous": *Reorganization Report*, p. 23.

208 Invited absentees: "Visiting Week."

208 "Black as midnight": Patterson, p. 42.

208 Induction by Dies: "Visiting Week"; Anderson.

208 Charm through a hose pipe: Leuchtenburg, "Second Life."

209 "Weekend charm school": "Visiting Week."

209 In biblical prose: Alsop and Catledge, pp. 114–115, 180–182.

209 Mailing the report: Leuchtenburg, "Second Life."

210 Strikes tapered off: "Number of Sit-down Strikes in 1937."

210 Poll results: Cantrill, p. 816.

210 "Come to Cape Cod": "The Bandwagon."

211 Court rulings against farmer aid: Swindler, p. 430.

211 Farm groups refuse: Alsop and Catledge, pp. 115–117.

211 AFL's lukewarm support: Ibid., p. 165.

211 Lewis's attitude: Ibid., p. 175.

212 Robinson's lieutenants: Ibid., p. 227.

213 Unveiling the plan: "Robinson's Compromise."

213 Polls on court packing: Cantril, pp. 149–151.

213 Long lines of citizens: "The Great Debate."

214 "I warn them now": *CR*, 75th Congress, 1st Session, July 6, 1937, pp. 6786–6798.

214 "For God sakes": Alsop and Catledge, p. 256.

214 "I am through!": "The Great Debate."

215 Pressure from the White House: Alsop and Catledge, pp. 262–265.
215 Sprawled next to his bed: Ibid., p. 267.
216 "Fight against God": NYT, July 15, 1937.
216 "Dear Alben": PPA, 1937, pp. 306–308.
216 Senate resentment: Alsop and Catledge, pp. 271–272.
217 The funeral train: "Caucus on Wheels."
217 "You are beat": Timmons, p. 222.
217 "Write your own ticket": Alsop and Catledge, pp. 283–288.
218 No roll call: Baker, pp. 220–221.
218 The bill's death throes: Alsop and Catledge, pp. 291–293; CR, July 22, 1937, pp. 7375–7381.
219 Provisions of reform law: McKenna, pp. 526–529; Buhite and Levy, p. 129.
219 "A meager performance": Swisher, p. 174.

10. ON THE ROPES

220 Perkins's new view: NYT, July 4, 1937.
221 Lewis unburdened himself: Ibid., September 4, 1937.
222 "There wasn't any": Dubofsky and Van Tine, p. 328, citing FDR Press Conferences, Transcripts, vol. 10, p. 196.
222 A brief visit: "What Do You Think?"
222 Fewer and farther between: Burns, pp. 350–351.
222 Labor tied to New Deal: Hamby, p. 342.
223 Public had been pro-union: NYT, September 4, 1937.
223 Labor lost public support: Ibid., October 28, 1937.
223 Economic collapse, McElvaine, p. 298; Hamby, pp. 354–355.
224 Not outstanding lawyer: Ickes, II, 191.
224 A great uproar: Davis, pp. 108–112.
224 Rebuking Roper: Farley, p. 101.
225 "Those moral controls": PPA, 1937, pp. 1–2.
225 "He is punch drunk": Ickes, II, 182.
225 Early legislative strategy: Alsop and Catledge, pp. 198–200.
226 The main items: PPA, 1937, pp. 429–435; Buhite and Levy, p. 103.
226 Plans turned to dust: "Five Weeks."
227 More to FDR's proposal: Hamby, p. 342.
227 A more modest version: "Ninth Inning Rally."
227 Dictatorship had arrived: CR, 75th Congress, 3rd session, p. 4641.
228 Disavowing dictatorship: "Midnight Mystery."
228 A facetious amendment: Leuchtenburg, p. 263.
229 Nine initial targets: Farley, pp. 123–124.
229 "A clear-cut issue": PPA, 1938, p. 399; Buhite and Levy, p. 134.
229 Farley's verdict: "It's a Bust."
229 New conservative alliance: Patterson, p. 282.

229 A narrow victory: Burns, p. 364.
230 Dies's background: *American Biography*.
230 Threat from foreign-born: Leuchtenburg, p. 280.
231 Witnesses against Murphy: Howard; "Dies and Duty."
231 FDR defends Murphy: *PPA*, 1938, pp. 559–561, 587.
231 Ickes and Jackson campaign: Howard.
231 "The most serious defeat": Ickes, II, 498.
231 GOP gains: "The 76th."
232 "The hookworm Democrats": Crawford.
232 "Effectively dead": Hamby, p. 366.
233 "A movement with no program": Burns, *Deadlock*, p. 166, citing Walter Millis, "The President's Political Strategy," *Yale Review*, September 1938.
233 "Dr. Win the War": *PPA*, 1943, pp. 569–575 (December 28, 1943); "Platform for 1944."
233 "A typical verdict": Davis, p. 99.
234 The 1940 destroyer deal: see Robert Shogan, *Hard Bargain: How FDR Twisted Churchill's Arm, Evaded the Law and Changed the Role of the American Presidency* (New York: Scribner, 1995), pp. 235–250.
235 "The big, easy smiling man": Tugwell, p. 247.
236 "Grilled millionaire": Burns, p. 367.
236 "A turning point": *PPA*, 1937, p. lxvi.
237 "The reactionary members": Ibid., p. lxi.
237 "No reasonable assurance": Ibid., p. lxv.
237 "Key to the whole program": "Death and Politics."
240 "Man and boy for forty years": Evans and Novak, p. 460.
240 "Government can't solve": *NYT*, January 20, 1978.
241 "Era of big government": *NYT*, January 23, 1996.

Bibliography

The following abbreviations are used throughout the Bibliography and Notes:

CR   *Congressional Record*
FDRL   Franklin Delano Roosevelt Library
GPO   Government Printing Office
NYT   *New York Times*

ARCHIVAL SOURCES

Diary of Homer Cummings. Papers of William Jett Lauch. Alderman Library, University of Virginia, Charlottesville, Va.
Papers of William Allen White. Library of Congress.
Diary of Henry Stimson. Sterling Library, Yale University, New Haven, Conn.

GOVERNMENT DOCUMENTS

U.S. Senate. Committee on the Judiciary. *Reorganization of the Federal Judiciary. Hearings.* 75th Congress, 1st Session. Washington: GPO, 1937 (cited in notes as *Reorganization Hearings*).
U.S. Senate Committee on the Judiciary. *Reorganization of the Federal Judiciary, Senate Report No. 711.* 75th Congress, 1st Session. Washington: GPO, 1937 (cited in notes as *Reorganization Report*).
U.S. Senate. Committee on Education and Labor, *West Virginia Coal Fields, Hearings,* Vol. I. 67th Congress, 1st Session. Washington: GPO, 1921.

BOOKS

Acheson, Dean. *Morning and Noon*. Boston: Houghton Mifflin, 1965.

Alinsky, Saul. *John L. Lewis: An Unauthorized Biography*. New York: Putnam, 1949, pp. 144–146.

Alsop, Joseph, and Turner Catledge. *The 168 Days*. Garden City: Doubleday, 1938.

Auerbach, Jerold S. *Labor and Liberty: The La Follette Committee and the New Deal*. Indianapolis: Bobbs Merrill, 1966.

Baker, Leonard. *The Duel Between FDR and the Supreme Court*. New York: Macmillan, 1967.

Bernstein, Irving. *Turbulent Years: A History of the American Worker 1933–1941*. New York: Houghton Mifflin, 1969.

Bird, Caroline. *The Invisible Scar*. New York: Pocketbooks, 1967.

Bowen, Catherine Drinker. *Miracle at Philadelphia*. Boston: Little, Brown, 1966.

Blum, John Morton. *Roosevelt and Morgenthau*. Boston: Houghton Mifflin, 1972.

Buhite, Russell D., and David W. Levy, eds. *FDR's Fireside Chats*. Norman: University of Oklahoma Press, 1992.

Burns, James MacGregor. *The Deadlock of Democracy: Four Party Politics in America*, rev. ed. Englewood Cliffs, N.J.: Prentice-Hall, 1963 (cited in notes as Burns, *Deadlock*).

———. *Roosevelt: The Lion and the Fox*. New York: Harcourt, 1956.

Byrnes, James F. *All in One Lifetime*. New York: Harper, 1958.

Campbell, James E. *The Presidential Pulse of Congressional Elections*, 2nd ed. Lexington: University Press of Kentucky, 1997.

Cantrill, Hadley. *Public Opinion, 1935–1946*. Princeton: Princeton University Press, 1951.

Caro, Robert. *The Years of Lyndon Johnson: The Path to Power*. New York: Knopf, 1982.

Cole, Wayne S. *Roosevelt and the Isolationists*. Lincoln: University of Nebraska Press, 1983.

Chace, James. *Acheson: The Secretary of State Who Created the American World*. New York: Simon and Schuster, 1998.

Creel, George. *Rebel at Large*. New York: Putnam, 1947 (cited in Notes as Creel, *Rebel*).

Cummings, e. e. Collected Poems. New York: Harcourt Brace, 1926.

Danielski, David J. *A Supreme Court Justice Is Appointed*. New York: Random House, 1964.

Davis, Kenneth S. *FDR: Into the Storm, 1937–1940*. New York: Random House, 1993.

De Caux, Len. *Labor Radical: From the Wobblies to the CIO*. Boston: Beacon Press, 1940.

Dictionary of American Biography. New York: Council of Learned Societies, various dates (cited in notes as *American Biography*).

Dubofsky, Melvin. *The State and Labor in Modern America.* Chapel Hill: University of North Carolina Press, 1994.

—— and Warren Van Tine. *John L. Lewis: A Biography.*

Evans, Rowland, and Robert Novak. *Lyndon B. Johnson: The Exercise of Power.* New York: New American Library, 1966.

Fairfield, Roy P., ed. *Federalist Papers,* 2nd ed. Garden City: Doubleday, 1966.

Farley, James. *Jim Farley's Story.* New York: McGraw-Hill, 1948.

Fine, Sidney. *Sit-Down: The General Motors Strike of 1936–1937.* Ann Arbor: University of Michigan Press, 1969.

Freedman, Max. *Roosevelt and Frankfurter: Their Correspondence, 1928–1945.* Boston: Little, Brown, 1967.

Freidel, Frank. *Franklin D. Roosevelt: The Ordeal.* Boston: Little, Brown, 1954.

Galbraith, John Kenneth. *The Great Crash.* Boston: Houghton Mifflin, 1961.

Graham, Otis, Jr., and Meghan Robinson Wander. *Franklin D. Roosevelt: His Life and Times.* New York: Da Capo, 1990.

Guide to U.S. Elections, 2nd ed. Washington, D.C.: Congressional Quarterly, 1985.

Hamby, Alonzo. *For the Survival of Democracy: Franklin Roosevelt and the World Crisis of the 1930s.* New York: Free Press, 2004.

Hatfield, Mark O., with the Senate Historical Office. *Vice Presidents of the United States, 1789–1993.* Washington: GPO, 1997.

Hofstadter, Richard. *The Idea of a Party System.* Berkeley: University of California Press, 1966.

Hurd, Charles. *When the New Deal Was Young and Gay.* New York: Hawthorne, 1965.

Ickes, Harold. *The Secret Diary of Harold Ickes: Vol I. The First Thousand Days.* New York: Simon and Schuster, 1953.

——. *The Secret Diary of Harold Ickes: Vol II. The Inside Struggle.* New York: Simon and Schuster, 1954.

Jackson, Robert. *That Man: An Insider's Portrait of Franklin D. Roosevelt.* New York: Oxford University Press, 2003.

Kempton, Murray. "Fathers and Sons," in *Part of Our Time: Some Monuments and Ruins of the Thirties.* New York: Dell, 1955.

Korson, George. *Coal Dust on the Fiddle.* Hatboro, Pa., 1965.

Kraus, Henry. *The Many and the Few: A Chronicle of the Dynamic Auto Workers,* 2nd ed. Urbana: University of Illinois Press, 1985.

Lash, Joseph P. *Dealers and Dreamers: A New Look at the New Deal.* New York: Doubleday, 1988.

Leuchtenburg, William. *Franklin D. Roosevelt and the New Deal, 1932–1940.* New York: Harper, 1963.

———. "The First Modern President," in Fred I. Greenstein, ed. *Leadership in the Modern Presidency.* Cambridge, Mass.: Harvard University Press, 1988.

Levinson, Edward. *Labor on the March.* New York: University Books, 1956.

Lorant, Stefan. *The Glorious Burden: The American Presidency.* New York: Harper and Row, 1968.

Louchhheim, Katie, ed. *The Making of the New Deal: The Insiders Speak.* Cambridge, Mass: Harvard University Press, 1983.

Maney, Patrick J. *The Roosevelt Presence.* New York: Twayne, 1992.

Mason, Alpheus T. *Harlan Fiske Stone: Pillar of the Law.* New York: Viking, 1956.

McElvaine, Robert S. *The Great Depression: America, 1929–1941.* New York: Times Books, 1984.

McKean, David. *Tommy the Cork: Washington's Ultimate Insider from Roosevelt to Reagan.* South Royalton, Vt.: Steerforth Press, 2004.

McKenna, Marian C. *Franklin Roosevelt and the Great Constitutional War: The Court-Packing Crisis of 1937.* New York: Fordham University Press, 2002.

Moley, Raymond. *After Seven Years.* New York: Harper, 1939.

Mooney, Booth. *Roosevelt and Rayburn: A Political Partnership.* Philadelphia: Lippincott, 1971.

Mooney, Fred. *Struggle in the Coal Fields: The Autobiography of Fred Mooney,* J. W. Hess, ed. Morgantown, W. Va.: West Virginia University Library, 1967.

Morris, Richard B. "George Washington's Farewell Address," in Daniel J. Boorstein, ed. *An American Primer.* New York: Mentor, 1973.

———. *Witness at the Creation: Hamilton, Madison, Jay and the Constitution.* New York: Holt, 1985.

Murray, Robert K. *The 103rd Ballot.* New York: Harper and Row, 1976.

Patterson, James T. *Congressional Conservatism and the New Deal.* Lexington: University of Kentucky Press, 1967.

Pearson, Drew, and Robert S. Allen. *The Nine Old Men.* Garden City: Doubleday, 1937.

Roosevelt, Franklin D. *Public Papers and Addresses, 1933–1945,* Samuel I. Rosenman ed. New York: Random House, Macmillan, Russell and Russell (cited in notes as *PPA*).

Rosenman, Samuel I. *Working with Roosevelt.* New York: Harper, 1955.

Schlesinger, Arthur M., Jr. *The Age of Roosevelt: Vol. I. The Crisis of the Old Order.* Boston: Houghton Mifflin, 1957.

———. *The Age of Roosevelt: Vol. II, The Coming of the New Deal.* Boston: Houghton Mifflin, 1959.

———. *The Age of Roosevelt: Vol. III, The Politics of Upheaval.* Boston: Houghton Mifflin, 1960.

Shannon, David A. *The Great Depression.* Engelwood Cliffs, N.J.: Prentice-Hall, 1960.

Sherwood, Robert E. *Roosevelt and Hopkins*. New York: Harper, 1948.
The Supreme Court in American Life. Washington, D.C.: Foundation of the Federal Bar Assocation, 1965.
Swanberg, W. A. *Citizen Hearst*. New York: Bantam Books, 1967.
Swindler, William E. *Court and Constitution in the 20th Century: The New Legality, 1932–1968*. Indianapolis: Bobbs-Merrill, 1970.
Swisher, Carl Brent, ed. *Selected Papers of Homer Cummings*. New York: Scribner, 1939.
Tugwell, Rexford G. *The Democratic Roosevelt*. Baltimore: Penguin, 1957.
Tully, Grace. *FDR: My Boss*. Chicago: People's Book Club, 1949.
Wechsler, James A. *Labor Baron: A Portrait of John L. Lewis*. New York: Morrow, 1944.
Wheeler, Burton K. *Yankee from the West*. Garden City: Doubleday, 1952.
Zevin, B. D., ed. *Nothing to Fear: The Selected Addresses of Franklin Delano Roosevelt, 1932–1945*. Boston: Houghton Mifflin, 1946.
Zieger, Robert. *The CIO: 1935–1955*. Chapel Hill: University of North Carolina Press, 1995 (cited in notes as Zieger, *CIO*).
———. *John L. Lewis, Labor Leader*. Boston: Twayne, 1988.
Zinn, Howard, Dana Frank, and Robin D. G. Kelley. *Three Strikes: Miners, Musicians, Salesgirls and the Fighting Spirit of Labor's Last Century*. Boston: Beacon, 2001.

PERIODICALS, JOURNALS, AND WEBSITES

Adamic, Louis. "Sitdown." *Nation*, December 5, 1936.
"Alarums & Excursions." *Time*, January 25, 1937.
"All at One Table." *Time*, February 15, 1937.
Anderson, Paul Y. "Investigate Mr. Dies!" *Nation*, November 5, 1938.
"Automobile Armageddon." *Time*, January 18, 1937.
"The Bandwagon." *New Republic*, August 4, 1937.
Blackwell, Jan. "The Governor Was a Thief." *Trentonian*, n.d. www.capital century.com.
Bliven, Bruce. "Sitting Down in Flint." *New Republic*, January 27, 1937.
Bork, William. "Massacre at Republic Steel." www. kentlaw.edu/ilhs/republic.htm
Brubaker, Howard. "Of All Things." *New Yorker*, September 21, 1935.
Buchanan, James M. "A Note on the 'Joe Cotton Story.'" *Supreme Court Historical Society 1981 Yearbook*.
"Caucus on Wheels." *Time*, July 26, 1937.
"The Chief Justice's Letter." *New Republic*, April 7, 1937.
Coleman, McAlister. "Hoffman of New Jersey." *Nation*, May 15, 1937.
Crawford, Kenneth. "Washington's Big Show." *Nation*, December 31, 1938.
Creel, George. "Looking Ahead with Roosevelt." *Collier's*, September 7, 1935.

"Deadlock at Detroit." *Time*, February 15, 1937.

"Death and Politics." *Nation*, July 24, 1937.

"Dies and Duty." *Time*, November 7, 1938.

Father Dahme murder trial: www.symes.tv/schubin.

Fast, Howard. "An Occurrence at Republic Steel." *Progressive*, July 17, 1937.

"Fighting Clothes." *Time*, May 24, 1937.

Fine, Sidney. "The General Motors Sit-Down Strike: A Re-examination." *American Historical Review*, vol. 70, no. 3 (April 1965) (cited in notes as Fine, "Re-examination").

"Five Weeks." *Time*, June 3, 1938.

"Forest vs. Trees." *Time*, June 14, 1937.

Gosset, William T. "The Human Side of Chief Justice Hughes." *ABA Journal*, vol. 59 (December 1973).

"The Great Debate." *Time*, July 19, 1937.

Greenfield, Jeff. "A Hero to His Valet." *Harper's*, November 2002.

Howard, J. Woodford Jr. "Frank Murphy and the Sit-Down Strikes of 1937." *Labor History*, vol. 1, 1960.

"It's a Bust." *Time*, September 26, 1938.

"John L. Lewis Discusses the General Motors Sit-Down Strike." *Labor History*, vol. 15 (1974) (cited in Notes as Fine, "Lewis Discusses").

"Joker's Heritage." *Time*, June 28, 1954.

Labor Hall of Fame: www.dol.gov/laborhalloffame.

Leuchtenburg, William E. "F.D.R.'s Court-Packing Plan: A Second Life, A Second Death." *Supreme Court Historical Society Yearbook*, 1988 (cited in Notes as Leuchtenburg, "Second Life").

———. "The Nine Justices Respond to the 1937 Crisis." *Journal of Supreme Court History*, vol. 1, 1997 (cited in notes as Leuchtenburg, "The Nine Justices").

———. "The Origins of Franklin Roosevelt's 'Court Packing' Plan." *Supreme Court Review*, 1966 (cited in Notes as Leuchtenburg, "Origins").

Levinson, Edward. "Bill Hutcheson's Convention." *Nation*, January 2, 1937.

Meijer, Hank. "Depression, Detroit and the New Deal of Sen. Arthur Vandenberg." Burton Memorial Lecture, 2003 Michigan Historical Conference. www.hsmichigan.org.

"Midnight Mystery." *Time*, April 11, 1938.

Moley, Raymond, and Celeste Jedel. "The Gentleman Who Does Not Yield: Hatton Summers, Dallas Diogenes." *Saturday Evening Post*, May 10, 1941.

"Ninth Inning Rally." *Time*, April 4, 1938.

"Number of Sit-Down Strikes in 1937." *Monthly Labor Review*, August 1938.

O'Rourke, Francis. "Sit-Down Strike Journal." http://community-zwebtv.net/uhhuhdotcom/dairyofasit-downer.

"Peace and Automobiles." *Time*, February 22, 1937.

"Platform for 1944." *Time*, January 10, 1944.

"President Lewis." *Time*, June 4, 1923.

Pringle, H. F. "The President." *New Yorker*, June 16, 1934.

"Quiet Crisis." Time, March 22, 1937.

"Rip Tide." *Time*, April 12, 1937.

Roberts, Owen J. "Office Memorandum." University of Pennsylvania Law Review, December 1955.

"Robinson's Compromise." *Time*, July 12, 1937.

"Robinson Will Not Do." *Nation*, May 29, 1937.

Sears, Stephen W. "Shut the Goddam Plant." *American Heritage*, April/May 1982.

"The Shape of Things." *Nation*, January 16, 1937.

Sofchalk, Donald G. "The Chicago Memorial Day Incident: An Episode of Mass Action." *Labor History*, vol. 6, Winter 1965.

"The 1936–37 Flint, Michigan, Sit-down Strike." www.bbc.co.uk/dna/h292.

"The 76th." *Time*, November 21, 1938.

"The Time Has Arrived . . ." *Time*, May 31, 1937.

"Three Whispers." *Time*, September 17, 1928.

Timmons, Bascom N. "John Garner's Story." *Collier's*, March 20, 1948.

"Truce at a Crisis." *Time*, August 14, 1933.

Tugwell, Rexford. "Franklin Roosevelt on the Verge of the Presidency." *Antioch Review*, Spring 1956.

"Visibility Poor." *Time*, February 22, 1937.

"Visiting Week." *Time*, July 5, 1937.

Vorse, Mary Heaton. "The Emergency Brigade at Flint." *New Republic*, February 17, 1937.

Walker, Charles. "Flint Faces Civil War." *Nation*, February 13, 1937.

Ward, Paul W. "Washington Weekly." *Nation*, October 31, 1936.

———. "Washington Weekly." *Nation*, February 20, 1937.

"Washington v. Detroit." *Time*, February 8, 1937.

"Washington Notes." *New Republic*, September 8, 1937.

Weir, Ernest T. "I Am What Mr. Roosevelt Calls an Economic Royalist." *Fortune*, October 1936.

Weller, Cecil Edward Jr. "Joseph Taylor Robinson: Keystone of Franklin D. Roosevelt's Supreme Court 'Packing' Plan." *Journal of Southern History*, vol. 7, 1986.

"What Do You Think?" *Time*, September 27, 1937.

MISCELLANEOUS

Linder, Walter. "The Great Flint Sit-Down Strike Against GM, 1936–37." Solidarity Pamphlet No. 31, published by Solidarity (North London), 1969.

Index

Reuther, Roy, 46, 47
Reuther, Victor, 46, 51, 99
Reuther, Walter, 46
Reventlow, Barbara Hutton
  Haugwitiz, 146
Richards, Gene, 44
Richberg, Donald, 75, 88
Ripley, William Zebina, 198
R. J. Reynolds Tobacco, 109
Roaring Twenties, 35
Roberts, Owen J., 24, 166, 185, 186,
  188
Robinson, Joseph, 84, 113, 120, 174,
  179, 200, 203, 223; background of,
  201; death of, 215, 216; FDR,
  relationship with, 202; funeral of,
  216, 217; and Supreme Court
  reform bill, 125, 204, 207, 209,
  212–15, 217; and sit-down strikes,
  150, 151, 154, 183
Roper, Dan, 109, 224
Roosevelt, Anna, 5
Roosevelt, Betsy Cushing, 3
Roosevelt, Eleanor, 11, 90; and civil
  rights, 126
Roosevelt, Franklin Delano, 18, 57,
  58, 59, 63, 65, 66, 68, 70, 90, 102,
  114, 130, 149, 175, 192, 240, 241, 242;
  Dean Acheson, firing of, 74;
  advisers of, 75; African Americans,
  support of, 126; attacks on, 20, 152;
  backlash against, 7; and banking
  crisis, 69; and big business, 7, 8,
  38, 118; and Brain Trust, 75; charm
  of, 11; clandestine approach of, 85;
  as communicator, 19; crisis,
  handling of, 176; defeats of, 219,
  220; deviousness, charges of, 236;
  dictatorial ambitions, disavowal of,
  227, 228; economy, collapse of, 223,
  224; election of, 3, 36, 44, 67; and
  farmers, 211; and First Hundred
  Days, 14; flexibility of, 10; and

General Motors strike, 91, 92, 93,
  104, 105, 109, 111; and gold-buying
  policies, 73, 74; iron will of, 10;
  Jefferson Island Club bash, 197,
  207, 208, 209; and Justice
  Department, 72, 73; and labor, 49,
  52, 55, 56, 60, 177, 179, 195, 196; as
  lame duck, 233; leadership of, 235;
  legacy of, 204, 239; legislative
  program, failures of, 225, 228; and
  John L. Lewis, 41, 42, 177, 211, 212,
  222; management style of, 76, 234;
  mistakes of, 238; and Frank
  Murphy, 54, 231; and New Deal,
  15, 28, 62, 233, 238, 239;
  newspapers, as enemy, 8; persona
  of, 27; personality of, 75;
  popularity, drop in, 226; power of,
  116; as power grabber,
  denouncement of, 123, 227;
  prestige, drop in, 227; and public
  utility holding companies, 116, 117;
  and racism, 126; self-assurance of,
  9; Senate purge of, as failure, 228,
  229; and sit-down strikes, 180, 182,
  206, 234; and Social Security Act,
  203; as successful, 234; and
  Supreme Court, 9, 14, 17, 22, 29,
  55, 61, 80–84, 89, 92, 115, 117, 119,
  157; Supreme Court, and
  constitutional amendment, 20, 42,
  77; Supreme Court, excoriation of,
  19; and Supreme Court packing
  plan, 7, 87, 120–21, 127, 132–35,
  142–43, 148, 154–55, 160, 174, 186,
  188–89, 197–99, 200, 204, 207,
  210–11, 216, 219, 233, 236–37;
  Supreme Court packing plan,
  defeat of, 226; Supreme Court
  packing plan, as devious, 121;
  Supreme Court, restraining of, 25,
  26, 76, 77, 131; swearing in of, 86;
  and tax code changes, 117, 118; toll

A NOTE ON THE AUTHOR

Robert Shogan is a former prizewinning national political correspondent for *Newsweek* and the *Los Angeles Times*. Born in New York City, he studied journalism at Syracuse University and after reporting for newspapers and magazines and writing books for more than forty years turned to teaching. He has been professional in residence at the Annenberg School of Communications of the University of Pennsylvania, and is currently adjunct professor of government at Johns Hopkins University while continuing to write books. Mr. Shogan's other books include *The Double-Edged Sword*, *The Fate of the Union*, *Hard Bargain*, *Riddle of Power*, *Bad News*, *Constant Conflict*, and *The Battle of Blair Mountain*. He lives with his wife in Chevy Chase, Maryland.